Reading this book is a pure joy. A breath of fresh air, *Cultural Apologetics* is one of the best books I've read in years. Paul Gould was meant to write it. His ideas having marinated, his prodigious teaching skills honed, his reading wide and deep, he was able to write with the fertile mind of a philosopher, capacious heart of a poet, vivid imagination of an artist, and the nimble hands of a passionate practitioner. This is essential reading for every actual or budding apologist; in fact, the book deserves a very wide readership among believers and skeptics alike. It is not a book to be read quickly but digested and savored. Read, relish, and reread it; use it in class; give it away as a gift. Culturally informed and sensitive, embodying what it extolls, eclectic in numerous respects, and punctuated with clever and telling illustration~ ~ ~ ~ ~bal and visual—this remarkable book makes a power^f^·~·~ ~ ~ologetic faithful to a true anthropology. It's ~ ~ ~ imagination of a disenchanted age. Every ~ ~ ~tion. At moments it's veritably sublime and e ~ ~ ~ ~ ~suasive, and moving as it is eminently practical. ~ ~ ~ ~ommend it enough.

David Baggett, professor of philosophy and apologetics, Rawlings School of Divinity, Liberty University, coauthor of *God and Cosmos* and *The Morals of the Story*

The world is flat. This claim is not about the shape of the earth. Rather, the world is flat in the experience of most secular people. They live an impoverished, empty existence. Their world has been thoroughly disenchanted. What they need is a fresh breeze of hope. What they need is for their world to be reenchanted with the reality of the living Christ. They need their vision cleared so they are able to see the good and the true and the beautiful.

Paul Gould's *Cultural Apologetics* tackles this disenchantment and calls believers to hold forth the gospel as a greater vision of life. This book is not simply another rehashing of apologetics. As the subtitle says, it develops a strategy for *Renewing the Christian Voice, Conscience, and Imagination in a Disenchanted World*. With wisdom and insight, Gould traces our human longings through literature, philosophy, film, and human relationships. He equips the reader to better move from these shared human experiences into conversations about the most important things. This is a truly important book.

Gregory E. Ganssle, professor of philosophy, Talbot School of Theology, author of *Our Deepest Desires*

Paul Gould nails it. *Cultural Apologetics* is, more than any book I've read, a strategic missionary map, defining and clarifying what the church must do to reach Western culture with the gospel in these strange, foreign days in which we live.

Tom Gilson, senior editor and ministry coordinator, *The Stream*

I often find myself distressed when I consider the current state of the church's witness to the world. How has the greatest story the world has ever known lost its credibility, its beauty, and its persuasive power? Not only does this book answer these questions with penetrating insight, but it also shows us a hopeful way forward. By giving us a holistic apologetic that brings together the mind, the conscience, and the imagination, Paul charts a thoroughly biblical course for the church's cultural engagement. Every Christian should read this book carefully, as it will effectively prepare us to bear witness to the truth, goodness, and beauty of the gospel of Jesus to a disenchanted culture.

Brett Kunkle, founder and president of MAVEN,
coauthor of *A Practical Guide to Culture*

Cultural Apologetics is a timely and balanced book. Although Gould addresses some big apologetics issues today, *Cultural Apologetics* is more of a practical roadmap for advancing the Christian message through reason, imagination, and conscience. I highly recommend this book not only for those interested in apologetics but for Christians interested in learning how to creatively bring the Christian voice into cultural conversations today.

Sean McDowell, associate professor of Christian apologetics, Talbot
School of Theology, a popular speaker, and author or coauthor
of over eighteen books, including *A New Kind of Apologist*

We live in a post-Enlightenment, disenchanted culture emptied of transcendence. For many, belief in God is unwelcome, unnecessary, and unimaginable. Paul Gould's *Cultural Apologetics* is as enjoyable to read as it is important in considering culturally relevant means of engaging our post-Enlightenment (i.e., postmodern) culture with the gospel of Christ. His broad reading in philosophy and Christian apologetics, as well as his background in campus ministry, helps him diagnose the problem to effectively reach toward a solvent model of cultural engagement in what he calls a "new lane" in Christian apologetics. Some may see Christianity as plausible but not desirable. Others see it as desirable but not plausible. The cultural apologist, Gould claims, seeks to show that Christianity is both plausibly true and satisfyingly desirable. This important book provides tools leading toward the pathway of reenchantment.

Corey Miller, president and CEO, Ratio Christi

I have long known that culture is a powerful means of spiritual formation. It is also a tacit means of shaping what people consider plausible, and what they feel to be true, good, and beautiful. Paul Gould's *Cultural Apologetics* works not a paradigm change so much as a paradigm expansion on our concept of what apologetics is and does, but it is nonetheless revolutionary for that. This is the book on apologetics for which I have long been waiting.

Kevin J. Vanhoozer, research professor of systematic theology, Trinity Evangelical Divinity School

Always be ready to give a reason for the hope that is in you, said the apostle Peter. Paul Gould in this fine book gives reasons for hope that are not just argumentative or propositional but narrative and personal, reasons that resonate with those hard-to-articulate but utterly essential components of life: mystery, beauty, holiness, and wholeness. Here is a clear, personable, heartening work, which I warmly recommend.

Michael Ward, fellow of Blackfriars Hall, University of Oxford, professor of apologetics, Houston Baptist University

CULTURAL APOLOGETICS

Renewing the Christian Voice, Conscience, and Imagination in a Disenchanted World

PAUL M. GOULD

ZONDERVAN

Cultural Apologetics
Copyright © 2019 by Paul M. Gould

ISBN 978-0-310-53049-7 (softcover)

ISBN 978-0-310-53050-3 (ebook)

Requests for information should be addressed to:
Zondervan, *3900 Sparks Dr. SE, Grand Rapids, Michigan 49546*

Cover design: Studio Gearbox
Cover photo: Shutterstock
Interior design: Kait Lamphere

Printed in the United States of America

HB 07.23.2022

To my energetic, inspiring, and delightful leadership team at the Two Tasks Institute—Lucas Shipman, Avery Earl, Courtney McClean, Neil Williams, and Chris Lee—thanks for being a source of encouragement and God's grace as we join together to help others see the brilliance and beauty of Jesus and the gospel story.

The people who walk in darkness
will see a great light.

Isaiah 9:2 NLT

CONTENTS

ARGUMENTS FOR GOD

FOREWORD

As I write this forward in the fall of 2018, we are living in a crazy, morally and spiritually chaotic culture that is slouching towards a deeply secular, morally and spiritually bankrupt Europe. As each day goes by, we are becoming increasingly secular. I have been a Christian for fifty years, and if you had told me fifteen years ago that we would be where we are today, I simply would not have believed it. For centuries, there have been those who thought Christianity was an irrational superstition. But the ethical teachings of the Bible, especially those of Jesus, were still considered the pinnacle of solid morality. No longer. A growing number of people consider Christianity not only foolish but also immoral due to its alleged intolerance and bigotry.

At the same time, record numbers of Christians—especially those thirty-five and under—are leaving the church and abandoning belief in God and Jesus Christ. Why? Are our worship services poorly done? Are we failing to love and enfold people into the church? Are we doing a bad job of fostering relationships and promoting a healthy congregational life? It may come as a shock to learn that none of these are the main reason. In a recent Barna poll, researchers tried to see why Millennials (those between twenty-two to thirty-seven years old) are abandoning the church and the faith. They identified six reasons for the exodus: (1) The church is overprotective and fails to expose people to anti-Christian ideas. (2) The church's teaching is shallow. (3) The church is antagonistic to science and fails to help believers interact with scientific claims. (4) The church treats sexuality simplistically and judgmentally. (5) The church makes exclusivist claims. (6) The church is dismissive of doubters.

Note that *every single reason involves a failure to engage the life of the mind and employ apologetics to answer people's questions.* Last spring, I received an email from someone I did not know. The gentleman shared that he and a few others were working with about twenty-five Millennials. Some were atheists, but most were Christians on a razor's edge in abandoning Christianity. When they shared their doubts in church, they were either dismissed (e.g., stop over-thinking things and get into the Word) or given weak answers. He asked me if I would come to his home and have a question-and-answer time with the group. I happily agreed, and the evening consisted of two and a half hours of question-and-answer with about twenty-five people. After our time, several shared with me that their faith had been restored by the evening.

Our greatest need is to reintroduce believers to the value and practice of apologetics and to equip them to engage our culture's ideas in a winsome and intelligent way. That is why I am so excited about professor Paul Gould's book *Cultural Apologetics*. I have known Paul for decades. He is a cherished and respected friend and co-laborer. And he is exactly the right person to write this book. For one thing, he has demonstrated by his lectures and writings that he is at home in the rigors of academic philosophy. He is a Christian who does philosophy and apologetics, not a philosopher who happens to be a Christian. In short, he knows his stuff and is a first-rate *Christian* scholar.

But that is not the end of the story. Professor Gould has been shaped by years of being on the staff of Cru, and he is a passionate lover of Jesus who is deeply committed to the Great Commission. He has the heart of an evangelist and equips believers to penetrate the culture with a Christian worldview.

This book is the result of years and years of passion and reflection on the material you are about to read. He is *the* man to write this book. And its release could not have come at a better time. However, keep in mind that this is not your typical apologetics book. Yes, it provides reasons for Christianity and responses to objections raised against it. But it emphasizes *cultural* apologetics. As Paul defines his project, "Cultural apologetics [is] the work of establishing the Christian voice, conscience, and imagination within a culture so that Christianity is seen as true and satisfying."

So be prepared for a fresh, new approach to penetrating our culture with a Christian worldview. You are about to learn a lot. Enjoy!

J. P. Moreland, distinguished professor of philosophy,
Talbot School of Theology, Biola University

ACKNOWLEDGMENTS

How does the gospel get a fair hearing in this day and age? In seeking an answer to this question, I've benefitted from the example, friendship, discussions, and writings of many. From my campus ministry days, thanks to Roger Hershey, Stan Wallace, Mark Brown, and the Faculty Commons staff. Your lives carry the fragrance of transcendence, modeling how to live for a story bigger than yourself. To my students over the past four years at Southwestern Seminary and Scarborough College, thanks for your spirited engagement and patience as I work out my views on culture and apologetics. It is a beautiful thing when men and women, students and professor, come together to love God and love people as truth seekers and agents of shalom. To my friends and colleagues who have read all or part of the manuscript, thanks for your invaluable insight, suggestions, and encouragement. Special thanks to Skip Holmes, Andy Chapin, Richard Brian Davis, Lucas Shipman, Travis McNeely, Rick Wade, David Baggett, Mike Austin, Brett Kunkle, Ross Inman, Brandon Rickabaugh, Corey Miller, Keith Loftin, and Travis Dickinson. Thanks to Chris Lee and Brandon Watts Tejedor for their research assistance and to Jacob Brunton for putting together the bibliography. While pictures might not be worth a thousand words, they do help us imaginatively understand the ideas developed in this book. I thank Russell Lightner for his creativity and skill in bringing the concepts developed in this book to life through graphic art. To Paul Maxwell, Ryan Pazdur, Matt Estel, and Elise Emmert, who read the manuscript and offered numerous improvements, thank you for your insight, encouragement, and patience. I could not have hoped for better editors or a better team at Zondervan. Thanks also to the editors of C. S. Lewis Institute's journal *Knowing and Doing* for permission to reproduce in chapter 2 part of my essay "Is Bigger Better? C. S. Lewis, Atheism, and the Argument from Size" from their Winter 2015 issue. To my children, thanks for putting up with a father who always pokes and prods with questions at the dinner table. I write this book so you might find your way in an increasingly disenchanted culture. Finally, to my wife, Ethel, thanks for being God's gift to me. I am a better person because of you. (The book is better because of you too—thanks for your skillful edits on every page.) Thanks for being my constant companion and champion as together we seek to live for Jesus and the gospel.

CHAPTER 1

WHAT IS CULTURAL APOLOGETICS?

From a humble beginning, its presence is now worldwide. It impacts all aspects of daily life, shapes life's rhythm, expands our possibilities, and creates even as it fulfills desire. Its banner is instantly recognizable; its reach is nearly universal. Am I describing the church or the cross of Christ? No, I'm talking about the fast-food giant McDonald's. A visit to the company's home page reveals its sense of manifest destiny: "Can you imagine a world without the Big Mac? Or Chicken McNuggets? Or Happy Meals? Luckily, back in 1954, a man named Ray Kroc discovered a small burger restaurant in California, and wrote the first page of our history."[1]

Yet even such an iconic American (and now worldwide) staple as McDonald's is not immune to difficulty. As concerns over the rise of obesity and obesity-related illnesses increase, the McDonald's image has become tarnished. McDonald's is now viewed as a part of the problem. Documentaries such as *Super Size Me*, in which Morgan Spurlock eats only Big Macs, Double Quarter Pounders, Egg McMuffins, and other McDonald's offerings for thirty days with devastating results, don't help.[2] Attempts to rebrand the fast-food chain as a healthy option have largely fallen on deaf ears. Silver bullet fixes (such as the 1991 introduction of the McLean Deluxe) have failed. Now McDonald's seems to be settling in for the long haul, attempting to refurbish its image through a

---

1. "Our Company," McDonald's, https://www.mcdonalds.com/bh/en-bh/ourcompany.html.
2. See also Spurlock's book that followed the 2004 documentary, *Don't Eat This Book: Fast Food and the Supersizing of America* (New York: Putnam, 2005). Spurlock's documentary has not gone unchallenged, however. See, for example, Ken Hoffman, "Ordering up Some Food for Thought," *Houston Chronicle*, January 15, 2008, http://www.chron.com/life/hoffman/article/Ordering-up-some-food-for-thought-1627633.php.

multitude of little changes. In the meantime, however, sales and profits have plummeted worldwide as upscale fast-casual restaurants such as Chipotle and Smashburger eat away at their market share.[3]

At a superficial level, Christianity and McDonald's have much in common. Christianity too had a humble beginning and now exerts worldwide influence. Christianity, like McDonald's, affects all aspects of daily life. Its banner—the cross—is as universally recognizable as the golden arches. Yet like McDonald's, Christianity suffers from an image problem. Scandals, affairs, and inflated egos in pulpits across America have diminished the church's credibility as a beacon of moral authority. Division within the church on issues such as abortion, race, same-sex marriage, how to help the poor and the immigrant, and gun control give the impression that the church is beholden more to the spirit of the age than the eternal Word of God. Alarmingly, youth are leaving the church in record numbers.

Our comparison between McDonald's and Christianity only goes so far. Christianity is often maligned and misunderstood, but the truth is that it has unequivocally been good for the world. For McDonald's food, the verdict is less conclusive.[4]

Around the world, interest in religion has increased in the twenty-first century. Yet our culture in the West is becoming increasingly post-, sub-, and anti-Christian. If these trends continue, people will grow more hostile to the gospel, incapable of understanding and embracing the good news. The problem is not simply "out there" in the culture. The church has grown anti-intellectual and sensate, out of touch with the relevancy of Jesus and the gospel to contemporary life. Marred by scandal, infighting, and a lack of conviction, the church's prophetic voice, once resounding with power on issues of slavery and human rights, is now but a whimper. The gospel no longer receives a fair hearing (the Christian *voice* is muted). Christians find themselves as morally fragmented as their non-Christian neighbors (the Christian *conscience* is muted). The collective imagination of Christian culture is focused on the mundane (the Christian

---

3. See Stephanie Strom, "McDonald's Seeks its Fast-Food Soul," *New York Times*, March 7, 2015, http://www.nytimes.com/2015/03/08/business/mcdonalds-seeks-its-fast-food-soul.html?_r=0.

4. I'm concerned here mainly with the quality and healthiness of its food, not with issues related to economics, such as the apparently good result that McDonald's provides gainful employment for thousands of people around the world, and through its suppliers even more, and thus is a source of economic flourishing for many, all of which is hotly debated.

imagination is muted). And the prospect of a genuine missionary encounter is diminished. All too often, Christianity is relegated to the margins of culture, viewed as implausible, undesirable, or both. Like the struggling fast-food giant, the church today has an image problem.

A GENUINE MISSIONARY ENCOUNTER IS NEEDED

In the year 1936, a twenty-seven-year-old man named Lesslie Newbigin set out from England for India to share Christ among the Hindus. Newbigin faithfully ministered in India for the next thirty-eight years. When he returned to his home country in 1974, he found it had become a drastically different country from the one he left. It was becoming increasingly a post-Christian nation, one in need of a fresh missionary encounter.

It was during this time that Newbigin wrote what is now considered a modern classic on mission, *Foolishness to the Greeks*. In his book, he explores the most crucial question of our time. He asks:

> What would be involved in a missionary encounter between the gospel and this whole way of perceiving, thinking, and living that we call "modern Western culture"?[5]

This is *the* question to be asked of any post-Christian culture. Newbigin is interested in how we can talk to others about Jesus in a way that is understood by those becoming further and further removed from Christianity's language and worldview. This is the "missionary encounter" Newbigin has in mind. And while Newbigin's question is essential for us to answer today, it also leads us to an even bigger question: What do you make of Jesus Christ? Newbigin understood that every person in every culture is shaped by what sociologist Peter Berger calls "plausibility structures." Berger says every culture has a collective mind-set, a collective imagination, and a collective conscience. This combined outlook shapes the culture's view of the world and what is judged within the

---

5. Lesslie Newbigin, *Foolishness to the Greeks: The Gospel and Western Culture* (Grand Rapids: Eerdmans, 1986), 1.

culture as plausible or implausible. Is this a genuine possibility . . . or just an outrageous idea?

Newbigin knew that we fail to have genuine missionary encounters if we fail to understand those we seek to reach with the gospel. Our words and our message must be understandable. In a post-Christian society, talk about Jesus is no different from talk about Zeus or Hermes. We sound foolish, and our beliefs appear implausible and meaningless.

How can we have a genuine missionary encounter in our culture? This is the question that drives the work of cultural apologetics. The term "cultural apologetics" itself has not been widely used until recently, but little has been written on how we are to understand this new kind of cultural engagement. Ken Myers, the producer and host of *Mars Hill Audio Journal*, offers the following definition:

> Traditional apologetics is concerned with making arguments to defend Christian truth claims, and has often addressed challenges to Christian belief coming from philosophical and other more intellectual sources. The term "cultural apologetics" has been used to refer to systematic efforts to advance the plausibility of Christian claims in light of the messages communicated through dominant cultural institutions, including films, popular music, literature, art, and the mass media. So while traditional apologists would critique the challenges to the Christian faith advanced in the writings of certain philosophers, cultural apologists might look instead at the sound bite philosophies embedded in the lyrics of popular songs, the plots of popular movies, or even the slogans in advertising ("Have It Your Way," "You Deserve a Break Today," "Just Do It").[6]

Notice that, according to Myers, the cultural apologist is concerned with truth, argument, and the plausibility of Christianity. The main point of contrast between the traditional apologist and the cultural apologist has to do with the kinds of evidence utilized in making a case for Christianity. For the traditional apologist, academic sources, such as philosophy, science, and history,

---

6. This excerpt is from a June 2005 fundraising letter by Ken Myers found in Michael Poor, "A Primer: Cultural Apologetics . . .," The Humanitas Forum on Christianity and Culture, November 7, 2013, http://humanitas.org/?p=2552.

are prioritized in providing evidence for arguments. But for the cultural apologist, cultural artifacts—illustrations from the world of music, art, sports, entertainment, social relations, and politics—are paramount.

Some are less enthusiastic about the emergence of cultural apologetics. William Lane Craig, a traditional apologist *par excellence*, claims cultural apologetics

> constitutes an entirely different sort of apologetics than the traditional model, since it is not concerned with epistemological issues of justification and warrant. Indeed it does not even attempt to show in any positive sense that Christianity is true; it simply explores the disastrous consequences for human existence, society and culture if Christianity should be false.[7]

According to Craig, the cultural apologist is not concerned with the truth, plausibility, or justification of Christianity, but merely with showing the disastrous consequences of a godless world. I disagree.

My proposed definition for the task of cultural apologetics is broader than, though still inclusive of, Myers's and far more positive than Craig's. I define cultural apologetics as the *work of establishing the Christian voice, conscience, and imagination within a culture so that Christianity is seen as true and satisfying.* How does this conception of cultural apologetics fit into the discipline of apologetics and relate to the debates over apologetic method, cultural engagement, and worldview analysis?

Regarding the question of apologetic method, my proposed definition of cultural apologetics is neutral, and I believe compatible, with many of the prominent approaches. One can be, for example, a classical apologist, an evidentialist, a cumulative case apologist, a presuppositionalist, or a Reformed Epistemologist and still employ the approach suggested in this book.[8] The method suggested here is more general and inclusive than the oft-debated question of which epistemology best fits apologetics.

Since the Enlightenment, apologetics has primarily been conceived as a

---

7. William Lane Craig, *Reasonable Faith: Christian Truth and Apologetics*, 3rd ed. (Wheaton, IL: Crossway, 2008), 65, cited in Mark Coppenger, *Moral Apologetics for Contemporary Christians: Pushing Back against Cultural and Religious Critics* (Nashville: B&H, 2011), 4.

8. For a lively debate over which of these apologetic methods is best, see Steven B. Cowan, ed., *Five Views on Apologetics* (Grand Rapids: Zondervan, 2000). See also Brian K. Morley, *Mapping Apologetics: Comparing Contemporary Approaches* (Downers Grove, IL: InterVarsity Press, 2015).

defense of the *reasonableness* of Christianity.[9] With the demise of Enlightenment rationality in the twentieth century, alternative models of apologetics have been proposed. Many of these newer proposals resist the reductionistic impulse of modernity, seeking a return to an integrated, and more ancient, way of conceiving the task of bearing witness. We now read of apologetics beyond reason, joy-based apologetics, imaginative apologetics, moral apologetics, sapiential apologetics, popologetics, and more.[10] With the flourishing of new ways of conceiving apologetics, it will be helpful to provide a taxonomy of the discipline in order to locate my proposal.

Approaches to apologetics that begin with (or focus primarily on) reason or the imagination or the human conscience are classified, accordingly, as rational, imaginative, or moral apologetics. Cultural apologetics acknowledges all of these approaches and integrates them into a vision of what it means to be an embodied human that shapes and is shaped by culture, offering what I think is a more realistic and compassionate approach to apologetics. The cultural apologist affirms man's rational nature, but situates it within a more comprehensive account of what it means to be human. I claim a new lane then for cultural apologetics as I conceive it (see figure 1.1).

In addition, a cultural apologist operates at two levels. First, she operates *globally* by paying attention to how those within a culture perceive, think, and live, and then she works to create a world that is more welcoming and thrilling and beautiful and enchanted.[11] Secondly, she operates *locally*, removing

---

9. Classic examples include John Locke's 1695 work *The Reasonableness of Christianity* (Oxford: Oxford University Press, 1999); and William Paley's 1802 work *Natural Theology* (Oxford: Oxford University Press, 2006). More recent works in this tradition include J. P. Moreland, *Scaling the Secular City: A Defense of Christianity* (Grand Rapids: Baker, 1987); and Craig's *Reasonable Faith*.

10. For a recent proposal of apologetics that moves beyond a purely rationalistic approach, see James W. Sire, *Apologetics beyond Reason: Why Seeing Really Is Believing* (Downers Grove, IL: InterVarsity Press, 2014); for more on "joy-based apologetics," see Randy Newman, *Bringing the Gospel Home: Sharing Your Faith with Family and Friends* (Wheaton, IL: Crossway, 2011), 57; for examples of imaginative apologetics, see Holly Ordway, *Apologetics and the Christian Imagination: An Integrated Approach to Defending the Faith* (Steubenville, OH: Emmaus Road, 2017); and Joseph D. Wooddell, *The Beauty of the Faith: Using Aesthetics for Christian Apologetics* (Eugene, OR: Wipf & Stock, 2011); for examples of moral apologetics, see David Baggett and Marybeth Baggett, *The Morals of the Story: Good News about a Good God* (Downers Grove, IL: InterVarsity Press, 2018); and Coppenger, *Moral Apologetics*; for sapiential apologetics, see Kevin J. Vanhoozer, *Pictures at a Theological Exhibition: Scenes of the Church's Worship, Witness, and Wisdom* (Downers Grove, IL: InterVarsity Press, 2016), ch. 10; for an energetic exploration of pop culture and apologetics, see Ted Turnau, *Popologetics: Popular Culture in Christian Perspective* (Phillipsburg, NJ: P&R, 2012).

11. For more on our role as *creators* and *cultivators* of the good, the true, and the beautiful, see Andy Crouch, *Culture Making: Recovering Our Creative Calling* (Downers Grove, IL: InterVarsity Press, 2008).

obstacles to, and providing positive reasons for, faith so individuals or groups will see Christianity as true and satisfying, plausible and desirable.

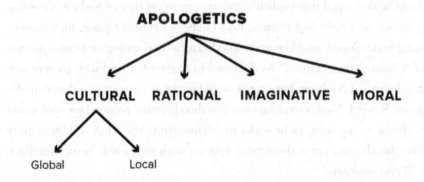

FIGURE 1.1: Cultural Apologetics and the Discipline of Apologetics

The global component to cultural apologetics needs to be distinguished, on the one hand, from the debate over Christ's relationship to culture, a debate framed largely by H. Richard Niebuhr's 1951 book *Christ and Culture*, and, on the other hand, the activity of worldview analysis championed by Francis Schaeffer, Nancy Pearcey, and James Sire.[12] Regarding the relationship between Christ and culture, the cultural apologist finds insight from all of Niebuhr's five possible postures (Christ against, of, above, in paradox with, and as the transformer of culture) yet need not endorse any one position as definitive. While I find taxonomies like Niebuhr's somewhat helpful, I do not explicitly endorse any one of his positions in this book. I think the actual relationship between Christ and culture is more nuanced than any of these five postures, and to adopt one over another is to risk painting with too broad a brush. I do think, however, that sociologist James Davison Hunter's "faithfully present within" is the most defensible approach or posture toward culture for the Christian as well as the cultural apologist.[13]

---

12. H. Richard Niebuhr, *Christ and Culture* (New York: Harper & Row, 1951). See also, D. A. Carson, *Christ and Culture Revisited* (Grand Rapids: Eerdmans, 2008). On the topic of worldview, see Francis Schaeffer, *How Should We Then Live? The Rise and Decline of Western Thought and Culture*, 50th anniv. ed. (Wheaton, IL: Crossway, 2005); Nancy Pearcey, *Total Truth: Liberating Christianity from Its Cultural Captivity* (Wheaton, IL: Crossway, 2004); and James Sire, *The Universe Next Door*, 5th ed. (Downers Grove, IL: InterVarsity Press, 2009).

13. Hunter unpacks his positive proposal toward culture in *To Change the World: The Irony, Tragedy, and Possibility of Christianity in the Late Modern World* (Oxford: Oxford University Press, 2010).

I adopt Hunter's "faithfully present within" culture approach, augmented by Andy Crouch's insight that Christians are called to be creators and cultivators of the good, true, and beautiful. Alternative accounts of cultural apologetics could be developed that explicitly endorse one or another of Niebuhr's possible positions on Christ and culture. Rod Dreher's *Benedict Option*, for example, suitably developed, could be understood as a cultural apologetic from a posture of "Christ against culture." As discussed in chapter 6, I find such an approach problematic. I do think, however, it would count as a version of cultural apologetics. Kevin J. Vanhoozer's sapiential or theodramatic proposal for apologetics is closest to my own, as he seeks to "demonstrate the truth of Christianity (the theodrama, not a theoretical system) with our whole being: intellect, will and emotions."[14]

The cultural apologist is also deeply interested in the many worldviews found within culture and how they find expression in the cultural goods produced and consumed by others. Each of these topics is important for the first task of the cultural apologist—the task of *understanding* culture. I do a fair amount of worldview analysis in chapters 2 and 3. Any cultural apologetic worth its salt will do likewise. The cultural apologist does not stop with understanding, however. As we shall see, the cultural apologist works to awaken those within culture to their deep-seated longings for goodness, truth, and beauty. Part of that process involves engaging with and working within the culture-shaping institutions—the university, the arts, business, and government—to help others see the reasonableness and desirability of Christianity. Worldview analysis is necessary but not sufficient for a cultural apologetic.

The cultural apologist works to *resurrect relevance* by showing that Christianity offers plausible answers to universal human longings. And she works to *resurrect hope*, creating new cultural goods and rhythms and practices that reflect the truth, beauty, and goodness of Christianity.[15] To summarize, cultural apologetics is defined as the *work of establishing the Christian voice, conscience, and imagination within a culture so that Christianity is seen as true and satisfying*, and it has both a global and local component. As we shall see,

---

14. Vanhoozer, *Pictures at a Theological Exhibition*, 233.
15. The phrase "resurrecting relevance" comes from S. Michael Craven, *Uncompromised Faith: Overcoming Our Culturalized Christianity* (Colorado Springs: NavPress, 2009).

this definition allows—even necessitates—the use of philosophy, science, and history as well as the creation of new cultural artifacts in making a case for Christianity. Broader than Myers's characterization of cultural apologetics, and contrary to Craig, cultural apologetics *is* concerned with the truth and justification of Christianity. Cultural apologetics must demonstrate not only the *truth* of Christianity but also its *desirability*.

Now that we have defined the problem facing Christianity in Western culture and have established a working definition of what we mean by cultural apologetics, the remainder of this book attempts to outline the contours of a model for how to proclaim and embody the gospel in ways understandable to particular human cultures. In this there is no better place to begin than by following the lead of the apostle Paul as he engages the Greeks in Athens.

PAUL ON MARS HILL

On his second missionary journey, after being run out of Thessalonica and Berea, Paul found himself in Athens waiting for the arrival of his companions, Silas and Timothy. Athens was one of the greatest cities of the ancient world, a center of intellectual and cultural achievement. Great philosophers such as Socrates, Plato, Aristotle, Zeno, Epictetus, and Epicurus lived there. Athens also produced famous playwrights such as Menander and Aristophanes, as well as important historians such as Thucydides. A walk through the agora (the marketplace) would reveal a pantheon of idols, indicative of the Athenians' religious devotion. One could find temples for the worship of Roman Caesars, Greek and Roman gods, and countless other shrines and idols. A novelist at the time wrote of Athens, a city of roughly 25,000 people, "It is easier to meet a god in the street than a human."[16] It is no wonder Paul was "greatly distressed" (Acts 17:16) as he walked the streets of Athens. He was confronted at every turn by multitudes of lifeless idols.

As Paul went about preaching Jesus and the resurrection, first in the synagogue and then in the marketplace (Acts 17:17), he was invited to address the

---

16. The quote comes from a character in the satirical novel the *Satyricon*, which was probably written by Roman courtier Petronius. See Paul Copan and Kenneth D. Litwak, *The Gospel in the Marketplace of Ideas: Paul's Mars Hill Experience for Our Pluralistic World* (Downers Grove, IL: InterVarsity Press, 2014), 30.

leaders of the city on Mars Hill. In his speech, we find a helpful model for engaging "our Athens" with the truth, beauty, and goodness of the gospel.[17]

First, Paul affirmed what he could affirm.

> Paul then stood up in the meeting of the Areopagus and said: "People of Athens! I see that in every way you are very religious. For as I *walked around* and *looked carefully* at your objects of worship, I even found an altar with this inscription: TO AN UNKNOWN GOD. So you are ignorant of the very thing you worship—and this is what I am going to proclaim to you." (Acts 17:22–23, italics added)

Notice that Paul did his homework. He "walked around" and meticulously examined the culture he sought to reach with the gospel. In his search, he found a starting point, a place where he could begin to build a bridge between something familiar to his audience and the gospel: their religiosity and their worship of an unknown god.

Second, Paul *outflanked the thinking of the Athenians*, showing them that the God they worshiped as unknown was actually true and knowable. "The God who made the world and everything in it is the Lord of heaven and earth and does not live in temples built by human hands" (Acts 17:24). Paul knew the Stoic and Epicurean philosophies of the day. He quoted their poets in order to show that this previously "unknown god" was the true God in whom "'we live and move and have our being.' As some of your own poets have said, 'We are his offspring'" (Acts 17:28). In quoting their poets, Paul demonstrated his intellectual credibility and challenged the audience to see the God he proclaimed as the God they were seeking all along (Acts 17:27).

Finally, Paul *confronted their rank idolatry*. In Acts 17:29 Paul moved the discussion out of the familiar world of the Greeks and into a distinctively Christian view of reality. In the past God overlooked ignorance. Now is the time to repent—to change one's beliefs and behavior—for God will one day judge the world in justice (Acts 17:30). Then Paul delivered his most controversial point: God gave "proof of this [gospel] to everyone by raising [Jesus] from the dead" (Acts 17:31).

---

17. This three-part framework of affirm, outflank, and confront is from N. T. Wright.

Paul's method in Athens is instructive. He understood the culture and employed that knowledge to identify a starting point for building a bridge to the gospel. We would be wise, like Paul, to consider "our Athens"—our own cultural context—as well as the kinds of bridges we can build between "our Athens" and the gospel. Lastly, we want to carefully consider the obstacles to bridge building that we must address along the way. Let's start by considering the "Athens" of our modern Western culture.

Our Athens

To frame our discussion, we can begin by following Newbigin and asking: what is the "whole way of perceiving, thinking, and living" in what we would today call modern Western culture (see figure 1.2)?

How does our culture *perceive* the world? In a word, we are *disenchanted*. The view of the world presented to us in the Bible is sacred and beautiful, yet our culture treats it as mundane, ordinary, and familiar. As a culture, we are "under a spell" of materialism. We assume concepts like beauty, goodness, and holiness, but they are disassociated from the wonder of receiving them as a gift from our Creator. Belief in God, faith, and religion are an embarrassment. Yet there is a universal longing for transcendence, a nostalgia for an enchanted

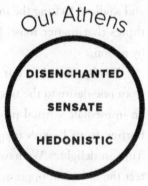

FIGURE 1.2: Our Athens

cosmos, something beyond the ordinary and mundane, that will not leave us. Modern culture is obsessed with "contraband transcendence"—a kind of spirituality and occultism that is antitheistic and antihumanistic. Moderns insist that everything is matter. At the same time, through their actions, they reveal a deep longing to connect to something beyond the material world. Some might call this spiritual pornography—a cheap substitute for the real and beautiful.[18] Human beings are created to worship that which is ultimate, but given the idolatry of the human heart in a disenchanted cosmos, the result is a shallow

---

18. See Peter Berger, "The Devil and the Pornography of the Modern Mind," in *Facing Up to Modernity* (New York: Basic Books, 1977), ch. 17; see also Berger's discussion of the "reality police-men" and their ban on any form of transcendence as "contraband goods" (202).

and ultimately unsatisfying attempt to find meaning, purpose, and identity in lifeless idols instead of in the transcendent God who created, sustains, judges, and redeems the world.

In addition to considering our culture's dominant way of perceiving, we also need to ask: How does our culture *think*? In a word, we are *sensate*. We are fixated on the physical, the sensory, and the material. As C. S. Lewis says through the words of the Senior Devil Screwtape, dispensing devilish advice to the Junior Devil Wormwood in the book *The Screwtape Letters*, our lives are focused on the "stream of experience" with little attention to universal matters.[19] Our whole education system trains us to fix our minds upon the material world. We become fixated on the here and now, with little thought of the there and then. The collective mind of our culture is largely anti-intellectual and shallow, lacking the intellectual categories or ability to think deeply about things that matter most. Many are guided more by feeling and desire than by reason.

Finally, how does our culture *live*? In a word, we are *hedonistic*. We move from one desire to the next, filling ourselves with bite-size pleasures that give an immediate sensual payoff, but end up enslaving us. We are captivated, to borrow from Lewis's imagery in *The Lion, the Witch, and the Wardrobe*, by Turkish delight.[20] We have a strong (and good) desire to advance justice, protect the poor and oppressed, and meet the needs of all people, but this desire ultimately falls short because we have a disenchanted view of reality and have embraced the corresponding "doctrines" of materialism, hedonism, and utilitarianism. The Christian virtues of faith, hope, and love have been replaced by the modern virtues of tolerance, personal autonomy, and progressivism (that is, a discarding of the oppressive ethical and religious view of the past).

Building Bridges to the Gospel

Given the reality of our postmodern "Athens," we discern at least three universal longings which can, following Paul, serve as starting points for building bridges to the gospel. The philosopher Peter Kreeft speaks of three longings of the human soul—truth, goodness, and beauty—and three prophets (or guides

---

19. C. S. Lewis, *The Screwtape Letters* (Westwood, NJ: Barbour, 1990), 11.
20. See Lewis, *The Lion, the Witch, and the Wardrobe* (New York: HarperCollins, 1998), where Edmund becomes addicted to Turkish delight at the instigation of the White Witch.

or capacities) of the human soul—reason, conscience, and the imagination. Each of these prophets can point to Jesus—the source of our longings for truth, beauty, and goodness, as revealed in the gospel (see figure 1.3).[21]

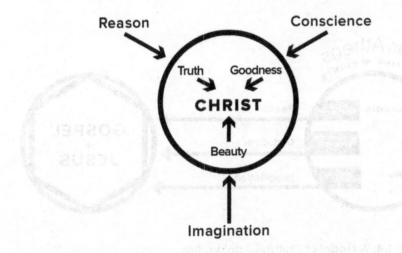

FIGURE 1.3: Christ the Source of Truth, Goodness, and Beauty

These three universal longings, for truth, goodness, and beauty, can serve as fitting starting points for a cultural apologetic, much like Paul's appeal to the Athenians' worship of an unknown God. Humanity was made to be nourished on them. These universal human longings cannot be eradicated. Unfortunately, they can be and often are muted and repressed. It's possible to settle for cheap counterfeits too. This is why God has provided guides within the human soul to help us on our journey. Reason guides us on the quest for truth. The conscience leads us to goodness. And the imagination transports us toward beauty. This is also why we have intellectuals, prophets, and artists. They can perform a priestly duty, leading us if we allow them toward the ultimate object of our soul's longing: Jesus Christ, the source of all truth, goodness, and beauty.

---

21. Peter Kreeft, *Back to Virtue: Traditional Moral Wisdom for Modern Moral Confusion* (San Francisco: Ignatius, 1992), 49. (Figure 1.3 is adapted from Kreeft's chart highlighting how all of goodness, truth, and beauty finds its source in Christ.) Cf. C. S. Lewis, *Miracles* (New York: Touchstone, 1996), who says, "The story of Christ demands from us and repays, not only a religious and historical but also an imaginative response. It is directed to the child, the poet, and the savage in us as well as to the conscience and to the intellect" (177n1).

If we utilize these three universal human longings as starting points from within culture to build bridges and connect them with the three "planks" of reason, conscience, and imagination, the following model of cultural engagement results (see figure 1.4):

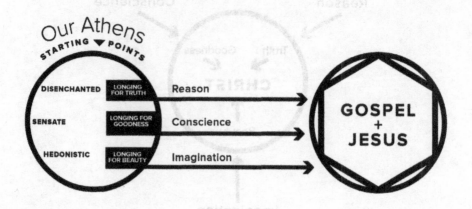

FIGURE 1.4: A Model of Cultural Apologetics

Let's briefly consider each universal longing and its quest for a fitting and satisfying object.

As rational animals, human beings naturally desire to know the truth about reality. As Aristotle puts it at the beginning of *The Metaphysics*, "All men by nature desire to know."[22] But this desire for the true knowledge of reality is often suppressed in our sensate culture. Part of the reason, as we shall see in chapter 2, has to do with the fact that when it comes to God, human beings often suppress the truth. Our job in seeking a missionary encounter with modern human beings is to reawaken the rational faculties of the soul to the reality of God and a God-bathed world. We want to help people see the truth clearly. One way to do this is to use the deliverances of philosophy, history, and science (prominent among other sources) to show there is such a thing as truth and that Christianity is the embodiment of that truth. How do we reawaken the rational sensibilities if they lie dormant today? Familiarity with evidence for belief in God, the historicity of the Gospels, and the resurrection of Jesus are

---

22. Aristotle, *Metaphysics* 980ᵃ21, in *The Complete Works of Aristotle*, vol. 2, ed. Jonathan Barnes (Princeton, NJ: Princeton University Press, 1984), 1552.

key. In ably articulating the truth of Christianity, we demonstrate intellectual credibility, humility, and our God-given call to love God with our minds.

Regarding the longing for goodness, we can consider that one tragedy of the fall is the loss of paradise. Our innate longings lead us, if we pay attention to them, to desire a better world, a world that has faded from conscious memory, yet that memory persists in our hearts. Deep within the human conscience, we find an unexplainable longing for wholeness, justice, and a meaningful life. We long to experience life "the way it was meant to be," even if we cannot explain why we think it should be that way. Because of sin, our efforts to attain happiness—the fulfillment of that inconsolable longing—have been frustrated. Our longing for goodness takes on specific form in our longings for wholeness, justice, and significance, all of which form contextual bridges to the gospel. By living lives of wholeness under the banner of Christ, finding Jesus as our greatest need and highest good, and seeking to be agents of shalom, of peace and reconciliation, in the world, we point others to the true object of this desire. Further, as we demonstrate (and articulate) a richer understanding of happiness, not as hedonistic, as contemporary caricatures suggest, but as "edenistic," we reawaken the human longing to live for something greater than self, something we once had in paradise but now have lost.[23]

Finally, the human longing for beauty is another plank we can use to begin building our bridge from "our Athens" to the gospel. Human beings are drawn to beauty. We are, as C. S. Lewis puts it, votaries "of the Blue Flower,"[24]—the mythical symbol, prevalent in German literature, of intense longing and desire for something that is on our horizon but remains elusive. This universal longing for beauty is nourished through the imagination. Our longing for beauty draws us to literature, film, music, and art; they entice us and awaken within us our desire for a world that dazzles and satisfies us. Like the apostle Paul in Athens, we can utilize the cultural narratives embodied in literature, film, music, and art to build bridges to the gospel.

What we find in Christianity is a perfect blending together of reason and romance, a comprehensive understanding of reality that speaks to both head and heart, rationality and experience. In a passage chronicling his preconversion

---

23. The idea of happiness as "edenistic" is from David Naugle, *Reordered Love, Reordered Lives: Learning the Deep Meaning of Happiness* (Grand Rapids: Eerdmans, 2008).

24. C. S. Lewis, *Surprised by Joy: The Shape of My Early Life* (Orlando: Harcourt, 1955), 7.

mind-set, Lewis wrote, "The two hemispheres of my mind were in the sharpest conflict. On the one side a many-island sea of poetry and myth; on the other a glib and shallow 'rationalism.' Nearly all that I loved I believed to be imaginary; nearly all that I believed to be real I thought grim and meaningless."[25] Lewis's discovery of the Christian story as true myth enabled him to bring the two parts of his mind together. He had found a place to stand and a story that understood him. As Lewis's spiritual story illustrates (see more in chapter 3), rich gospel themes are easy to find in the literature, films, music, and art produced by our culture. As cultural apologists part of our job as bridge builders is to find those points of common interest and make the gospel connections.

Addressing Barriers to the Gospel

As we seek a missionary encounter in our culture, we must address the barriers to belief (see figure 1.5).

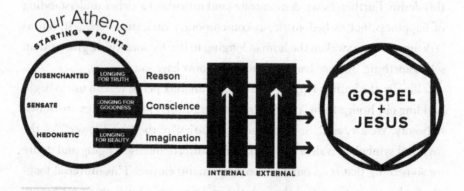

FIGURE 1.5: Barriers to Jesus and the Gospel

Sometimes these barriers are internal, erected by those within the church. At other times these barriers are external, caused by those outside the church. Throughout this book we will examine several barriers along the way as we unpack a model of cultural engagement. For now, we will briefly consider a few examples of how these internal and external barriers can thwart genuine missionary encounters.

---

25. Lewis, *Surprised by Joy*, 170.

One of the first barriers we find is internal, namely that Christians often view Jesus through the lens of their own culture. Christians tend to give Jesus moral and spiritual authority in their lives, but when it comes to gaining other kinds of knowledge, Christians tend to follow the rest of the culture in looking to scientists or Hollywood instead. Jesus is not often thought of as someone with intellectual virtue who is able to speak with authority on everything. Because of this attitude, Jesus is often seen as irrelevant in the Western world, especially on matters related to the acquisition of knowledge. By implication, those who follow him are viewed as amateurish, not to be taken seriously.

How do we challenge this barrier? It begins by revising how we see and present Christ to others. *As Christians, we must see Jesus as brilliant, a person of wisdom, and an expert on all matters.* Our incongruent view of Jesus contradicts the biblical witness. The Bible presents Jesus as rational, the sustainer of the universe, and the exact representation of God's being. He is the one in whom treasures of wisdom and knowledge are hidden (John 1:3; Col. 1:15–17; 2:3; Heb. 1:3). To put it plainly, Jesus is smart. Even more, he is brilliant. When Christians begin to regard Jesus not only as beautiful but as brilliant and wise, it will shift the way he is perceived in our culture.

In addition, *we must view (and defend) Christianity as public truth.* Today, religious claims generally and Christian claims specifically are viewed as subjective claims. The truth claims of Christianity are not understood as claims pointing to an objective, mind-independent reality. Rather they are viewed as private, subjective beliefs held by a few faithful individuals. As subjective beliefs, these claims are viewed as irrelevant to the so-called public marketplace of ideas. Christianity is marginalized and ignored since the claims Christians make are treated as a personal preference, not as something publicly testable, and not as claims that can compete for the mantle of "public truth." Our task in addressing this external barrier is to reassert Christianity as a knowledge tradition, a religion that makes claims about the world that can be tested and judged as true or false.

Further, we must recognize that there are culture-shaping institutions that exert an inordinate influence on the Western world. Our universities and educational institutions, the media, the arts, the business world, and the institutions of government each influence culture and can shape our understanding of what is true and good. As James Davison Hunter points out, "The work of world-making and world-changing are, by and large, the work of elites: gatekeepers who provide creative direction and management within spheres of social life."[26] As already noted, a missionary encounter requires Christians to engage both "upstream" within these centers of cultural influence and "downstream" where culture is largely consumed.

What should we hope to achieve by this? If a genuine missionary encounter between Christianity and Western culture were to happen, and the church could bridge the gap by pointing to the truth, goodness, and beauty the culture longs for, I believe it would lead to the reestablishment of the Christian imagination, mind, and conscience. Ultimately, this is possible only through the work of the Holy Spirit, but the Spirit will accomplish this work through human means, using human longings and desires to convict and redeem.

In this book, we will unpack a model of cultural apologetics inspired by Paul's speech on Mars Hill. I hope it will be *inspiring*, awakening within you your God-given desire to live for a cause greater than yourself, and *practical*, providing guidance for how you can influence those around you and the culture at large so that the gospel would take root in people's lives.

---

26. James Davison Hunter, *To Change the World: The Irony, Tragedy, and Possibility of Christianity in the Late Modern World* (Oxford: Oxford University Press, 2010), 41.

CHAPTER 2

DISENCHANTMENT

Oh yeah, life goes on. Long after the thrill of living is gone.

John Cougar Mellencamp

The eye is the lamp of the body. If your eyes are healthy,
your whole body will be full of light. But if your eyes are
unhealthy, your whole body will be full of darkness. If then
the light within you is darkness, how great is that darkness!

Matthew 6:22–23

The locus of human mystery," writes Marilynne Robinson, "is perception of this world. From it proceeds every thought, every art."[1] As I write that sentence, flames crackle off neatly cut logs as they burn in our family room fireplace. The aroma of burnt oak fills the air. My dog sleeps contently at my feet while my son plays a video game. The digital cheers of pixilated soccer fans join the chorus of background noises. My younger boys are upstairs playing games; occasionally, a golf-ball-turned-grenade careens down the stairwell, detonating against the door on the bottom floor. My daughter labors at her schoolwork, tapping her pencil on the desk to the beat of music pumping through her earphones. Our nine baby chicks, a birthday gift for our youngest son, chirp away in the laundry room. We are all awaiting my wife's return later in the day from a much-needed break in Florida. A person looking at us would

---

1. Marilynne Robinson, "Freedom of Thought," in *When I Was a Child I Read Books* (Thorndike, MA: Center Point, 2012), 27.

find nothing special about our leisurely Sunday afternoon. Yet, for those who have eyes to see, this moment is sacred. It possesses deep beauty and mystery. In the best sense of the word, it's magical.

Consider this: Who conjured the fire from the void, giving it light and power to destroy and bless, to consume and comfort? And what minds lie behind and beyond the pixelated images in my son's video game? What kind of intelligence creates such artifacts? To my boys playing make-believe upstairs, what is this precious gift we call imagination? How can two boys transport themselves from a twelve-by-twelve room in North Texas to the Wild West and a world of adventure, all at the snap of a finger? My daughter learning in the next room, a husband longing for his wife, a child aspiring to be a hero— what kind of creatures are we that we learn, hope, and long, transcending the necessities of bare survival? "What are mere mortals" the psalmist asks, "made . . . only a little lower than God" (Ps. 8:4–5 NLT)?

Or consider the beasts with us, the creatures who live in our home. Nine chicks a-chirping, one dog a-sleeping . . . yes, I'm breaking into song. Watching my son care for and play with these animals is itself a thing of beauty. This is a world that cries out to be examined and understood.

There is far more going on in my family room than a casual observer might see.

The grandeur of heaven is on display, if we have eyes to see. The music of heaven sings praise to God, if we have ears to hear. The aroma of heaven invites us to a feast, if we have the nose to smell.

"The locus of human mystery is perception of the world." Robinson speaks of a twofold mystery. There is the mystery of how our minds *connect with the world* in order that we might live in it, theorize about it, and re-present it to others in language, art, and music. And there is the mystery of how, in this world created, sustained, and loved by God, we *fail to see reality* in its proper light. It is a tale of two perceptions, two ways of perceiving the world.

TWO WAYS OF PERCEIVING

In C. S. Lewis's novel *The Magician's Nephew*, we read the story of the creation of Narnia, a fantastical world of talking animals that exists parallel to our own world.[2] Aslan, its creator, sings this magical world into being, and Digory and Polly, two human beings who arrived in Narnia at the moment of its creation, are filled with awe, joy, and delight. Yet also present at the creation event are Uncle Andrew, a self-serving occultist, and the wicked Queen Jadis. Unlike Digory and Polly, they look on Aslan's act of creation with horror and disgust.

Lewis intends to make a point here. He wants us to consider why Digory and Polly view the creation of Narnia so differently than Uncle Andrew and the wicked Queen Jadis. Lewis offers us an answer: "For what you see and hear depends a good deal on where you are standing: it also depends on what sort of person you are."[3] Through his imaginative fiction, Lewis wants us to consider two questions related to our perception. First, *where are you standing?* What story, of all the possible stories that give meaning to life, have you embraced? And related to this, *what sort of person do you want to be?* Do you want to live for small things, like Uncle Andrew, who saw one good thing about Narnia—the financial opportunity involved in turning broken parts into fully functioning lamps? Or do you wish to live for something greater than yourself?[4]

In the story, Lewis presents Uncle Andrew and Queen Jadis as individuals who cannot conceive of something more important than themselves. Lewis concludes from this that they were unable to *truly see* the world before them.[5] We might say they were blinded by their own pride and self-aggrandizement. Their self-absorption limited their visions, their perception of reality.

On the other hand, characters like Digory and Polly are open to a world beyond themselves, and as such, they see the creation of Narnia in its true light. Lewis uses this fictional story to contrast two ways of perceiving the world, a *disenchanted* way (Uncle Andrew and the wicked Queen Jadis) and an *enchanted* way (Digory and Polly).

Suzanne Collins portrays a similar contrast between two ways of perceiving in her bestselling book *The Hunger Games*.[6] In the novel, the Gamemakers call upon the main character, Katniss, to demonstrate her "skill" for the upcoming "hunger game," a survival-of-the-fittest competition with a single

2. C. S. Lewis, *The Magician's Nephew* (New York: HarperCollins, 1983).

3. Lewis, *The Magician's Nephew*, 136.

4. Thanks to David K. Naugle for this insight found in his *Worldview: The History of a Concept* (Grand Rapids: Eerdmans, 2002), 2.

5. Wesley A. Kort, *C. S. Lewis: Then and Now* (Oxford: Oxford University Press, 2001), 33.

6. Suzanne Collins, *The Hunger Games* (New York: Scholastic, 2008).

surviving winner. Katniss draws her bow and effortlessly hits her intended targets, receiving nothing but a nod from the Gamemakers.[7] They largely ignore her because they are enticed and distracted by the aroma of a newly arrived roast pig. Knowing that her life is on the line, Katniss shoots another arrow—right toward the Gamemakers, piercing the snout of the pig they are about to eat. Having secured their full attention, she bows and walks away.

Collins uses this scene to portray the sacredness of life through Katniss's will to live, juxtaposing it with the dead pig and the apathy of the Gamemakers, who are responsible for making life and death decisions but are unable to see beyond their own stomach. In the novel, Collins criticizes attempts to reduce the value of human life to spectacle and entertainment, emptying life of its sacredness.

Notice the connection between what we love and our perception. As people and things are drained of intrinsic value and become commodities to use instead of gifts to be cherished, our perception of the world shifts. As we devalue human life, we experience a corresponding struggle to "see" the evidence God has provided us of his existence.

Consider the common mantra of those who don't believe in God. They pose this challenge: "If God exists, then why doesn't he make himself more obvious? If there was any evidence for God, then I'd believe in him." Really? Is it that simple? This common challenge is problematic for two reasons. First, it wrongly assumes that no evidence for God exists and that God's existence *isn't* obvious. And second, it assumes that if the evidence for God were available, belief would automatically follow. But what if the problem goes deeper? What if there is a problem with our perception itself? What if the disease that hinders our belief distorts how we see?

As the philosopher Stephen Evans notes, given God's desire for humans to flourish in a loving relationship with him, we would expect the evidence for God to be *widely available*. At the same time, since God wants the relationship that humans enjoy with him to be freely and joyfully accepted, evidence for his existence would also be *easily resistible*.[8] For the evidence of his existence to be easily resistible, God must make the evidence for himself less than compelling.

---

7. Collins, *The Hunger Games*, 180–82.
8. C. Stephen Evans, *Natural Signs and Knowledge of God: A New Look at Theistic Arguments* (Oxford: Oxford University Press, 2010), 12–17.

As Evans suggests, "It might, for instance, be the kind of evidence that requires interpretation, and include enough ambiguity that it can be interpreted in more than one way."[9]

To be clear, I agree that the evidence for God is widely available. In fact, I would argue that we encounter millions of signposts pointing to God's existence, available for anyone with eyes to see.[10] As John Calvin famously says of the created universe,

> The final goal of the blessed [i.e., happy] life, moreover, rests in the knowledge of God. Lest anyone, then, be excluded from access to happiness, he not only sowed in men's minds that seed of religion of which we have spoken but revealed himself and daily discloses himself in the whole workmanship of the universe. As a consequence, men cannot open their eyes without being compelled to see him.[11]

Calvin connects our knowledge of God, which is available to all through his creation, to our longing for human happiness. As Lewis eloquently states, "God wills our good, and our good is to love Him (with that responsive love proper to creatures) and to love Him we must know Him: and if we know Him, we shall in fact fall on our faces."[12] God reveals himself because he wants us to flourish, and we will only truly flourish as our love for him grows.

God does not force himself upon us. He desires genuine love, and thus the evidence for his existence can, and often is, missed by those who think there is nothing outside themselves more important than themselves. As Blaise Pascal observes, "Wishing to appear openly to those who seek him with all their heart and hidden from those who shun him with all their heart, he has qualified our knowledge of him by giving signs which can be seen by those who seek him and not by those who do not."[13] Consider the religious leaders during the

---

9. Evans, *Natural Signs and Knowledge of God*, 15.

10. James W. Sire, *Apologetics beyond Reason: Why Seeing Really Is Believing* (Downers Grove, IL: InterVarsity Press, 2014), 24.

11. John Calvin, *Institutes of the Christian Religion*, ed. John T. McNeill, trans. Ford Lewis Battles, 2 vols. (Louisville: Westminster John Knox, 1960), 1:51–52.

12. C. S. Lewis, *The Problem of Pain* (San Francisco: HarperCollins, 1996), 46.

13. Blaise Pascal, *Pensées*, cited in Evans, *Natural Signs and Knowledge of God*, 16. Elsewhere Pascal says, "What can be seen on earth indicates neither the total absence, nor the manifest presence of divinity, but the presence of a hidden God. Everything bears this stamp." Pascal, *Pensées*, trans. A. J. Krailsheimer (New York: Penguin, 1995), 142, cited in Sire, *Apologetics beyond Reason*, 24.

time of Jesus. They were eyewitnesses to his miracles, able to talk with him and measure his claims and character against the plumb line of the Torah and prophecies about the coming messiah, yet they did not see him clearly or understand his mission. As John reports, "Even after Jesus had performed so many signs in their presence, they still would not believe in him" (John 12:37). Yet it was not just the Jews who were blind to God's reality. In Romans chapter 1, we learn that God provides evidence of his existence to everyone, yet many suppress this truth and worship idols instead of the one true God (Rom. 1:18–23).

What we find, in Scripture and in life, is that it is possible for two people to look at the same object or event and *see and understand it differently*. Our choices have a role in our perception. Will we be like Uncle Andrew and assume there is nothing important beyond ourselves? If we value ourselves above all else, we will perceive the world as harsh, flat, and nasty. Or will we be like Digory and Polly and choose to receive the things of this world in creaturely delight, looking beyond ourselves for clues to meaning and purpose?

What we see and understand depends, to some degree, on our perception of reality. To the extent that our primary way of perceiving the world is one of disenchantment, which is common in modern, materialist conceptions of reality, God's existence will be muted. The gospel message will seem implausible and, often, undesirable.

A MODEL FOR REENCHANTMENT

God wants to be known. And as God reveals himself to us through the storyline of the Bible, we learn that he pursues us in love, even as we run from him. "Love always wants to be known," Dallas Willard reminds us, and "God wants to be present to our minds with all the force of objects given clearly to ordinary perception."[14] Yet most of us don't experience God in such a concrete, ordinary way. Something seems to be missing from the equation. According to the Bible, what's missing is the work of the Holy Spirit. With the help of the Holy Spirit, we begin to see God and the world the way Jesus does and then to

---

14. Dallas Willard, *The Divine Conspiracy: Rediscovering Our Hidden Life in God* (New York: HarperCollins, 1998), 76–77.

invite others to see God in the same way. In other words, reenchantment is a work of the Holy Spirit.

But reliance upon the Holy Spirit should not prevent us from asking questions to diagnose the problem and seek a solution. In seeking a model of reenchantment that is both true to the way the world is and the way the world ought to be, we should ask how the world became disenchanted. What are the chief characteristics of our disenchantment? How can we join with God's Spirit to help others see the world in its proper light? The story of Scripture, several ancient thinkers (who hail from a more enchanted age) such as Saint Augustine and Thomas Aquinas, and modern writers like C. S. Lewis and Dallas Willard are helpful guides in answering these questions for our contemporary context.

In the Bible we find not only the greatest story ever told but the greatest *possible* story ever told.[15] It features man's tragedy, a divine comedy, and a fairy-tale ending.[16] It's an inviting story that points us, relentlessly, to the deep and abiding love of a God who creates, pursues, redeems, and restores all that he has made. We will explore this story in greater depth in the final chapter. For now, let's look at a simple plotline of the biblical story.

One of the most common ways to describe the plotline of Scripture is *creation—fall—redemption—restoration*.[17] There are countless variations on this movement, each emphasizing different metaphors, each one following the same progression. My preferred framework for understanding the story of the Bible uses the metaphor of home and moves in three parts: *home—away—home again*.[18] Essentially, part one involves God creating a place, then a people, and giving those people a purpose. This is the world as it should be (Gen. 1–2). We are *home*. Early in the story a conflict is introduced, and the people God creates decide to meet their needs apart from God. The result is catastrophe (Gen. 3), the second part of the storyline. We fall *away*. Yet God does not give up on the world he has made. He relentlessly pursues humanity through a grand narrative

---

15. See, e.g., the philosopher Alvin Plantinga and his argument that any best world would be a world that contains incarnation and atonement. See Plantinga, *Where the Conflict Really Lies: Science, Religion, and Naturalism* (Oxford: Oxford University Press, 2011), 59.

16. Frederick Buechner, *Telling the Truth: The Gospel as Tragedy, Comedy, and Fairy Tale* (New York: HarperCollins, 1977).

17. A helpful book on the overall storyline of the Bible is Vaughn Roberts, *God's Big Picture: Tracing the Storyline of the Bible* (Downers Grove, IL: InterVarsity Press, 2002).

18. This understanding of the biblical plotline is from Stephen Kirk, who was my pastor in West Lafayette, Indiana, when I was a graduate student in philosophy at Purdue.

spanning thousands of years. The story culminates in the act of God becoming a human being, taking on a human nature. God does this so human beings might find forgiveness for their sins and true happiness as God had originally intended. This is the third part of the story (Gen. 4–Rev. 22). We go *home again*. Some include a fourth part, though it is really an extension of the third, emphasizing that one day all will be restored and made new again. Notice the general pattern present in the movements of the story: from God to God, from creation to new creation, *exitus-reditus*, wander and return (see figure 2.1).

FIGURE 2.1: Exitus-Reditus

This pattern gives shape to the common storyline of individual lives. We see this pattern of wander and return in the life of Saint Augustine, for example. Augustine lived in the fourth century, and he chronicled his personal story in his spiritual autobiography, *Confessions*.[19] His story begins with these jarring words:

> You stir man to take pleasure in praising you, because you have made us for yourself, and our heart is restless until it rests in you.[20]

For a decade of his life, Augustine followed Manicheism, a pagan cult that believed God and evil were two equal forces dueling for the fate of the world. Yet despite his honest search for knowledge, his restless heart did not find peace or truth in Manicheism. As a young adult, Augustine came to believe that Christianity was true. In a dramatic event described in his autobiography, he bent his knee and became a follower of Christ. The longings of his heart for truth, goodness, and beauty found the proper object of their quest.

Augustine believed that his own story was a microcosm of *the* story. All things come from God and return to God. Reality is deeply valuable—alive at the core—and lovingly created and sustained by God for human well-being.

---

19. Saint Augustine, *Confessions*, trans. by Henry Chadwick (Oxford: Oxford University Press, 1998).
20. Augustine, *Confessions* 1.1 (p. 3).

For those who have eyes to see, reality is *the* story, and the Author bids us to "awake" and "enter in." In doing so we find rest for our weary souls. We come home to a place where we are loved, known, and belong.

Another of history's great minds, Thomas Aquinas was a theologian and philosopher who lived in the thirteenth century. Aquinas, like Augustine, believed reality is best understood in terms of wandering and returning. To capture the dynamic nature of God's unfolding story, Aquinas structured his monumental *Summa Theologiae* through the lens of this familiar scheme. The *Summa* begins with God, then moves to creation, man, Christ, the church, and last things. As Aquinas summarizes at the outset of his work:

> The principal aim of this sacred teaching is to convey knowledge of God, not only as he is in himself, but also as the origin and end of things, especially rational creatures. Accordingly, our exposition will proceed thus: we will first discuss God; second, the movement of rational creatures toward God; and third, Christ, who, as human, is the way for us to strive for God.[21]

Aquinas, like Augustine, believed we are all part of a larger, ongoing story. This story begins and ends with God. The pages of the story turn each day as we make our mark in this world.

In a little-known essay called "Talking about Bicycles," C. S. Lewis notes the four stages of enchantment each of us goes through (or should go through) with respect to "nearly everything" that exists.[22] He invites us to consider a bicycle. As a very young child, the bike means nothing to us. It is simply part of the world of grown-up gadgets. But once a child is old enough to ride a bike for the first time, the child looks at the bike very differently. The bike enchants us. We happily pedal around the neighborhood, exalting in our newfound freedom. Soon, however, the riding of bicycles becomes a chore. It is tiring, monotonous, uninspiring. Most people, according to Lewis, never move from this third stage, the disenchanted stage, onto the fourth. Yet a few, if they press through the third stage, experience a new and more profound appreciation of

---

21. Aquinas, *Summa Theologiae* 1.2, quoted in *The Treatise on the Divine Nature: Summa Theologiae I 1–13*, trans. Brian J. Shanley, OP (Indianapolis, IN: Hackett, 2006), 17–18.

22. C. S. Lewis, "Talking about Bicycles," *Present Concerns: Journalistic Essays*, ed. Walter Hooper (New York: Harcourt, 1986), 68.

the gift of bicycles in which "the fact of riding brings back a delicious whiff of memory."[23]

Lewis proceeds to name these four stages: "They are the Unenchanted Age, the Enchanted Age, the Disenchanted Age, and the Re-enchanted Age."[24] Lewis believed that while most people are stuck in a disenchanted age, the possibility of reenchantment is very real. These four stages can be applied broadly to our experience as individuals and to our culture. If we follow Lewis, the third stage of disenchantment becomes the worst of humanity's wandering from God, the result of man's tragic sin and rebellion against a loving Creator. Yet despite our disenchantment, God is alive and working to draw individuals (and groups of individuals) to himself, and he invites his followers to participate in that mission of redemption and restoration. The potential for reenchantment, given God's intention for humanity, remains a genuine possibility.

Putting together the insights gathered from Scripture, Augustine, Aquinas, and Lewis, I propose the following model of reenchantment to help us understand where we are, how we got here, and how we ought to proceed as cultural apologists (see figure 2.2). The model follows the pattern of wander and return.

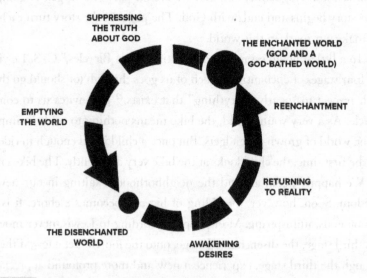

FIGURE 2.2: Model for reenchantment

---

23. Lewis, "Talking about Bicycles," 67.
24. Lewis, "Talking about Bicycles," 68.

Beginning with the enchanted world created by God, we move to stage two where human beings suppress the truth about God, emptying the world of all meaning, purpose, and beauty, and leaving us with a disenchanted world (stage three). The missionary work of the church, then, is conceived as a return to enchantment—a reenchantment of reality through the awakening of desires and a "return to reality."

In the rest of this chapter, we shall explore the descent into disenchantment. In the next chapter, we will explore the possibility of return.

SUPPRESSING THE TRUTH ABOUT GOD

The first step toward disenchantment is the suppression of truth about God. But what does it mean to suppress the truth?

We are shaped by what we value as great and good. We are moved by what we think lovely. We run to that which we think will satisfy our desire.[25] If we live for small things or for ourselves, we will not recognize the God-given signs of his existence and loving care. Distracted by what is infinitely less important, we fail to glorify God as God. We fail to give him thanks for his provision (Rom. 1:21). As Paul unpacks in the first chapter of his letter to the Romans, those who suppress the truth about God become "futile" in their thinking, "darkened" in their hearts, and foolish idolaters. They exchange "the glory of the immortal God for images made to look like a mortal human being and birds and animals and reptiles" (Rom. 1:23). As the theologian Norman Wirzba observes, "Idolatry is one of humanity's great sins because it encourages us to see and represent reality as, and thus limit reality to, the sphere of human power and convenience. It prompts us to reduce the world and God to the level of human appetite and expectation."[26]

When we fail to acknowledge God, this failure has catastrophic effects, corrupting our perception of reality. Everything goes wrong. Reality is turned on its head, and the "world as a whole is put out of joint."[27] This is why A. W.

25. Thanks to Rick Hove for this idea.
26. Norman Wirzba, *From Nature to Creation: A Christian Vision for Understanding and Loving Our World* (Grand Rapids: Baker Academic, 2015), 54.
27. N. T. Wright, *Paul for Everyone: Romans Part One; Chapters 1–8* (Louisville: Westminster John Knox, 2004), 16.

Tozer's statement rings true: "What comes into our minds when we think about God is the most important thing about us."[28] Tozer was speaking of individuals, yet his point is just as true of our broader cultural values. Our cultural beliefs regarding God's existence and nature are determinative factors in our culture's ability to see reality clearly. And our unwillingness to *know* and *worship* God as God is the first step of our descent into disenchantment.

EMPTYING THE WORLD

The ancients inhabited a world drastically different from ours. Populated with gods and goddesses, nymphs and dryads, monsters and spirits, heroes and lawgivers, their world was not tame or dull. Life was a colorful adventure, a battle between opposing forces. The world was supernaturally imbued with personalities and powers. At any moment, you might be in the presence of a god. Divine judgment for sins was a constant worry. The human experience of the world was one of mystery, enchantment, and sacredness.

Not so today. The world has been emptied of the divine and the sacred. Our experience of the world is diminished. This emptying of the world, as C. S. Lewis notes, has been a one-way progression ever since we began to try and make sense of our existence:

> At the outset the universe appears packed with will, intelligence, life, and positive qualities; every tree is a nymph and every planet a god. Man himself is akin to the gods. The advance of knowledge gradually empties this rich and genial universe: first of its gods, then of its colours, smells, sounds and tastes, finally of solidity itself as solidity was originally imagined.[29]

We have rejected knowledge of God and his purposes for creation, and our experience of the world has changed considerably. Yet as the inhabitants of the world were sifted through the caldron of this reductionist impulse, they rallied, making a comeback by transferring "to the subjective side of the account:

---

28. A. W. Tozer, *The Knowledge of the Holy* (New York: Harper & Row, 1961), 1.
29. C. S. Lewis, "The Empty Universe," *Present Concerns: Journalistic Essays*, ed. Walter Hooper (New York: Harcourt, 1986), 81.

classified as our sensations, thoughts, images or emotions."[30] We no longer believed that gods and goddesses existed, except perhaps in our minds,[31] and the same can be said for goodness, truth, and beauty. Values once thought to be the essential furniture of the world's living room, now only exist in the realm of the human mind. Once set on this trajectory, the emptying of the world could not be stopped: "While we were reducing the world to almost nothing we deceived ourselves with the fancy that all its lost qualities were being kept safe (if in a somewhat humbled condition) as 'things in our own mind.'"[32]

Over the last three centuries especially, as the richness of the sacred world was replaced by the barren desert of materialism, those same processes began to work on the human subject. The subject—the human individual—had become "gorged, inflated, at the expense of the Object."[33] Like an overinflated balloon ready to explode, man's sense of dignity, destiny, and value was poked and prodded by the steel point of unbridled pride until it eventually burst. Modern humanity, emptied of its soul, collectively sighed as sacredness vaporized into the crisp, cold air of this disenchanted age. As Lewis concludes, "In emptying out the dryads and the gods (which, admittedly, 'would not do' just as they stood) we appear to have thrown out the whole universe, ourselves included."[34]

As the world was emptied of the divine, space and time were drained of significance. Space is viewed today as nothing more than an empty container for particles in motion. The heavens are viewed by many as "chiefly, a vast empty space with a humanoid God and a few angels rattling around in it, while several billion human beings crawl through the tiny cosmic interval of human history on an oversized clod of dirt circling an insignificant star."[35] God or the gods, if they exist at all, are silent and distant. Time is divested of meaning and viewed as a commodity greedily dispensed only if a perceived benefit, usually a personal pleasure or accomplishment, ensues. It is little wonder that modern man, in such a universe, has aptly been described as an "empty self."[36]

30. Lewis, "The Empty Universe," 81.

31. As A. O. Balcomb describes the descent into disenchantment, "God was God in the world, then God was God of the gaps in the world, then God was pushed out of the world," in "Re-Enchanting a Disenchanted Universe: Post Modern Projects in Theologies of Space," *Religion and Theology* 16 (2009): 84.

32. Lewis, "The Empty Universe," 83.

33. Lewis, "The Empty Universe," 81.

34. Lewis, "The Empty Universe," 85.

35. Willard, *The Divine Conspiracy*, 74.

36. Philip Cushman, "Why the Self Is Empty," *American Psychologist* 45 (May 1990): 599–611.

EXCURSUS: PHILOSOPHICAL CAUSES
OF DISENCHANTMENT

Thus far, I've argued that the culture's descent into disenchantment is driven by a form of idolatry that elevates self to the place of God and sees any value the natural order might have as existing apart from a divine source. While I don't think that ideas alone move history as if severed from the networks of individuals, artifacts, and institutions that possess, embody, and propagate them, it is nonetheless illuminating to identify the root philosophical causes of disenchantment.[37] In understanding intellectual history as well as the junctures where the dominant thought patterns of culture began to veer from the path of truth, the cultural apologist can more effectively call others back to an integrated understanding of the natural and supernatural. While philosophers, theologians, and historians disagree over the details, they tend to agree that the unraveling of what Hans Boersma calls the "sacramental tapestry"[38] of the world can be traced to at least three philosophical ideas: nominalism, mechanism, and empiricism.[39]

Until roughly five hundred years ago, most people saw the world as sacred. Social orders reflected heavenly realities, that which could be observed by the senses did not exhaust all that exists, and the created world participated in some sense in the divine life. One important element in the history of the Christian church is the idea, adapted from Plato, that Forms or Ideals exist

---

37. For more on the erroneous view that ideas alone move the world, see James Davison Hunter, *To Change the World: The Irony, Tragedy, and Possibility of Christianity in the Late Modern World* (Oxford: Oxford University Press, 2010), 24–27.

38. Hans Boersma, *Heavenly Participation: The Weaving of a Sacramental Tapestry* (Grand Rapids: Eerdmans, 2011).

39. I am of course simplifying a long and complicated story. Charles Taylor asks, "How did [disenchantment] arise? There were many causes. People cite: Renaissance humanism, the scientific revolution, the rise of the 'police state', the Reformation. All of these are right." Taylor, *A Secular Age* (Cambridge, MA: Belknap, 2007), 61. Taylor goes on to argue that the root cause comes earlier, in the late medieval period, and the "rage for order" that expressed itself in the desire and attempt to close the gap between the church leadership and the commoner in terms of piety and religious practice (61–89). Hans Boersma speaks of "the medieval revolt of nature" that set the stage for disenchantment. These precursors to disenchantment include, according to Boersma, the juridicizing of the church under Pope Gregory VII (1073–85), the rediscovery of Aristotelian philosophy in the twelfth and thirteenth century, the increasing separation of the authority of Scripture and the church in the fourteenth and fifteenth century, and the sixteenth-century controversy over the separation of nature and the supernatural. Each of these episodes contributed to the eventual severance of the supernatural from the natural (*Heavenly Participation*, 52–67). For a helpful summary of the philosophical ideas that contribute to disenchantment as outlined here, see Jeffrey Koperski, *The Physics of Theism: God, Physics, and the Philosophy of Science* (Malden, MA: Wiley-Blackwell, 2015), 12–25.

as mind-independent realities.[40] Consider my son's pet chicken, Rosie. What makes Rosie a chicken instead of an oak tree or monkey? The answer is that Rosie, in addition to her matter (feathers, carbon atoms, organs, etc.) has a chicken *nature* or *essence*—a substantial form—that determines the kind of thing Rosie is and gives her the capacity to act. Rosie is a form-matter composite.[41] There are other chickens in our pen too. They are distinct things, having their own bits of matter. They also share something in common with Rosie and each other. The thing all chickens share that makes them chickens and gives them the capacity to act is their substantial form. These shareable forms are called, in the medieval debate, *universals*. Chickenhood is not the only universal, however. Arguably, for every natural thing we find in the world—chickens, armadillos, giraffes, goats, humans—there is a universal, a mind-independent substantial form or essence, that grounds the thing's character and abilities.

This picture of the world began to unravel in the late medieval period. One important consequence of *realism*, the view that mind-independent universals exist, is that the structure of the world imposes limits on what is possible, even for God. Even God can't change Rosie into an alligator. What God could do is cause Rosie to cease to exist and in her place create an alligator. What God can't do, however, is cause Rosie the chicken to be an alligator. After all, Rosie is a chicken. Moreover, God too has an essential nature that imposes limits on his ability to act (for example, traditionally God cannot do the logically impossible or anything inconsistent with his essential goodness, such as evil acts).

Some fourteenth century theologians didn't like the idea of God being restricted by his own essence or the essence of things in the world. William of Ockham (1287–1347) argued that God can do whatever he wants. God's power is absolute. Extreme versions of what is called voluntarism allow that God could command murder as morally right, make contradictions logically true, or bring about four-sided triangles. For God to have this kind of power, essences had to be removed from the world. Ockham argued for a view called *nominalism*.

---

40. Boersma, *Heavenly Participation*, 80.

41. For an excellent discussion of the debate over the nature of substance, understood in terms of matter and form, see William M. R. Simpson, "Knowing Nature: Beyond the False Dilemma of Reduction or Emergence," in *Knowing Creation: Perspectives from Theology, Philosophy, and Science*, ed. Andrew B. Torrance and Thomas H. McCall (Grand Rapids: Zondervan, 2018), 237–59.

Nominalists reject belief in universals. There are no shareable essences in the world. Whatever traits chickens have in common can be explained without an appeal to universals. So too for every other creature in the world, including humans. They share things in "name" (*nomen*) only in virtue of the absolute and free will of an omnipotent God. This "fateful doctrine of nominalism," wrote the historian Richard M. Weaver, "was the crucial event in the history of Western culture; from this flowed those acts which issue now in modern decadence."[42]

Nominalism removed form, and formal causation, from the world. The medieval picture of the cosmos as an organism that strives toward some end, as well as the Aristotelian idea of final causation, soon crumbled too. "The nominalist rejection of universals," writes the philosopher Michael Gillespie, "was thus a rejection not merely of formal but also of final causes."[43] The nature-as-organism picture of the world was soon replaced with a nature-as-mechanism view.[44] Without substantial forms, matter—now understood as corpuscles—became the fundamental substance of the universe. Causal powers were no longer located within substances. Rather, immutable laws of nature governed the behavior of inert microphysical pieces of matter. By the sixteenth and seventeenth century, the universe was understood as a great clock, a mechanism, fully describable in terms of matter in motion. Henry Oldenburg (c. 1619–77), the first secretary of the Royal Society in London, complimented the mechanistic philosopher Robert Boyle (1627–91) for having "driven out that drivel of substantial forms," which "has stopped the progress of true philosophy [science], and made the best of scholars not more knowing as to the nature of particular bodies than the meanest ploughmen."[45] By the eighteenth century, occult qualities and substantial forms had all but disappeared from mainstream philosophy and science.[46] The cosmos could be understood in its entirety in terms of matter and empirically discoverable laws of motion.

42. Richard M. Weaver, *Ideas Have Consequences* (Chicago: University of Chicago Press, 1948), 3. The root crisis of modernity then has its roots in theology and this particular conception of omnipotence. For more, see Michael Allen Gillespie, *The Theological Origins of Modernity* (Chicago: University of Chicago Press, 2008); and Boersma, *Heavenly Participation*, 20.

43. Gillespie, *The Theological Origins of Modernity*, 24.

44. Koperski, *The Physics of Theism*, 16.

45. Henry Oldenburg, *Correspondence*, ed. and trans. A. R. Hall and M. B. Hall (Madison: University of Wisconsin Press, 1965), 3:67, quoted in Simpson, "Knowing Nature," 246.

46. Simpson, "Knowing Nature," 246.

This changing conception of nature and the natural led to advances in experimental science, which in turn secured the ascendancy of empiricism as the dominant epistemology. According to David Hume (1711–76), if we are going to arrive at a true account of human nature and our place in nature, then "the only solid foundation we can give to this science itself must be laid on experience and observation."[47] The only truths that can be known according to empiricism are those that come from the senses. As Nancy Pearcey summarizes, in late modernity "a biblically informed respect for empirical fact, which had inspired science to begin with, was replaced by empiri*cism*, a philosophy that elevates the senses to the sole source of truth."[48] The stage was set for the forces of decreation to purge the world of its riches.[49] Immaterial minds, sacred order, and moral and aesthetic values were about to be emptied from the universe as presumptuous and chimerical postulations of a bygone era.

The moves from realism to nominalism, from nature-as-organism to nature-as-mechanism, and from a healthy respect for empirical facts to empiricism each helped set the stage for the nineteenth-century ascendancy of Marx, Nietzsche, and Darwin and the complete severance of the sacred order from the natural (and social) order. The resultant disenchantment and "the notion of a culture that persists independent of all sacred orders," writes Philip Rieff, "is unprecedented in human history."[50] The materialism, reductionism, scientism, naturalism, Darwinism, and nihilism of our day find their roots in the changing philosophical and cultural scene of the late medieval and early modern period.[51]

---

47. Hume, David. *A Treatise of Human Nature*, eds. David Fate Norton and Mary J. Norton (Oxford: Oxford University Press, 2005), 4.

48. Nancy Pearcey, *Saving Leonardo: A Call to Resist the Secular Assault on Mind, Morals, and Meaning* (Nashville: B&H, 2010), 108.

49. The language of *decreation* and *decreators* is from Philip Rieff, *My Life among the Deathworks: Illustrations of the Aesthetics of Authority* (Charlottesville, VA: University of Virginia Press, 2006).

50. Rieff, *My Life among the Deathworks*, 13.

51. To cite but two examples of contemporary heirs of Hume, Nietzsche, Darwin, and their horde, consider the late philosopher David Lewis and the theoretical physicist Sean Carroll. According to David Lewis, the world is composed of a "vast mosaic of local matters of particular fact, just one little thing and then another. . . . And that is all." Lewis, introduction to *Philosophical Papers*, vol. 2 (Oxford: Oxford University Press, 1986), ix. Sean Carroll's understanding of our empty world is bold and unapologetic too: "Categories such as "male" and "female" are human inventions—stories we tell because it helps us make sense of our world. The basic stuff of reality is quantum wave function, or a collection of particles and forces—whatever the fundamental stuff turns out to be. Everything else is overlay." Carroll, *The Big Picture: On the Origins of Life, Meaning, and the Universe Itself* (New York: Dutton, 2017), 142.

CHARACTERISTICS OF DISENCHANTMENT

What began as the suppression of truth about God has led to, in the West at least, disenchantment. Emptied of transcendence, the human experience of the world fades to grey. Moral distinctions between right and wrong, good and evil, are erased, and aesthetic evaluations of what is beautiful and what is horrid begin to blur. Everything once held dear and valued as sacred is now up for grabs. This even extends to the very concepts of goodness, truth, and beauty themselves. Without an underlying vision of the world as magical or mysterious, life is utterly mundane. The divine fabric that holds together the warp and woof of reality is severed: "When mankind no longer lives spontaneously turned toward God or the supersensible world—when, to echo the words of Yeats, the ladder is gone by which we would climb to a higher reality—[we all] must stand face to face with a flat and inexplicable world."[52] The world as perceived and experienced today by individuals in modern, Western culture is disenchanted, purged of the sacred and transcendent.

So how should thoughtful Christians respond to and engage those who perceive the world in this manner? Before we land on a model for engagement, we must first understand the four characteristics of our world's disenchantment: the felt absence of God, a consumer culture, blindness and foolishness, and idolatry.

The "Felt Absence of God"

A highlight of my time as a graduate student at Purdue University was teaching philosophy classes. In the crucible of the classroom, I transitioned from learning about philosophy to becoming a philosopher. My students pushed and prodded me to articulate, clarify, and defend my positions. Is there a God? What is the meaning of life? Can we know anything? What is truth?

At the beginning of each semester I assign my students a worldview paper where they answered, without any additional research, these core, perennial questions. Over the course of the semester we would engage, one by one, each question by exploring the intellectual options, probing the strengths and weaknesses of each view, and seeking together to find the truth. At the end of the

---

52. William Barrett, *Irrational Man: A Study in Existential Philosophy* (New York: Anchor, 1962), 49, quoted in Pearcey, *Saving Leonardo*, 170.

semester, students would rewrite this worldview paper utilizing the arguments and evidence they had learned to justify and defend their views.

After spending six weeks of the class discussing the question of God, invariably I noticed that most students moved from unbelief or nonbelief to a firm conviction that God existed. They found the traditional arguments for God (ontological, cosmological, teleological, and moral) strong and compelling. When I first witnessed this shift from unbelief to belief in God I was elated, reasoning that if you accept that God exists, everything else changes after that acceptance. But I was wrong. I began to notice a disturbing pattern. Though students shifted from unbelief or nonbelief to belief in God, almost all of them responded to this newfound belief with a shrug and a sigh. "God exists. So what? Pass the beer and pizza." Apathy was the common denominator, not conversion and faith. But why? Why such a lackadaisical response to belief in God?

Five hundred years ago, a similar response of apathy toward God would have been virtually unthinkable. But the disenchantment of Western culture over the past five centuries has changed much. The modern lives comfortably in an empty world devoid of moral or aesthetic absolutes, a world without fixed meaning or clear purpose. We've found a way to sneak meaning in without appealing to transcendence, inconsistently borrowing from the language and thought of the enchanted world, while denying the foundations of that world. Hollow at our core, we've become insulated to the reality of our own fragmentation and incoherence. The goal of life in our modern culture is no longer virtue oriented toward an end (as the Greeks argued) or religion oriented toward the divine (as the medievals argued). Rather, the goal of life is entirely subjective. It is found *within* the self. To be specific, the defining goal of an individual's life in this disenchanted age is the satisfaction of their personal desires. If God can help us achieve that goal, then by all means add him to the mix. But God must meet us on our own terms. God, if he exists, remains an outsider, a genie in the bottle, on call until needed, and not a sovereign who makes demands upon our lives. As Paul describes in Romans 1:21, although they knew God, they did not honor him as God. This is how our culture accommodates belief in God, as a tool for us to use. In this, we fail to honor God as God, even if we admit he exists.

The felt absence of God characteristic of this disenchanted age led to the apathetic responses of my students. According to Norman Wirzba, Nietzsche's famous declaration that God is dead "has never simply been about the murder and burial of a divine being."[53] The death of God is the end of reality as we knew it. *Everything* dies when God dies, including our link to the wisdom of the ancient world and to the established conceptions of human meaning, purpose, and value. Merely adding God back, as a character who matches the modern furniture of our disenchanted reality, is insufficient. Given enough time in the darkness, "straying through an infinite nothing," we can no longer see what's lost and therefore can't recognize our own lostness.[54]

The felt absence of God is the defining feature of our day. In a disenchanted age, belief in God is unwelcome, unnecessary, and unimaginable.[55] God is *unwelcome* in the boardroom, bedroom, courtroom, classroom, and (even) in many of our churches. Thomas Jefferson, elected president of the United States in 1804, felt justified in applying a razor to passages in the Gospels "with even a whiff of supernaturalism."[56] More recently, liberal arts professor Stanley Fish, speaking to religious professors who might be tempted to evangelize their Christian convictions within the secular academy, stated:

> If what you really want to do is preach, or organize political rallies, or work for world peace, or minister to the poor and homeless, or counsel troubled youth, you should either engage in those activities after hours and on weekends, or, if part-time is not enough time, you should resign from the academy . . . and take up work that speaks directly to the problems you feel compelled to address.[57]

The university exists, according to Fish, "[for] the transmission of knowledge and the conferring of analytic skills."[58] And since religious claims have already been predefined and excluded as knowledge claims, religion has no place in the academy. Christians can believe what they want, but they must keep it to themselves. If they want to save the world, they must do it on their own

---

53. Wirzba, *From Nature to Creation*, 6.

54. Wirzba, *From Nature to Creation*, 8. The quote "straying through an infinite nothing" is from Friedrich Nietzsche, *The Gay Science*, trans. Walter Kaufmann (New York: Vintage, 1974), 181.

55. "For God to die, all that is necessary is for people to imagine and implement a world in which God is an unwelcome, unnecessary, or unimaginable hypothesis." Wirzba, *From Nature to Creation*, 7.

56. Stephen Prothero, *American Jesus: How the Son of God Became a National Icon* (New York: Farrar, Straus and Giroux, 2003), 25.

57. Stanley Fish, *Save the World on Your Own Time* (Oxford: Oxford University Press, 2008), 81.

58. Fish, *Save the World on Your Own Time*, 79.

time. Unfortunately, Fish's views are shared by many in the academy today, among both non-Christian *and* Christian educators. Even more pernicious is the reality that God is often unwelcome in the church today. Youth groups regularly attempt to draw kids into their programs with loud music, fun (but pointless) games, food, and teaching focused on felt needs. While nothing is wrong with these things in themselves, all too often they are offered as a *substitute*, a replacement for substantive biblical teaching and serious attention to the cultivation of spiritual disciplines (prayer, solitude, Scripture reading) that aim to draw people into an ever-deepening relationship with the living God.[59]

We are also told that belief in God is *unnecessary* to make sense of the world. Science offers a new hope of eternal life and scientists are the new priests, prophets, and kings of the modern world. Staunch atheist Richard Dawkins, with obvious sarcasm, illustrates a common perception about those who think God is necessary to explain some portion of our world:

> If you don't understand how something works, never mind: just give up and say God did it. . . . Please don't go to work on the problem, just give up, and appeal to God. Dear scientist, don't *work* on your mysteries. Bring us your mysteries, for we can use them. Don't squander precious ignorance by researching it away. We need your glorious gaps as a last refuge for God.[60]

Dawkins is saying that appeals to God shut down the process of gaining knowledge. Why is this the case? Because Dawkins assumes that science will one day be able to explain everything without appealing to the divine.

The felt absence of God also makes belief in God *unimaginable*. This is commonly raised as an objection given the intensity, distribution, and amount of horrific pain and suffering in the world. A good God would never allow the Holocaust or the pogroms or the death of millions from tsunamis and

---

59. Sociologist Christian Smith conducted a survey of 267 American teens that identify as Christians, exploring their religious beliefs and practices. Smith's conclusion is that the religious view of the youth in America's churches is best described as a kind of "Moralistic Therapeutic Deism." On this view, God exists in the periphery of our lives, wants us to be good, and is there to make us feel happy when we need him. See Christian Smith and Melinda Lundquist Denton, *Soul Searching: The Religious and Spiritual Lives of American Teenagers* (Oxford: Oxford University Press, 2005).

60. Richard Dawkins, *The God Delusion* (New York: Mariner, 2008), 159.

tornadoes. To think there is a God who cares is inconceivable: humanity exists on a little blue speck hurtling through space in a vast universe filled with billions of planets, stars, and galaxies. Given the immensity of the universe and the smallness of earth, it seems foolish to think we are somehow the focus of God's creative activity, the pinnacle of his love, and the image of his very character. It is far more likely, argues the atheist, that humanity is merely the accidental and lucky product of chance and necessity over time. While reflecting on an image taken by Voyager 1 in 1990 showing earth from four billion miles away, the astronomer Carl Sagan drives the point home: "Our planet is a lonely speck in the great enveloping cosmic dark. In our obscurity, in all this vastness, there is no hint that help will come from elsewhere to save us from ourselves."[61] Newton's model of a mechanistic universe delivered a knockout blow atrophying our collective imagination. We no longer see a charged cosmos, a world infused with the supernatural. God, if he ever existed, is no longer home. We are cosmic orphans, and somehow we must find our way forward alone.

In a disenchanted age, no beliefs are left untouched. Not only is nonbelief in God a genuine possibility, it becomes far more difficult to believe in God. Doubt, angst, and the felt absence of God characterize contemporary religious life. Religion is reduced to external behaviors—dance steps—while God's grace and presence—the music of the gospel—are noticeably absent in the believer's everyday life.[62] The religious person is not all that different from his secular counterpart. Both have learned to live on their own. Within the church, we give lip service to God, but our actions betray us.

The collective sigh of my students, upon realizing God exists, is no longer a shock to me. Many of us do the same thing. Once the momentary awareness of God has passed, we shrug our shoulders and get on with life.

A Consumer Culture

Hand in hand with our diminished experience of the world is what some have referred to as "the systematic degradation of the world."[63] The ancients

---

61. Carl Sagan, *Pale Blue Dot: A Vision of the Human Future in Space* (New York: Random House, 1994), 9.

62. For an excellent discussion on learning how to hear the music of the gospel, see Keith E. Johnson, "Hearing the Music of the Gospel," in *White Papers Critical Concepts Series*, vol. 1 (Orlando: CruPress, 2008), https://www.cru.org/content/dam/cru/legacy/2012/02/Music_of_the_Gospel.pdf.

63. Wirzba, *From Nature to Creation*, 5.

were vulnerable to the gods and at the mercy of the world around them. Moderns have rejected God and seek to manipulate and control the world through science and technology. The ancients "experienced a profound level of engagement or vital participation"[64] with the world. Moderns disengage from the world—mind separates from body, the individual from society, the spiritual from the material, the personal from the cosmic—and stand apart from and objectivize nature in order to subdue it.[65]

Our disengagement from and objectivization of nature is a fundamental shift, which moves us from seeing things and people as gifts to viewing them as commodities for use and consumption.[66] In this new, immanent framework, meaning resides in our individual appetite and the "good life" is identified with our consumption. The satisfaction of pleasure (hedonism) rules the day, as we move from one taste to the next in a perpetual search for more. Sex trafficking, the porn industry, and the Walmartization of America are driven by the same impulse: to find meaning and significance in the satisfaction of our unfettered desire. The world is now a "vast storehouse of commodities" in which everything is for sale.[67] Everything is reinvested with meaning, which is now defined by the market value.

As Wirzba observes, in a consumer culture "a new kind of person develops . . . a person who relates to others more impersonally and without a felt need to honor the social and ecological memberships that he or she is a part of and necessarily lives through."[68] As James K. A. Smith notes, a consumer culture "births in us a desire for a way of life that is destructive of creation itself; moreover, it births in us a desire for a way of life that we can't feasibly extend to others, creating a system of privilege and exploitation. . . . [A consumer culture] fosters habits and practices that are unjust, so it does everything it can to prevent us from asking [questions such as, 'Where does all this stuff come from?'] Don't ask; don't tell; just consume."[69] Smith's larger point is that the level of

---

64. Balcomb, "Re-Enchanting a Disenchanted Universe," 79.

65. Balcomb, "Re-Enchanting a Disenchanted Universe," 80.

66. Wirzba, *From Nature to Creation*, 139. As Roger Scruton observes, even our music has become "machinelike, not in its sound only, but in its mode of production. . . . It is a music of objects, from which the subjects have been excluded." Scruton, *The Soul of the World* (Princeton, NJ: Princeton University Press, 2014), 151. Lest you doubt, Scruton points us to Technohead and their 1995 single 'I Wanna Be a Hippy' as exhibit A.

67. Wirzba, *From Nature to Creation*, 139.

68. Wirzba, *From Nature to Creation*, 142.

69. James K. A. Smith, *Desiring the Kingdom: Worship, Worldview, and Cultural Formation* (Grand Rapids: Baker, 2009), 101.

production and consumption we see in the West is unsustainable, leading to the exploitation of the "have nots" by those that "have," to disintegration, abuse, and an ever-widening economic stratification. Like Lewis's Uncle Andrew, who found in the raw beauty of Narnia only financial opportunity, moderns live for small things that will never satisfy their hunger. Ruled by our consumption we become a small, flattened people: consumed by the things we aim to exploit and alienated from God, the world, each other, and even ourselves.

Blindness and Foolishness

In our consumer culture, the absence of God coupled with the felt absence of meaning leads to the third characteristic of disenchantment: a failure to see reality in its proper light, or *blindness*, which is followed by foolishness run amok. The world has been turned upside down. The barbarians have toppled the gates. As Paul described those who have suppressed the truth of God due to their wickedness and ungodliness, "their thinking became futile and their foolish hearts were darkened" (Rom. 1:21).

It doesn't take much effort to spot the foolishness that pervades our disenchanted age. My Facebook newsfeed has this article, for example: "Michigan School Let Students Pick Gender, Name, and Bathroom."[70] Do we really think it's wise to give children near absolute autonomy to choose their identity, orientation, and even their name without guidance on how to properly "conform the soul to reality"?[71] As Wirzba sagely notes, "The naming and narrating of the world is no trivial thing . . . because *the way we name and narrate the world [and ourselves] determines how we are going to live in it*."[72] The *Journal of Medical Ethics* has an essay, "After-Birth Abortion: Why Should the Baby Live?" which argues that infanticide should be permissible in all cases where abortion is permissible.[73] The conclusion of this essay is so repugnant it defies common sense that such an essay can find acceptance in a peer-reviewed

70. Peter Hasson, "Michigan School Let Students Pick Gender, Name, and Bathroom," The Daily Caller, (March 21, 2016). http://dailycaller.com/2016/03/21/michigan-schools-to-let-students-choose-gender-name-and-bathroom/#ixzz43YnMWaV0.

71. C. S. Lewis, *The Abolition of Man* (New York: HarperCollins, 2001), 77.

72. Wirzba, *From Nature to Creation*, 18–19.

73. The abstract for the article is as follows: "Abortion is largely accepted even for reasons that do not have anything to do with the fetus's health. By showing that (1) both fetuses and newborns do not have the same moral status as actual persons, (2) the fact that both are potential persons is morally irrelevant and (3) adoption is not always in the best interest of actual people, the authors argue that what we call 'after-birth abortion' (killing a newborn) should be permissible in all the cases where abortion is, including cases

academic journal on ethics.[74] Or consider the political discourse in America (as witnessed by the 2016 election cycle). We've been reduced to schoolyard name-calling, featuring "my wife is better looking than your wife" tweets. I realize we live East of Eden, and things have never been perfect this side of the fall, but the disenchantment of reality has ushered in a "malaise of immanence,"[75] which has seeped into the pores of an emptied world, heightening humanity's desperate attempt to find an overarching story that offers meaning and purpose on our own terms.

As we narrate the story of our lives and embody habits that are motivated by misplaced desire, our character (de)forms, and our perception of the world changes. We become blind and foolish. Money, entertainment, excess, gluttony—the litany of vices and her spoils—blind us to goodness and beauty. This blindness and foolishness lead to the fourth characteristic of disenchantment: idolatry.

Idolatry

As Paul noted in Athens, human beings are inherently religious (Acts 17:16, 22). We all worship something: either the true God or some created portion of reality. "Idolatry is inherently a rejection of God's authority and a quest for self-definition, self-importance, and self-fulfillment *on our own terms.*"[76] In a disenchanted culture, our restless hearts and minds seek satisfaction, solace, or love in anything other than God. This is modern idolatry. Believers and nonbelievers in every culture and time have struggled with idolatry, but disenchantment contributes to the *pervasiveness* and *entrenchment* of our idolatry. The temptation to engage in false worship is especially strong for us today because it is possible to orient one's entire life without any appeal to transcendent reality.[77]

---

where the newborn is not disabled." See Alberto Giubilini and Francesca Minerva, "After-Birth Abortion: Why Should the Baby Live?," *Journal of Medical Ethics* 39, no. 5 (May 2013): 261–63.

74. Unfortunately defending infanticide is nothing new, argued forcibly by notable philosophers such as Peter Singer and Michael Tooley. See, e.g., Peter Singer, *Practical Ethics*, 2nd ed. (Cambridge: Cambridge University Press, 1993); and Michael Tooley, "Abortion and Infanticide," *Philosophy and Public Affairs* 2, no. 1 (1972): 37–65.

75. The phrase is from Taylor, *A Secular Age*, ch. 8.

76. Paul K. Moser, "Cognitive Idolatry and Divine Hiding," in *Divine Hiddenness: New Essays*, ed. Daniel Howard-Snyder and Paul K. Moser (Cambridge: Cambridge University Press, 2002), 130.

77. For more on my own struggle with idolatry, see *The Outrageous Idea of the Missional Professor* (Eugene, OR: Wipf & Stock, 2014), 70–76.

Idolatrous living takes many forms. Some pursue the so-called "lower pleasures"—sex, money, and entertainment—creating a world, as John Stuart Mill sees it, fit for pigs.[78] Others are more refined, pursuing "higher pleasures"—intellectual and artistic—as they hobnob with social elites at charity balls, poetry readings, and suburban country clubs. Idolatry is found everywhere, from the Khayelitsha slums in Cape Town to Martha's Vineyard just south of Cape Cod and everywhere in between.

As we moderns preoccupy ourselves with self-appeasement, we become a shell, a wraith of our best selves, hollow at the core, and blind to the world around us.[79] People and things are seen as disposable commodities to be used and discarded. Idolatry affects how we live, which in turn affects what we see. The relentless pursuit of these lower or higher goods as God-substitutes diminish our ability to see things and people fully and truly as gifts, as sacred. Our vision of the giver of all good things blurs too. The result of an idolatrous way of living is moral bankruptcy and disintegration. The result of an idolatrous way of perceiving is an inability to see reality correctly. The disenchanted perceiver "assumes that when it comes to knowledge and meaning, we are at the top of the tree, and whatever we cannot see when we look down does not exist."[80] As Wirzba summarizes, in living [and perceiving] idolatrously, "we lose both God and the world."[81] And in losing the world, we lose ourselves too.

SIGNS OF TRANSCENDENCE

We are told by today's "reality police," elite groups of university professors, journalists, Hollywood producers, lawmakers, and others who define reality

---

78. Mill said, "It is better to be a human being dissatisfied than a pig satisfied; better to be Socrates dissatisfied than a fool satisfied." John Stuart Mill, *Utilitarianism*, ed. George Sher (Indianapolis: Hackett, 2001), 10. Perhaps. But wouldn't it be even better if all our desires—for God, truth, goodness, beauty, pleasure—could find a fitting object in their quest for satisfaction? I shall argue that there is a fitting object of all our longings: Jesus and the gospel story he bids us to enter into. While utilitarianism as a theory of living (and therefore perceiving) is neither true nor ultimately satisfying, Christianity is. This is good news indeed!

79. The allusion to being preoccupied with a very small object, namely himself, is from Alex de Tocqueville, *Democracy in America*, ch. 18, cited in Andrew Pinsent, "Humility," in *Being Good: Christian Virtues for Everyday Life* (Grand Rapids: Eerdmans, 2012), 261.

80. Paul Tyson, *Returning to Reality: Christian Platonism for Our Times* (Eugene, OR: Cascade, 2014), 7.

81. Wirzba, *From Nature to Creation*, 54.

for the rest of us, that transcendence has been declared "inoperative."[82] In other words, any appeal to something beyond the ordinary, beyond that which can be captured by science, is ruled out of bounds and therefore unacceptable. For anyone desiring to be rational, and scientistic as we shall see in chapter 7, there is incredible pressure to be naturalistic and materialistic. There is nothing beyond nature. There is nothing more to reality than the material. There are two pressing problems for these "official reality-definers,"[83] who desperately want us to think reality is secular and materialistic.

The first problem is that this modern scientific worldview is boring.[84] A disenchanted world is without meaning, purpose, or objective values. There is no deep story that governs the cosmos or our lives. There is no Author, no play. Birth, life, death—that's it. As G. K. Chesterton is reported to have observed, "Modernity has given ultimate authority to the world view of a slightly sleepy businessman right after lunch."[85] This boredom has fueled the modern obsession for experiences that provide momentary escape: movies, video games, drugs, alcohol, sex, sports, mindless trolling on social media—anything will do, as long as they do not point beyond the material world to some transcendent or supernatural reality. Yet our obsession with so-called "contraband transcendence"[86] betrays us. As we shall explore in chapter 3, many today are obsessed with the occult, the paranormal, and the spiritual. This obsession is at odds with what the reality police tell us exists. We long for more, even as we are told there is nothing but the material and material pleasures. We have become like Plato's tyrants, who "never taste any stable or pure pleasure. Instead, they always look down at the ground like cattle, and, with their heads bent over the dinner table, they feed, fatten, and fornicate."[87] The architects of our disenchantment have created a genuine mess. Human beings were not meant to live like cattle, and a life solely focused on sensual experience will never satisfy us. And those who become disillusioned with the ho-hum manna provided by modernity will end up in a state of despair.[88]

---

82. Peter L. Berger, *Facing Up to Modernity* (New York: Basic Books, 1977), 202.

83. As reported by Berger in *Facing Up to Modernity*.

84. Berger, *Facing Up to Modernity*, 210.

85. As quoted in Berger, *Facing Up to Modernity*, 210.

86. Berger, *Facing Up to Modernity*, 210.

87. Plato, *The Republic*, trans. G. M. A. Grube (Indianapolis: Hackett, 1992), bk. 9, 586a.

88. Atheist Bertrand Russell, for example, put it as follows: if God does not exist, and humanity is just the "outcome of accidental collocations of atoms," then all we can do is build our lives on "the firm

A second pressing problem, highlighted by the prevalence of so-called contraband transcendence, is that we long for things the material world cannot provide, and these longings refuse to go away quietly.[89] God and a deep spiritual reality are still there. He didn't leave. He still upholds us, even if we refuse to acknowledge him. Transcendence has a way of breaking forth. It erupts through the cracks of our experience and the byways of creation and points to something fundamental. The transcendent "bites us from behind in our daydreams and nightmares, in our fantasies and bored despair, in moments of extremity and disorientation, in experiences of startling delight, or in revelations of beauty, goodness, and truth, which the so called 'real world' has no words for."[90]

The signs of transcendence are everywhere. They litter the sides of the Texas highway every spring in the form of thousands upon thousands of bluebonnet flowers. They can be found in a moment of shared intimacy with a spouse or friend over dinner. They can be seen in the laughter of a child and the tearful embrace of a loved one in need. These experiences of beauty, communion, laughter, and love, however brief and small, help me see the world in a different light. They help me understand and imagine a world of deep meaning and the promise of a day when all will be set right again.

Peter Berger describes a signal of transcendence as follows:

> To speak of a signal of transcendence is neither to deny nor to idealize the often harsh empirical facts that make up our lives in the world. It is rather to try for a glimpse of the grace that is to be found "in, with, and under" the empirical reality of our lives. In other words, to speak of a signal of transcendence is to make an assertion about the presence of redemptive power in this world.[91]

There is a kind of restlessness and unease to life in a disenchanted world. We long for something more even as we are told there is nothing beyond. The universe *feels* haunted. Something presses within and upon us. These stirrings

---

foundation of unyielding despair." Russell, "A Free Man's Worship," in *Why I Am Not a Christian* (New York: Touchstone, 1957), 107.

89. Berger, *Facing Up to Modernity*, 203.
90. Tyson, *Returning to Reality*, 4–5.
91. Berger, *Facing Up to Modernity*, 212.

jar us. They offer the promise of hope, of redemption. They point to a power beyond the world that *can* and, hope against hope, *will* make things right one day.

"Christ plays in ten thousand places," as Gerard Manley Hopkins colorfully observes.[92] The signs of transcendence are often hidden in plain sight. By way of concrete example, Berger, in his excellent book *A Rumor of Angels*, notes five signals of transcendence from our everyday experiences.[93] First, there is the human propensity for *order*. Every society is burdened with the task of bringing order out of chaos. Even such commonplace acts as mowing the lawn, cleaning the kitchen after a meal, and a mother assuring her upset child that "everything will be all right" point to humanity's faith in order. What best explains the observable human propensity to order reality? If there is no God, if there is nothing *beyond* nature, then everything is *not* in order, everything is not all right.[94] Yet we take it upon ourselves to represent reality as being orderly and trustworthy. "This representation," Berger argues, "can be justified only within a religious (strictly speaking a supernatural) frame of reference."[95]

Second, Berger notes the pervasiveness of *human play*. In play, time is suspended. The seriousness of the world is set aside, and a separate universe of intense joy and delight is created and entered. The experience of joyful play can be readily found in ordinary life even as it points beyond to a world where all is as it should be, the good triumphs over evil, and everyone is known by his or her true name.

Third, there is the unconquerable human propensity to *hope*. Humanity is essentially future directed, looking forward to the fulfillment of desire, to a day when the difficulties of the here and now will be no more.[96] We think infinite happiness is really there. We hope that one day we will reach the rainbow's end. Such hope is absurd if there is no God and no afterlife. As C. S. Lewis famously argued, "If I find in myself a desire which no experience in this world can satisfy, the most probable explanation is that I was made for another world."[97]

---

92. Gerard Manley Hopkins, "As Kingfishers Catch Fire," in *Poems of Gerard Manley Hopkins*, ed. W. H. Gardner, 3rd ed. (New York: Oxford University Press, 1948), 95.

93. Peter Berger, *A Rumor of Angels: Modern Society and the Rediscovery of the Supernatural* (New York: Anchor, 1970), 61–94.

94. Berger, *A Rumor of Angels*, 69.

95. Berger, *A Rumor of Angels*, 71.

96. Berger, *A Rumor of Angels*, 76.

97. C. S. Lewis, *Mere Christianity* (New York: HarperCollins, 2001), 136–37.

The human characteristic hope points beyond itself and this world. It is a signal of transcendence.

Fourth, in the face of horrendous evils, such as the massacre of the innocent, rape, or murder, there is the human demand for not only condemnation but *damnation*. In our hearts we curse the perpetrators of such monstrous evils. No human punishment seems enough. Only eternal banishment of the guilty from God seems appropriate. Horrendous evil "raises the question of the justice and power of God. It also, however, suggests the necessity of hell—not so much as a confirmation of God's justice, but rather as a vindication of our own."[98] Both the human gesture of protective reassurance and the countergesture of damnation point to something beyond this world.

Finally, there is the reality of *humor*. Life is full of the unexpected, the unforeseen. Who would have expected to find the great and serious philosopher Socrates hanging in a basket, contemplating the air (as Aristophanes portrays him in the Greek comedy *The Clouds*)? Who would have foreseen Wile E. Coyote run over by a truck, emerge unharmed? The comic points to a discrepancy between our understanding of the world and another possible interpretation of it. We are forced to ask: Which picture of the world is true? Berger argues that at its most fundamental level, the comic reflects the "imprisonment of the human spirit in the world" and "implies that this imprisonment is not final but will be overcome."[99] Comedy is a foretaste of things to come and as such another signal of transcendence.

To these five we could add the reality of cosmic wonder, morality, beauty, music, death, the directedness or "aboutness" of our mental lives, religious experience of the divine, and more.[100] The basic idea is this: everything that exists—every truth discovered, every beauty (and every corruption of beauty), and every good (and perversion of good)—points to and illuminates the divine. Since God creates everything that exists, everything bears his stamp. Each of

---

98. Berger, *A Rumor of Angels*, 86.

99. Berger, *A Rumor of Angels*, 87–88.

100. For an excellent discussion of the concept of a theistic natural sign, see Evans, *Natural Signs and Knowledge of God*. For a sustained argument that the surface features of our lives—glances, a kiss, a smile, the real presence of another—point to transcendence, see Scruton, *The Soul of the World*. For a discussion of beauty as a sign of transcendence, see Ryan West and Adam C. Pelser, "Perceiving God through Natural Beauty," *Faith and Philosophy* 32, no. 3 (July 2015): 293–312. Finally, for a helpful discussion of religious experience, see William Alston, *Perceiving God: The Epistemology of Religious Experience* (Ithaca, NY: Cornell University Press, 1991).

these signals of transcendence also point to the gospel story as the true story of the world. For in the gospel we find an enchanted, supernatural world where love is eternal, death is overcome, victory is snatched out of the hands of defeat, and all turns out for the good in the end. The world, if we pay attention, points to God and a God-bathed reality.

We must begin to see everything in its proper light, not as ordinary, mundane, and familiar, but as sacred, holy, and a gift from our Creator. In doing so, like John the Baptist in the Gospels, we will point others to the King and Creator.

The process of reenchanting the world begins, with the help of the Holy Spirit, by awakening those under the spell of disenchantment from their slumber. Reenchantment is possible. While man's desire for truth, goodness, and beauty has become distorted, the desire remains. Part of our job as cultural apologists is to help reawaken these universal and natural human desires and redirect them toward their proper end. In the next chapter, we consider the possibility of return.

CHAPTER 3

REENCHANTMENT

You have awaked the noble urge in me
To gaze into the wide world's soul and meaning.

Novalis[1]

Come out, look back, and then you will see . . . this astonishing
cataract of bears, babies, and bananas: this immoderate
deluge of atoms, orchids, oranges, cancers, canaries, fleas,
gases, tornadoes and toads. How could you ever have
thought this was the ultimate reality?

C. S. Lewis[2]

As a child I learned to play the piano. I had a natural ear for music and could play Beethoven's "Für Elise" with precision and Billy Joel's "Piano Man" with passion. I could play both parts of "Chopsticks" at the same time. I even composed a couple of songs that would later woo and impress my future wife on our first dates together. I was captivated by the beauty of a well-placed harmony. It moved me and awoke longings within me.

As a teenager, the classical music I'd played no longer moved me as it had. My interests were sports and girls. Piano was now an obstacle to those interests—both time-consuming and somewhat boring. My parents caved under my pressure to quit. I no longer cared to play. I'd grown deaf to the

---

1. Novalis, *Henry von Ofterdingen*, trans. Palmer Hilty (Long Grove, IL: Waveland, 1990), 12.
2. C. S. Lewis, *Miracles* (New York: Touchstone, 1996), 89–90.

beauty of Bach and had forgotten the subtlety of Mozart. Instead, I'd discovered Michael Jackson, Madonna, and Led Zeppelin.

I didn't stop playing, though. My musical ability became a means of exploring meaning and purpose in my teenage search for significance. Like others my age, I started a band. We practiced in my basement, working on cover songs to "I Melt with You" by Modern English or "Mony Mony" by Billy Idol. We knew we were amazing. But after a few gigs at our high school, my hopes of fame and fortune met cold, hard reality. There were no groupies, no girls, no pot of gold.

My relationship with music in those years reveals an important lesson about human nature: we are creatures driven by our longings and loves. We are *desiring animals*. As James K. A. Smith puts it, "To be human is to be animated and oriented by some vision of the good life, some picture of what we think counts as 'flourishing.' And we *want* that. We crave it. We desire it. This is why our most fundamental mode of orientation to the world is love. We are oriented by our longings, directed by our desires."[3] As a teen, my idea of the good life was sensual pleasure, fame, and fortune. The classical music of my earlier years didn't fit with that vision, so I dropped it and reoriented my world to other interests in order to satisfy my immediate desires.

Over time my ability to appreciate the beauty of a well-placed harmony atrophied. The music that had once enchanted me no longer held my attention. I'd become dead to the echo of transcendence within much of classical music. But my desire for beauty never abated. Rather, it was redirected. These new interests satisfied me to a certain extent. Like C. S. Lewis's "Disillusioned 'Sensible Man,'" I learned to lower my expectations. I'd "given up chasing the rainbow's end."[4] And I certainly didn't think God had anything to do with the good life I longed to live.

Many today don't see how God is related to our happiness. If anything, God is seen in contrast to human happiness, opposed to our joy. If there is happiness to be found, it will be found on human terms, free from limitations on our desires. Peter Kreeft notes that *sloth*, a spiritual lethargy or a failure to recognize our inherent longing for God, is a distinctively modern

---

3. James K. A. Smith, *You Are What You Love: The Spiritual Power of Habit* (Grand Rapids: Brazos, 2016), 11.

4. C. S. Lewis, *Mere Christianity* (New York: HarperCollins, 2001), 136.

sin.[5] The universal thirst for God, recognized across cultures and throughout history, has been muted. Today, people feel the longing, but we cannot recognize it as a divine call. We revel in our unhappiness and disillusionment. As Pascal notes, "There are only three sorts of people: those who have found God and serve him; those who are busy seeking him and have not found him; those who live without either seeking or finding him. The first are reasonable and happy, the last are foolish and unhappy, those in the middle are unhappy and reasonable."[6] Given disenchantment, things are not quite as simple as Pascal thinks. It is increasingly difficult for those who are found, let alone the seeker and nonseeker, to believe or even understand that happiness should be understood in terms of friendship with God. As Smith rightly notes, our fundamental orientation toward the world is love, yet our loves are often grossly disordered. Traditionally, love has been understood as a theological virtue. In exercising the theological virtue of love, chiefly for God and secondarily for neighbor, we experience inner peace and joy. In a disenchanted age, the demand of love, with its call for personal transformation from selfishness to selflessness, is difficult and unappealing.

This resistance to love's call and the offer of happiness through friendship with God and participation in the divine life has traditionally been understood as a moral sin, the vice of sloth. Sloth or spiritual apathy, according to Aquinas, "consists of boredom or sadness regarding a spiritual and interior good" and is "contrary to charity."[7] As Rebecca Konyndyk DeYoung explains,

> Sloth's main target is our love relationship with God, in the context of a life in which we take our likeness to God to be our defining identity and loving communion with God to be our main vocation as human beings. The slothful person resists this relationship and the like-naturedness to God that she must accept and cultivate to sustain it.[8]

---

5. Peter Kreeft, *Back to Virtue: Traditional Moral Wisdom for Modern Moral Confusion* (San Francisco: Ignatius, 1992), 153.

6. Blaise Pascal, *Pensées*, trans. A. J. Krailsheimer (New York: Penguin, 1995), §160 (p. 52), cited in Kreeft, *Back to Virtue*, 153–54.

7. Thomas Aquinas, *On Evil*, ed. Brian Davies, trans. Richard Regan (Oxford: Oxford University Press, 2003), 363, 368.

8. Rebecca Konyndyk DeYoung, "Sloth: Historical Reflections on Laziness, Effort, and Resistance to the Demands of Love," in *Virtues and Their Vices*, ed. Kevin Timpe and Craig A. Boyd (Oxford: Oxford University Press, 2014), 189.

Many today have been lulled to sleep. The traditional vice of sloth has been transformed into a new virtue, the virtue of apathy toward God and the things of God (see figure 3.1). This slide toward sloth is contagious. Many people today are like the zombies in *The Walking Dead* who mindlessly walk around, often in "herds," looking for another pound of flesh to devour. A bite wound from a zombie is sufficient to turn those still living, who long for a "far-off country,"[9] into mindless devouring animals. The world of *The Walking Dead* is not safe. Neither is our disenchanted world. Still, there are pockets of life. Most importantly, there is Jesus. There is hope of reenchantment. The first step toward reenchantment is to reawaken within ourselves and others the deeper desires of the heart for truth, goodness, and beauty, which in turn will arouse the heart's deepest desire—a desire and love for God.

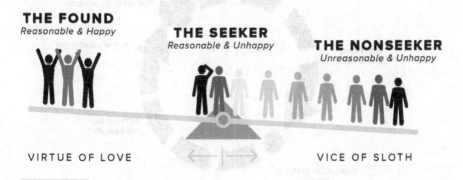

FIGURE 3.1: Three Kinds of People and the Slide toward Sloth in a Disenchanted World

AWAKENING DESIRE

In chapter 2 we considered how Western culture wandered from God first by suppressing the truth about God and then by emptying the world of transcendence. As illustrated on the left-hand side of figure 2.2 (reproduced below), the collective journey of humanity away from God has resulted in this disenchanted age. In this chapter, we will consider the possibility of return, as illustrated on

---

9. C. S. Lewis, *The Weight of Glory* (New York: HarperCollins, 2001), 29.

the right-hand side of figure 2.2. It's important to note that we are after a *re-*
enchantment of the world, not a return to the way things were. We can never
go back. We can help others see Christianity as plausible and desirable, if we
embody a faith that "carries whiffs of transcendence,"[10] and entice and invite
others to see Jesus and the gospel as true and beautiful. In reenchanting the
world, we join with the Holy Spirit in turning the world right-side up.[11] We
step out in faith, assured that all things will one day be united under Christ
(Eph. 1:10). "Righting" the world begins with reawakening innate desires,
including the desire for the divine.

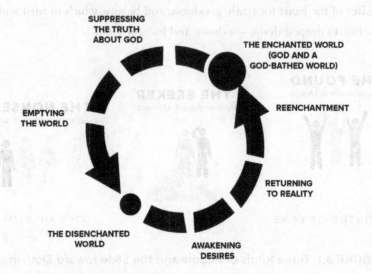

FIGURE 2.2: Model for reenchantment

Some are acutely aware of their hearts' deepest desire; they are fully cognizant of the restlessness of their heart apart from God. They find joy in the
longing and delight in union with the object of their longing. King David,
for example, opines,

---

10. Smith, *You Are What You Love*, 102. Consider also Smith's claim that "now that the whole world has
been disenchanted and we have been encased in a flattened 'nature,' I expect it will be forms of reenchanted
Christianity that will actually have a future" (102).

11. "But in this world everything is upside down," C. S. Lewis, *Letters to Malcolm Chiefly on Prayer*
(Orlando: Harcourt, 1992), 93.

> O God, you are my God;
>   I earnestly search for you.
> My soul thirsts for you;
>   my whole body longs for you
>   in this parched and weary land
>   where there is no water. (Ps. 63:1 NLT)

Similarly, after wrestling with God over the disparity between the wicked who seem to prosper in this life and the faithful who often struggle, Asaph cries out to God, exclaiming, "I desire you more than anything on earth" (Ps. 73:25 NLT). There are those like David and Asaph who crave God above all else. Unfortunately, their tribe is small. We even have a name for this little band of heavenly minded heroes: saints.[12] Yet sainthood remains unattainable for most. The problem isn't primarily one of moral defect; rather, it's one of longing and loves: many simply do not desire God above all else, or even at all.

Disenchantment, the loss of transcendence, changes everything. While the heart desires God, many are *unaware* of this deep longing.[13] Awareness comes in degrees and can be clouded by repression, self-deception, spiritual pride, and a host of other issues that prevent transparency of the heart. The modern self is fragmented. The desires that shape action in the world often remain elusive, and conflicting desires pull people helter-skelter in opposing directions. Many feel as if life is one giant treadmill: always moving, never arriving; always striving, never attaining.

Moreover, the desire for God can be partly *repudiated*. We exercise considerable control over our desires, albeit indirectly. I once had a strong desire to eat Twinkies. Anyone who has tasted these delicacies will know why. But I also had a desire to be healthy. Given my deeper desire for good health, I knew that I needed to change the way I ate. My greater desire for health and wellness trumped my desire for the Twinkie. Part of me still wanted the Twinkie, but at the same time, I knew I didn't want to eat it anymore. I muted my desire for Twinkies by removing them from sight, finding healthy replacements,

---

12. Theologically speaking, all Christians are saints. The word is often used, however, to pick out those few among us that live an exemplary moral life. I am using the word in this second sense in this paragraph.

13. For a helpful discussion of the web or network of desires within the human heart, as well as how we can fail to be aware of certain desires, including our deepest heart desire for God, see Eleonore Stump, *Wandering in Darkness: Narrative and the Problem of Suffering* (Oxford: Clarendon, 2010), 438–50.

and focusing on my desire for a healthy body. Over time, my desire for Twinkies dissipated and atrophied. It's not entirely gone. I walk a step slower when I pass the Hostess counter at the grocery store. But it's no longer a desire that moves me to act. I'm able to exert considerable control over the desires of my heart, in this case at least.

Whether it's to a Twinkie or to the God who created us, the human heart responds the same to habits and disciplines. If someone doesn't want to acknowledge God, that innate desire for God can be repudiated, to some degree. Since it is innate, the desire cannot be stamped out, but it can be suppressed and muted. The pacification of our innate desires is possible.

In our disenchanted culture, the universal longing for transcendence is either unnoticed or suppressed. As Alison Milbank observes, "Part of our problem in presenting the Faith is that our world deadens desire, and many people do not know that they are missing anything."[14] Cultural apologists need to be aware of this. Disenchantment redirects and channels man's desires toward the mundane. The spell has been cast and the world remains in a stupor. Our task is to reawaken in human hearts a longing for more, for that "far-off country." To that end, there are at least three ways we can join with the Holy Spirit in awakening desire in those we seek to reach with the gospel: the way of imagination, the way of reason, and the way of morality.

The Way of Imagination:
Heroic Escape and the Invitation Home

One of the best ways to begin reawakening the religious impulse is through imagination. Art, music, poetry, and story can awaken a desire for transcendence by "[shocking] people into engagement with reality."[15] Neither the initial stirring nor the medium need to be explicitly religious, nor must they carry the label of Christian (e.g., Christian movies, music, or books). As a child, my heart was stirred as Luke Skywalker watched the setting of two suns on his home planet in *Star Wars: Episode IV—A New Hope*. Like Luke, I craved a life of significance. As I grew older, reading about Narnia and Middle-earth awakened

---

14. Alison Milbank, "Apologetics and the Imagination: Making Strange," *Imaginative Apologetics: Theology, Philosophy and the Catholic Tradition*, ed. Andrew Davison (Grand Rapids: Baker Academic, 2012), 35.

15. Milbank, "Apologetics and the Imagination: Making Strange," 38.

within me a desire for another world. For many children today, the world of Harry Potter has engaged those longings. Watching the British drama *Poldark*, my heart stirs as the story's hero gallops along the cliffs near the seaside city of Cornwall. The Holy Spirit woos us through the beauty and imaginative stories depicted in these works of art. Ultimately this quest can only be satisfied with Jesus and the gospel. These stirrings in art and media provide a means of escape that is, according to J. R. R. Tolkien, heroic.[16] They remind us of our homeland and invite us to embark on an epic journey toward the object of our longing.

In the spiritual autobiography *Surprised by Joy*, C. S. Lewis describes three early experiences where his imagination awakened a longing for the divine.[17] His first experience of intense longing was "the memory of a memory."[18] As he stood beside a currant bush on a warm summer day there suddenly arose within him "the memory of that earlier morning at the Old House when my brother had brought his toy garden into the nursery."[19] Earlier in his memoir, Lewis had described the toy garden as "the first beauty I ever knew."[20] As Lewis stood staring out at the countryside, a sensation akin to the "'enormous bliss' of Eden" stirred within him.[21] His memory of that earlier memory awakened in him a primal longing for beauty.

Lewis's second episode of intense desire occurred when he read Beatrix Potter's *Squirrel Nutkin*. As he read the story, Lewis was troubled "with what I can only describe as the Idea of Autumn."[22] Again, his thoughts and his longings were lifted toward something beyond himself, an inexpressible desire for something lost, something missing from his life. A third glimpse of imagination came through poetry, awakening his desire for the divine. As he idly flipped through Longfellow's *Saga of King Olaf*, he stumbled upon these words:

> I heard a voice that cried,
> Balder the beautiful
> Is dead, is dead—[23]

---

16. J. R. R. Tolkien, "On Fairy-Stories," *The Tolkien Reader* (New York: Ballantine, 1966), 79.
17. C. S. Lewis, *Surprised by Joy: The Shape of My Early Life* (New York: Harcourt, 1955).
18. Lewis, *Surprised by Joy*, 16.
19. Lewis, *Surprised by Joy*, 16.
20. Lewis, *Surprised by Joy*, 7.
21. Lewis, *Surprised by Joy*, 16.
22. Lewis, *Surprised by Joy*, 16.
23. Lewis, *Surprised by Joy*, 17.

Lewis notes, "I knew nothing about Balder; but instantly I was uplifted into huge regions of northern sky, I desired with almost sickening intensity something never to be described (except that it is cold, spacious, severe, pale, and remote)."[24] While these experiences were specific to Lewis and might not awaken similar desires in anyone else, they all had something in common, that is, "an unsatisfied desire which is itself more desirable than any other satisfaction. I call it Joy."[25] Notice that Lewis's longing for the transcendent (what he calls Joy) was aroused through imagination—a memory of a toy garden, a story, and a poem. Later, as a teenager, Lewis read George MacDonald's *Phantastes* for the first time and began to understand the idea of sacredness. Writing of this experience, he says, "My imagination was, in a certain sense, baptized; the rest of me, not unnaturally, took longer. I had not the faintest notion what I had let myself in for by buying *Phantastes*."[26]

Our imagination moves us in a way that nothing else does. As James K. A. Smith puts it, "Our orientation to the world begins from, and lives off of, the fuel of our bodies, including the 'images' of the world that are absorbed by our bodies."[27] We are captured by that which captivates our imagination, and once hooked, *we're* hooked.[28] It may take time for the rest of us—our mind and will—to assent to what has captured our imagination, as it did for Lewis. But without the imagination the mind lacks the "raw materials" needed to judge something as true or false. The will possesses nothing to judge as worthy or unworthy of our devotion.[29] Often it is the "aesthetic currency of the imagination—story, poetry, music, symbols, and images"[30] that God uses to awaken our desire.

---

24. Lewis, *Surprised by Joy*, 17.
25. Lewis, *Surprised by Joy*, 17–18.
26. Lewis, *Surprised by Joy*, 181.
27. James K. A. Smith, *Imagining the Kingdom: How Worship Works* (Grand Rapids: Baker Academic, 2013), 17.
28. James K. A. Smith, *Desiring the Kingdom: Worship, Worldview, and Cultural Formation* (Grand Rapids: Baker, 2009), 54.
29. As Michael Ward notes, for Lewis the imagination is the "organ of meaning," and reason is the "natural organ of truth." Moreover, both the imagination and reason serve the will, functioning as guides in the will's decision to accept or reject the vision of the good life presented to it. See Michael Ward, "The Good Serves the Better and Both the Best: C. S. Lewis on Imagination and Reason in Apologetics," in Davison, *Imaginative Apologetics*, 59–78.
30. Smith, *You Are What You Love*, 129.

The Way of Reason: The Argument from Desire

Along with the imagination, human reason, the powers of the mind to draw inferences and assess statements as true or false, plays a vital role in awakening desire. By examining the nature of our deepest desire, along with the human predicament, we can even formulate an argument that God exists. C. S. Lewis famously presents a version of this argument from desire in his chapter on "Hope" in *Mere Christianity*. Lewis reasons as follows: "Creatures are not born with desires unless satisfaction for those desires exists. A baby feels hunger: well, there is such a thing as food. A duckling wants to swim: well, there is such a thing as water. Men feel sexual desire: well, there is such a thing as sex."[31] Lewis is noting that whenever humans have a natural desire for something, there is a corresponding object that satisfies the desire. Lewis continues: "Most people, if they had really learned to look into their own hearts, would know that they do want, and want acutely, something that cannot be had in this world."[32] The desire Lewis has in mind is that same universal longing for joy to which he earlier referred. It's the longing for transcendence. We long for God and a magical—a *super*natural—world full of deep mystery, beauty, holiness, and wholeness, a reality behind the material cosmos. We can summarize the argument with two premises:

1. Our natural desires have a corresponding object that satisfies them.
2. There exists in us a natural desire, the desire for transcendence, that nothing in the material cosmos can satisfy.

From premise (1) and (2) it follows that

3. There exists some object beyond the material cosmos that can satisfy this desire.

But what is the nature of this transcendent object? Plato had Forms, others have had gods and goddesses or a pantheistic deity. But Platonic Forms, being inert, impersonal, nondivine abstract objects such as goodness or justice or love,

---

31. Lewis, *Mere Christianity*, 136.
32. Lewis, *Mere Christianity*, 135.

cannot satisfy the deepest human longing to be known and loved by a supernatural reality. Pagan gods and goddesses, as personal supernatural agents, are an improvement, but they are finite, fickle, and often malevolent—hardly the sort of things that humans long to be united with. Pantheism denies all distinctions between good and evil, knower and thing known, desirer and thing desired. That leaves us with the God of theism, a personal agent, worthy of worship, who lovingly creates and sustains the material cosmos. This leads to a conclusion:

4. The transcendent object of our longing is God.

From which it follows straight away that

5. God exists.

The argument establishes that God exists, that our deepest desire will find satisfaction in union with God, and that there is a world beyond the material cosmos.

Peter Kreeft thinks the argument from desire is, next to Anselm's ontological argument, "the single most intriguing argument in the history of human thought."[33] Yet the argument, like all philosophical arguments, is not unassailable.[34] Objections have been raised against each of its premises.

To support premise (1), Lewis offers inductive evidence based on our experience of *some* natural desires in order to generalize that *all* natural desires have a corresponding object. But Erik Wielenberg demurs, arguing the inductive generalization in support of this premise is not justified. Wielenberg points out that "throughout human history, people have had desires involving all kinds of entities that do not belong to the known natural universe, and it is clear that the vast majority of these desires involve objects that do not exist."[35] In other words,

---

33. Peter Kreeft, *Heaven: The Heart's Deepest Longing* (San Francisco: Ignatius, 1989), 201.

34. For extended critical discussions of C. S. Lewis's argument from desire, see John Beversluis, *C. S. Lewis and the Search for Rational Religion* (Grand Rapids: Eerdmans, 1985); and Erik J. Wielenberg, *God and the Reach of Reason: C. S. Lewis, David Hume, and Bertrand Russell* (Cambridge: Cambridge University Press, 2008), 108–20. For extended discussions defending Lewis's argument from desire, see Robert Holyer, "The Argument from Desire," *Faith and Philosophy* 5, no. 1 (1988): 61–71; Kreeft, *Heaven*, 201–32; and Joe Puckett Jr., *The Apologetics of Joy: A Case for the Existence of God from C. S. Lewis's Argument from Desire* (Eugene, OR: Wipf & Stock, 2012).

35. Wielenberg, *God and the Reach of Reason*, 113.

he is suggesting that our longing for transcendence is, in many cases, simply not capable of satisfaction.

However, all that Wielenberg's objection establishes is that we can, and often do, misidentify the object of our longing. We may misidentify the object of our natural longings, but it does not follow that we lack a corresponding object to satisfy our natural desire, including our longing for God. We all crave happiness. Suppose that someone, let's call him Gully, thinks happiness is constituted by discovering the Fountain of Youth. Gully searches the entire world yet fails to find the Fountain of Youth. The fountain does not exist. What should Gully conclude from this: that nothing will match his desire for happiness, or that the satisfaction of his happiness is not answered by the Fountain of Youth? It seems more reasonable to conclude that Gully has misidentified the true nature of happiness. His happiness is not to be found in the discovery of the Fountain of Youth but in something he has not yet identified.

In the same way, while many people throughout human history have desired and believed in transcendent yet nonexistent things, it does not follow that there are *no* transcendent objects that satisfy the natural longing for transcendence. All Wielenberg has shown is that people fail to identify the proper object of their universal longing.

The strongest objection to the argument from desire comes from the field of evolutionary psychology. Evolutionary psychology suggests that our longing for transcendence exists because it either enhances our fitness for survival or is a by-product of something that does. In other words, the longing for transcendence is best understood as a natural desire, yet no object satisfies the longing. If this is true, then premise (1) is false, since the longing exists merely to enhance something else, namely our natural desire to survive. And if the longing for transcendence is best understood as a nonnatural desire, nothing but a by-product of a desire to live and survive, then premise (2) of the argument is false. Either way, evolution combined with naturalism (the idea that only the material cosmos exists) undercuts the argument from desire.

In response, we should notice that the objection from evolutionary psychology does not deny the existence of our natural desires. It simply attempts to explain that desire in terms of another natural desire. Our natural desire for God is explained in terms of our natural desire for survival. This seems to work, until the nature of desires themselves are considered.

To put it simply, the problem is that our desires are intrinsically *for* things.[36] We speak of having a desire *for* God or *for* survival or *for* happiness. This intrinsic feature of desires, what philosophers call the "intentionality" or "directedness" of certain features of our mental life, is difficult to accommodate if naturalism is true. Purely material things do not possess this intrinsic intentionality. My brain state is not intrinsically for or about anything. My chair is not intrinsically for or about anything. However, my mental life *is* intrinsically intentional. My thoughts, beliefs, hopes, and desires are directed toward something in a way that purely material things aren't. Naturalism struggles to explain the phenomenon of intentionality in a way that theism does not. Human minds and the intentionality of the mental life can be plausibly explained if a cosmic mind—namely God—exists, because reality is not confined to the material cosmos alone.

Even if the evolutionary story can explain our longing for transcendence, the argument from desire has not failed. The very nature of desire itself is best explained by theism, not naturalism. Erik Wielenberg is wrong to assume they are equals. He argues, "What we have are essentially two competing 'just so stories' [evolutionary psychology and theism]. If that is right, then we have a stalemate. And a stalemate in this context means failure for the argument from desire."[37]

Evolutionary accounts of the longing for transcendence are implausible. For example, Wielenberg argues that restlessness contributes to survival by driving people to succeed in life. Contentment, on the other hand, leads to stagnation, "which in turn breeds reproductive failure. . . . Evolutionarily speaking, a good strategy is never to be entirely satisfied with one's lot in life."[38] Thus, according to Wielenberg, restlessness does not point to a God-shaped hole in the human heart. Rather, restlessness contributes to the survival of the human species.

We can agree that if happiness is found in material things or accomplishments or this-worldly pleasures alone, then contentment can lead to stagnation. Eventually, a person would become disillusioned and recognize that worldly goods cannot satisfy. Yet for those who believe happiness is found in

---

36. For a nice discussion of how evolutionary naturalism cannot accommodate the intentionality of desires, see Conor R. Anderson, "Desire and the Failure of Evolutionary Naturalism," *Philosophia Christi* 17, no. 2 (2015): 369–82.

37. Wielenberg, *God and the Reach of Reason*, 118.

38. Wielenberg, *God and the Reach of Reason*, 117.

otherworldly goods, namely, in union with God, contentment is never stagnation. Throughout history, those who live for something greater than themselves and greater than worldly desires have contributed immensely to the advancement of education, culture, and the common good. For those who accept the offer of "infinite joy,"[39] contentment is obtained, and a powerful purpose for living is found. "Godliness with contentment is great gain" (1 Tim. 6:6 ESV), as Paul notes to Timothy, his protégé in the faith. True contentment does not lead to stagnation, as Wielenberg argues; rather, it indicates a flourishing life.

I conclude that the objection from evolutionary psychology is unsuccessful. The argument from desire is a good argument for God. We've considered one desire, the longing for transcendence, which is found within every human heart. By examining its texture and feel, we've seen that this desire reasonably and naturally points to God as a fitting object. There are countless additional longings that can awaken and set others on the journey of faith—the longing of the human heart for justice, love, beauty, goodness, truth, order, play, comedy, and many more longings that ultimately find their source in God. We could look at each longing like we examined the desire for transcendence, in order to discover their texture and feel and then ask what would best satisfy that longing. In asking and answering this question, using the power of the mind, reason can play a role in awakening the longing for God. Unpacking the argument from desire invites us to embark or reembark on a quest. Reason can shine light into the crevices and hidden corridors of the human heart, awakening longing and prompting a search that ends at the foot of the cross.

The Way of Morality: The Longing for Happiness and the Dialectic of Desire

As noted in chapter 2, everyone longs for truth, goodness, and beauty, transcendent values that ultimately find their source in Jesus. When it comes to the cultural apologist's task of awakening longing, there can be several starting points. We've explored how the imagination and reason can awaken longing. God has also provided humanity with a conscience that longs for goodness. This reality provides another starting place from which to awaken longing. We may ask of those we seek to reach for Jesus, "What good do you long for?"

---

39. Lewis, *The Weight of Glory*, 26.

Almost invariably, the answer is "to be happy."[40] Pascal observes, "All men seek happiness. There are no exceptions. . . . This is the motive of every act of every man, including those who go and hang themselves."[41] This profound statement rings true. We are *obsessed* with being happy. We pursue it with a sense of fervency and urgency—"if only I could have this experience, or that job, or this relationship, or that thing then . . ."—which should tip us off to the fact that something has gone awry.

As cultural apologists, one way for us to awaken desire in others is to point out this universal longing for happiness while admitting that it remains elusive. We can explore how this longing for happiness points to something we've lost. The longing awakens us to the fact that our world isn't the way it ought to be and suggests a time when humankind was truly and completely happy, now only a distant memory.[42] The elusive nature of happiness also exposes our helplessness and hopelessness apart from God. Again, Pascal notes, "This [longing for happiness] he tries in vain to fill with everything around him, seeking in things that are not there the help he cannot find in those that are, though none can help, since this infinite abyss can be filled only with an infinite and immutable object; in other words by God himself."[43] People today are confused about where to find happiness, seeking it in this-worldly goods or religious works instead of in the gospel and in union with God. But as Pascal concludes, "God alone is man's true good."[44] Only when we are united with God will we find true happiness. Cultural apologetics involves drawing attention to this universal longing for happiness and the fruitless efforts of humanity to attain happiness through self-effort or created things. By taking this approach, we can help others become more aware of their heart's deepest longing for God.

C. S. Lewis illustrates how we learn to pay attention to our desires. He describes the process as a kind of dialectic, an investigation into the source of our desires:

---

40. Willian C. Mattison II, "Hope," in *Being Good: Christian Virtues for Everyday Life*, ed. Michael W. Austin and R. Douglas Geivett (Grand Rapids: Eerdmans, 2012), 110–11. Lewis's longing for joy can be understood more generally in this way too: joy, as Lewis understood it, consists in union with God as we enjoy the gifts of God in creaturely response. This is the happiness that God gives to creatures.

41. Pascal, *Pensées*, §148 (p. 45).

42. As Pascal puts it, the longing for happiness shows "there was once a man of true happiness, of which all that now remains is the empty print and trace." Pascal, *Pensées*, §148 (p. 45).

43. Pascal, *Pensées*, §148 (p. 45).

44. Pascal, *Pensées*, §148 (p. 45).

It appeared to me therefore that if a man diligently followed this desire [i.e., the longing for happiness], pursuing the false objects until their falsity appeared and then resolutely abandoning them, he must come out at last into the clear knowledge that the human soul was made to enjoy some object that is never fully given—nay cannot even be imagined as given—in our present mode of subjective and spatio-temporal experience. . . . The dialectic of Desire, faithfully followed, would retrieve all mistakes, head you off from all false paths, and force you not to propound, but to live through, a sort of ontological proof.[45]

The process Lewis describes is a well-trodden path. We tether our hope to a false object, then untether it and retether to another false object, again and again, until the true object of desire is found. Consider the Olympic swimmer Michael Phelps. Phelps is one of the most accomplished athletes of all time. He has won more Olympic medals than anyone in history. Yet after the 2012 Olympics in London, Phelps admitted to struggling with despair, turning to alcohol and drugs, and even contemplating suicide. He checked into a rehab facility where he was encouraged by his friend Ray Lewis (a Christian and NFL star) to read Rick Warren's *Purpose Driven Life*. Phelps stated in an interview with ESPN that the book "turned me into believing there is a power greater than myself and there is a purpose for me on this planet."[46] Phelps lived through the dialectic of desire, and he experienced the emptiness of worldly success attained apart from God. He returned to the 2016 Olympics in Rio with a renewed purpose, a desire to live for something bigger than himself, even as he continued to add to his medal count.

In this example, Ray Lewis played the role of a cultural apologist, helping his friend navigate the awakening of his longings. He simply reached out to Phelps, challenged him to fight for his life, and gave him a book that carried within its pages the "whiffs of transcendence." Undoubtedly, there is more to the story, but it illustrates a point about the process of reenchantment and assisting people in their return to God. We do not act alone. When we are attentive

45. C. S. Lewis, *The Pilgrim's Regress* (Grand Rapids: Eerdmans, 2002), 204–5.

46. Hazel Torres, "Legendary U. S. Swimmer Michael Phelps Reveals How 'Purpose Driven Life' by Rick Warren Saved Him from Suicide," *Christian Today*, August 3, 2016, http://www.christiantoday. com/article/legendary.u.s.swimmer.michael.phelps.reveals.how.purpose.driven.life.by.rick.warren.saved. his.life/92191.htm.

to the Holy Spirit's promptings and step out in obedience to those promptings, the transcendent breaks forth into the mundane. Lives are changed. The journey back to God is possible—both for individuals and for our Western, twenty-first-century culture. As cultural apologists we must be cognizant of the Holy Spirit and attentive to his promptings as we point others to their longing for God through imagination, reason, and the conscience.

RETURNING TO REALITY

So far in this chapter I've given some hints that reenchantment is possible. The first step on the path to reenchantment is the awakening of desire. The next step is a return to reality. By "returning to reality" I mean that Christians ought to (1) see and delight in reality in the same way that Jesus sees and delights in reality and (2) invite others to see and delight in reality in the same way. This reenchantment is not the political takeover of culture or the reestablishing of the Christian Right or a new Christian Left. Our call is to be curators of culture in the hope that Christianity will be seen as plausible and desirable.[47] We "cultivate" the soil so that the "seed" of the gospel will take root in the lives of those we seek to reach (Mark 4:1–9).

However, as some become open to this reenchantment, a danger lurks. False reenchantments are possible too. In the next section, we will explore the process of return, paying careful attention to some of the potential ditches, redirects, and other distractions that can stall or even thwart us along the way.

Seeing Reality as Jesus Does

For Jesus, nothing is mundane. The world is God-bathed, full of wonder and delight. The world is God-permeated. God does not exist in some unreachable domain separated from earth by vast, empty space. God is an ever-present reality. As Dallas Willard puts it, "Nothing—no human being or institution, no time, no space, no spiritual being, no event—stands between God and those

---

47. For a helpful discussion of God's call for Christians to care for and cultivate culture, see Makoto Fujimura, *Culture Care: Reconnecting with Beauty for Our Common Life* (Downers Grove, IL: InterVarsity Press, 2017).

who trust him."[48] This is why Jesus's public ministry commenced with the proclamation to "repent, for the kingdom of *heaven* is at hand" (Matt. 4:17 ESV, italics added). His good news was that heaven is *here*. God is *here*, and lovingly sustains and cares for all he has made. Willard explains,

> Jesus' good news about the kingdom can be an effective guide for our lives only if we share his view of the world in which we live. To his eyes this is a God-bathed and God-permeated world. It is a world filled with a glorious reality. . . . It is a world that is inconceivably beautiful and good because of God and because God is always in it. . . . Until our thoughts of God have found every visible thing and every event glorious with his presence, the word of Jesus has not yet fully seized us.[49]

When we see the world as Jesus does, we see the world in its proper light. We receive it as a gift, as sacred. By perceiving the world as enchanted, we savor it, and find sustenance in it too. We learn to "eat the only food that the universe grows," enjoying the "happiness that God gives" as we "share in His goodness in creaturely response."[50]

The path of return to God lies *through* creation itself. We can't return to this God-infused reality (transcendence) by denying or devaluing the material world. All that God has made is good (Gen. 1:31). All is intrinsically valuable and sacred, even as it is broken and bent. Creation is haunted. *Numen inest.*[51] Cultural apologetics involves cultivating spiritual perception, recognizing that creation itself offers glimpses of the divine. Even more, creation ushers us into God's presence as we learn to see God in and through all that he lovingly has made.

The writings of Pulitzer Prize–winning novelist Marilynne Robinson are infused with a sacramental theology. Her writing helps us see and savor the divine in the midst of the mundane. In an oft-cited passage, she invites readers to consider the ordinary—in this instance water—from a new vantage point.

---

48. Dallas Willard, *The Divine Conspiracy: Rediscovering Our Hidden Life in God* (New York: HarperCollins, 1998), 67.

49. Willard, *The Divine Conspiracy*, 67.

50. C. S. Lewis, *The Problem of Pain* (San Francisco: HarperCollins, 1996), 47.

51. The phrase comes from Ovid's *Fasti*: "Under the Aventine there lay a grove black with the shade of holm-oaks; at sight of it you could say, 'There is a spirit here [*numen inest*].'" Ovid, *Fasti*, iii.294–96, trans. James George Frazer (Cambridge, MA: Harvard University Press, 1959), 141–43.

In *Gilead*, the Congregationalist minister John Ames knows his time on earth is coming to an end, so he writes a series of letters to his young son. Ames shares a memory of an earlier time when he watched a young couple stroll along on a leisure morning:

> The sun had come up brilliantly after a heavy rain, and the trees were glistening and very wet. On some impulse, plain exuberance, I suppose, the fellow jumped up and caught hold of a branch, and a storm of luminous water came pouring down on the two of them, and they laughed and took off running, the girl sweeping water off her hair and her dress as if she were a little bit disgusted, but she wasn't. It was a beautiful thing to see, like something from a myth. I don't know why I thought of that now, except perhaps because it is easy to believe in such moments that water was made primarily for blessing, and only secondarily for growing vegetables or doing the wash. I wish I had paid more attention to it. My list of regrets may seem unusual, but who can know that they are, really. This is an interesting planet. It deserves all the attention you can give it.[52]

The laughter and exuberance of the young couple, the sun sparkling off the "luminous" water, and the holiness of the moment are beautifully portrayed by Robinson. In that moment, the world holds its breath as this young couple and the watching minister pull back the curtain and glimpse reality as it really is. This wonderfully inviting picture is infused with longing. As a writer, Robinson sees and delights in reality, and she invites others to see and delight in it as well. Inviting others to see the sacredness and beauty of creation is not a task limited to Pulitzer Prize–winning authors. God wants each of us involved in this work. But what does it look like? How do we invite others to see the world as Jesus does, as a world infused with God-given beauty and meaning?

Inviting Others to See Reality as Jesus Does

In Lystra the apostle Paul healed a man crippled from birth. As the man picked himself up and began to walk, the crowd was amazed. They began to worship Paul and Barnabas, saying, "The gods have come down to us in the

---

52. Marilynne Robinson, *Gilead* (New York: Farrar, Straus and Giroux, 2004), 27–28.

likeness of men!" (Acts 14:11 ESV). The Lycaonians believed Paul was Hermes and Barnabas was Zeus, and in response to this misunderstanding, Paul and Barnabas tore their garments. They implored the crowd to stop worshiping them, since they too were mere men (Acts 14:12–15a ESV). Never one to miss an opportunity, Paul began to proclaim the good news, inviting them to "turn from . . . vain things" (i.e., idols) to "a living God, who made the heaven and the earth and the sea and all that is in them" (Acts 14:15b ESV). Paul points to the world and then argues that the living God is its Creator. But what he says next is unexpected.

Paul doesn't point his listeners to human sinfulness and their need for forgiveness (although that is important and a necessary part of ultimately understanding and embracing the gospel). Rather, he draws their attention to all the good and delightful things God has given to his creatures: "In past generations he allowed all the nations to walk in their own ways. Yet he did not leave himself without witness, for he did good by giving you rains from heaven and fruitful seasons, satisfying your hearts with food and gladness" (Acts 14:16–17 ESV). Paul calls his listeners to take note of the created things that yield pleasure—food, rain, the seasons of growth and fruitfulness. He implores them to see God as the giver of these things. This is significant because it suggests that *the good and pleasurable things in this world witness to God, who is good and delights in all that he has made.* Granted, we can be led astray by our pleasures, but understood properly, they are generous gifts from God.

Paul's invitation to the people is instructive as a model for helping others return to reality. He implores his listeners first to repent, to turn from idolatry and believe in and worship the true God. Second, he urges them to see everything they enjoy as gifts from God, signs that God exists and lovingly sustains and cares for that which he has made. This model is useful in our context as well, as we invite others to see and delight in God's gifts and to participate in a "life-world rebellion,"[53] where the old, disenchanted ways of seeing are abandoned in favor of a new way of seeing. Paul's example suggests one way to do this: to point to the things we all enjoy and help others see that delight is not found *in* them but comes *through* them.[54]

---

53. Paul Tyson, *Returning to Reality: Christian Platonism for Our Times* (Eugene, OR: Cascade, 2014), 182.

54. C. S. Lewis, *The Weight of Glory* (New York: HarperCollins, 2001), 30. Lewis speaks of the beauty found in books or music, but the point generalizes to the delight we experience in all things we enjoy: they beckon us toward something beyond the thing itself. They also awaken longing.

When the pleasures of this world become the ultimate objects of our longing, they are idols. But when pleasures evoke delight and longing for "the scent of a flower we have not found, the echo of a tune we have not heard, news from a country we have never visited,"[55] they produce a willingness to be enchanted.[56] As we build a bridge from "our Athens" or "our Lystra" to Jesus and the gospel, we invite others to see and delight in reality as Jesus does.

As mentioned earlier, openness to enchantment doesn't ensure return. False reenchantments are possible. There are many pitfalls and potholes that can trip up those we seek to reach with the gospel. Three false reenchantments are particularly appealing in our culture.

False Reenchantment 1: Contemporary Humanism

The French philosopher Luc Ferry rejected materialism, the view that only matter and the material cosmos exists, because he felt it inadequately accounted for the reality of transcendence. According to Ferry, transcendence is the idea "that there is within us something in excess of nature or history."[57] Despite this move toward transcendence, Ferry does not believe in the type of transcendence we've been discussing here, where there is a supernatural being who exists beyond and is responsible for this world. Rather, Ferry opts for a "here and now" transcendence that he calls contemporary humanism. According to contemporary humanism, reality is transcendent because there are things that exist in this world that are beyond our ability to comprehend. For Ferry, transcendent moral values are patently real and discoverable, yet "they are housed in concrete experience, not in a metaphysical fiction," such as God, a Platonic heaven, or society.[58] Values, beauty, mathematical truths, and concepts like love are "at once beyond me, yet nowhere to be found except within me, manifest only inside my consciousness and conscience."[59]

---

55. Lewis, *The Weight of Glory*, 31.

56. Alan Jacobs says this about C. S. Lewis and his posture toward reality: "Lewis's mind was above all characterized by a willingness to be enchanted," and in him was "an openness to delight, to the sense that there's more to the world than meets the jaundiced eye, to the possibility that *anything* could happen to someone who is ready to meet that anything. For someone with eyes to see and the courage to explore, even an old wardrobe full of musty coats could be the doorway into another world." Alan Jacobs, *The Narnian: The Life and Imagination of C. S. Lewis* (New York: HarperCollins, 2005), xxi.

57. Luc Ferry, *A Brief History of Thought: A Philosophical Guide to Living* (New York: Harper Perennial, 2011), 227.

58. Ferry, *A Brief History of Thought*, 236–37.

59. Ferry, *A Brief History of Thought*, 238.

Ferry's contemporary humanism is a step in the right direction in its rejec-tion of materialism. His world is not entirely disenchanted. Ferry creates room for beauty, goodness, and truth. Still, his version of "transcendence within immanence" is both unsustainable and unsatisfying, as he attempts "to confer rigorous meaning to human experience as formulated by a humanism freed from the illusion of metaphysics."[60] Ferry's contemporary humanism postulates a material world and objective moral values. These are straightforward *meta-physical* claims about the nature of reality. Assertions to the contrary, Ferry's contemporary humanism is not "freed from the illusion of metaphysics." On the other hand, Ferry's contemporary humanism is freed from *supernatural* meta-physics. Contemporary humanism has all the advantages of theft over honest toil, embracing the grandeur of the religious worldview while refusing to provide an explanation for its reality.[61] In stubbornly refusing to explain *how* there is objective beauty, love, justice, and truth, it buries its head in the ground like an ostrich.[62]

More importantly, contemporary humanism is unsatisfying. The "beam supporting the entire philosophical edifice of a secular humanism," according to Ferry, is the possibility of loving another, even if only for a moment.[63] In loving another, we experience a moment of exhale, a glimpse of life free from pain and suffering, an "eternal instant" or a moment of grace "where the fear of death . . . is itself removed."[64] Life becomes temporally bound—an acknowl-edgment that we all will die—but also life is meaningful since we can, for a time, love. Yet in settling for the glimpse—the moment of exhale when life is experienced as it ought to be—contemporary humanism turns the sign into the sacrament. The glimpses we have of heaven in the midst of this earthly reality were never intended to wholly satisfy us. A sign whets the appetite and awakens desire for the true object of our longing: God himself.

---

60. Ferry, *A Brief History of Thought*, 236.

61. As the philosopher Bertrand Russell quipped in a different context, "The method of 'postulating' what we want has many advantages; they are the same as the advantages of theft over honest toil. Let us leave them to others and proceed with our honest toil." Russell, *Introduction to Mathematical Philosophy* (London: Routledge, 1919), 71.

62. Not all atheists are ostrich humanists. Some do attempt to explain how there can be objective values in a godless universe. See in particular the Platonic atheist Erik J. Wielenberg, "In Defense of Non-Natural Non-Theistic Moral Realism," *Faith and Philosophy* 26, no. 1 (2009): 23–41; and Wielenberg, *Robust Ethics: The Metaphysics and Epistemology of Godless Normative Realism* (New York: Oxford University Press, 2014). I will discuss Wielenberg's Platonic atheism further in ch. 6.

63. Ferry, *A Brief History of Thought*, 254–55.

64. Ferry, *A Brief History of Thought*, 260.

The "glimpse" is no longer a portal to another world. Rather, the glimpse itself becomes a lifeless idol, an iron cage, which on its own can never fully satisfy and ultimately enslaves.

False Reenchantment 2: Augmented and Virtual Realities

Technology has long been viewed as a means of salvation from pain and death, and today it offers us a new experience of transcendence through augmented and virtual reality. Consider augmented realities, such as the video game *Pokémon Go*, which combines its world of fictional animals with physical reality. In the summer of 2016, *Pokémon Go* captured the imagination of millions of Americans, filling streets, museums, parks—and even churches—with people staring at their phones as they tried to catch the mythical creatures appearing (through the phone's video screen) in real, physical locations. Virtual realities offer a similar promise of transcendence. Popular video games, such as *Second Life* and its spin-offs, allow people to create second selves, or avatars, to live out an alternative life in an imaginary universe. Trans- and posthumanist movements take the promise of transcendence to another level altogether. The 2014 movie *Transcendence* starred Johnny Depp as Dr. Will Caster, an expert in artificial intelligence. Before his death, Caster's mind was successfully uploaded to a virtual reality where his life continued as a bodiless virtual being.[65]

Transhumanism and posthumanism have also found enthusiastic support beyond Hollywood screenwriters.[66] Backed by organizations such as Google and NASA, transhumanist and posthumanist institutions such as Humanity+ are working to usher in the next stage of human evolution.[67] New technologies will help "eliminate aging and . . . greatly enhance human intellectual, physical, and psychological capacities."[68] The underlying hope is that death itself will be overcome. As the futurist Ray Kurzweil (who is currently the director of engineering at Google) describes it,

---

65. See also Zoltan Istvan, *The Transhumanist Wager* (Reno, NV: Futurity Image Media, 2013). Istvan's novel is an attempt to express the transhumanist vision in a fictional story.

66. Andrea Vicini, SJ, and Agnes M. Brazal, "Longing for Transcendence: Cyborgs and Trans- and Posthumans," *Theological Studies* 76, no. 1 (2015): 155.

67. You can find out more about Humanity+ at www.humanityplus.org.

68. Hava Tirosh-Samuelson, "Transhumanism as a Secularist Faith," *Zygon* 47 (2012): 716, cited in Vicini and Brazal, "Longing for Transcendence," 156.

Up until now, our mortality was tied to the longevity of our *hardware*. . . .
As we cross the divide to instantiate ourselves into our computational
technology, our identity will be based on our evolving mind file. We
will be software, not hardware. . . . As software, our mortality will no
longer be dependent on the survival of the computing circuitry. . . . Our
immortality will be a matter of being sufficiently careful to make fre-
quent backups.[69]

The promise of science is a new utopia where transformed humanity will live
free of pain and free of constraint, free to do and be whatever we wish.

These technological offers of reenchantment and transcendence appeal
to our longings, but they cannot deliver on their promise. Augmented and
virtual realities do not provide genuine reenchantment because they fail to
help us see and delight in the real world. When we enter a virtual reality the
technologically fabricated fiction we have created further removes us from
the real world. Moreover, these augmented and virtual realities reflect the
dominant, and fallen, structures of the real world. There is no virtual door
providing a way of escape from the brokenness, alienation, and loneliness of a
disenchanted world.

Trans- and posthumanism makes for good science fiction, but they will
never deliver on what they promise. Human nature is not endlessly malleable,
and there are limits to what science and technology can offer to us. Downloading
human consciousness is possible only if the mind is reducible or identical to the
brain (purely material and physical). But if the mind is immaterial, it would
be impossible to "download" one's thoughts, beliefs, hopes, and dreams onto a
physical hard drive.[70] These dreams create false hope, perpetuating the lie that
we can save ourselves. The result is the same as it has always been: a path to
eternal misery.

---

69. Ray Kurzweil, *The Age of Spiritual Machines: When Computers Exceed Human Intelligence* (New
York: Penguin, 1999), 129, emphasis original, cited in Vicini and Brazal, "Longing for Transcendence," 157.

70. For an excellent discussion on the biblical teaching related to anthropology (the doctrine of man),
see John W. Cooper, *Body, Soul, and Life Everlasting* (Grand Rapids: Eerdmans, 2000); for a nice introduction
to the debate over whether the mind is identical to the brain, see J. P. Moreland, *The Soul: How We Know
It's Real and Why It Matters* (Chicago: Moody Press, 2014), where it is argued that we are souls (immaterial
substances) that have material bodies; for what it means to be created in the image of God, see John F. Kilner,
Dignity and Destiny: Humanity in the Image of God (Grand Rapids: Eerdmans, 2015).

False Reenchantment 3: Neopaganism

In the 1960s, sociologists predicted the imminent demise of religion. Scholars predicted by the twenty-first century our society would become entirely secular, abandoning religious superstition. Then, precisely the opposite happened. Sociologists admit they were wrong, telling us we now live in a post-secular age where religion is poised to play a dominant role in the unfolding of the twenty-first century.[71]

While many individuals in the global East and South have been turning to Christ as the answer to their longings, many in the West have faltered on the path of return, settling for neopaganism, a new spiritualism that is often atheistic, individualistic, and experiential. In neopaganism, as distinct from the secular world that preceded it, reality is not completely flat, nor is humanity completely buffered or protected from the supernatural. Instead, humanity is vulnerable to unexplained powers, perhaps even gods and goddesses, the paranormal, or the occult.

Yet neopaganism is another false reenchantment. It provides the trappings of transcendence while reconfiguring human desires, aspirations, and passions away from the good, true, and beautiful toward the evil, false, and horrific. We find evidence of the appeal of neopaganism in the frenzy of interest in and consumption of books, television series, and movies that celebrate and elevate the occult or paranormal. Recent examples include *The Twilight Saga*, *Underworld*, *Grimm*, *American Horror Story*, *Stranger Things*, and *The Magicians*, to name a few.[72]

To be clear, the emergence of neopaganism is more of a broader cultural response than an organized movement. When I refer to neopaganism, I'm speaking of a kind of postmodern spirituality that embraces the experiential over the doctrinal, the occult over the divine. Neopaganism is not the same as

---

71. Douglas Jacobsen and Rhonda Hustedt Jacobsen, "Postsecular American: A New Context for Higher Education," *The American University in a Postsecular Age*, ed. Douglas Jacobsen and Rhonda Hustedt Jacobsen (Oxford: Oxford University Press, 2008), 10.

72. I'm not saying that all of these movies and television series are bad. Rather, I'm simply pointing out that the culture is obsessed with the paranormal, the occult, and the mythical. Both television series on the list that I've actually watched—*Grimm* and *Stranger Things*—I enjoyed. Moreover, I think these kinds of stories *can* play a role in reenchanting the world. However, in this section, I am concerned with a kind of spirituality—what I am calling neopaganism—that embraces the paranormal or occult as the stopping point for the transcendent. For an excellent article on *Stranger Things* and the possibility of reenchantment, see Alissa Wilkinson, "How 'Stranger Things' Re-Enchants the World," *Christianity Today*, July 26, 2016, http://www.christianitytoday.com/ct/2016/july-web-only/stranger-things.html?start=1.

ancient paganism. C. S. Lewis, in contemplating the possibility of reenchantment, believed that ancient paganism could be a potential first step for people on the path of return.[73] Paganism offers us, as Lewis puts it, "good dreams," those "queer stories scattered all through the heathen religions about a god who dies and comes to life again and, by his death, has somehow given new life to men."[74] The ancient stories are "good dreams" because they point us to the true story of the world and help resacramentalize nature.

Neopaganism, on the other hand, shocks and tantalizes, pointing to an unseen reality that is finite and malevolent. Neopaganism calls out to our awakened longing, putting those longings, once captured, under its curse. Neopaganism is a false reenchantment because it does not evoke the pleasure of a dream, but that of a nightmare, where we are trapped in a world that is magical, but not good. It is a hopeless world, devoid of love and joy, without a moral order. Immortality, if it can be had at all, becomes a kind of hell.

ENCHANTMENT AND THE BARRIER TO UNBELIEF

Disenchantment has made unbelief possible and belief in God difficult. Some today, such as Luc Ferry, long for God but find Christianity too implausible: "I find the Christian proposition infinitely more tempting—except for the fact that I do not believe it. But were it to be true I would certainly be a taker."[75] Others, such as the atheist philosopher Thomas Nagel, find Christianity (or theism in general) plausible, but not desirable: "I don't want there to be a God; I don't want the universe to be like that."[76] A cultural apologist seeks to help others see Christianity as *both* plausible and desirable.

73. "I sometimes wonder whether we shall not have to re-convert men to real Paganism as a preliminary to converting them to Christianity. If they were Stoics, Orphics, Mithraists, or (better still) peasants worshipping the Earth, our task might be easier." C. S. Lewis, "Modern Man and His Categories of Thought," in *Present Concerns: Journalistic Essays*, ed. Walter Hooper (New York: Harcourt, 1986), 66.

74. Lewis, *Mere Christianity*, 50.

75. Ferry, *A Brief History of Thought*, 263.

76. Thomas Nagel, *The Last Word* (New York: Oxford University Press, 1997), 130. See also Nagel, *Mind and Cosmos* (Oxford: Oxford University Press, 2012), where he argues that materialist accounts of life, consciousness, reason, and value fail. He argues that the only two plausible contenders to explain these phenomena are theism and panpsychism. But, since he doesn't want theism to be true, he opts for panpscyhism, the view that reality is fundamentally conscious. For a helpful review of Nagel's *Mind and Cosmos*, see J. P. Moreland, "A Reluctant Traveler's Guide for Slouching toward Theism," *Philosophia Christi* 14, no. 2 (2012): 429–38.

To this point, we've sought to diagnose the problem, namely, the disenchantment of our Western culture. In the chapters that follow we will unpack a holistic approach to life and ministry that addresses disenchantment. All too often Christians try to fit Jesus into our own agendas, treating him like a genie instead of Lord and Savior. All too often our apologetic efforts focus on the plausibility of Christianity without much attention to its desirability. But Christianity's plausibility is not the only or even the most significant obstacle to belief in a disenchanted age. People question the goodness of God, the attractiveness of the church, the beauty of Jesus, and the sufficiency of the gospel to meet human needs and longings of the heart. A cultural apologetic of return calls the church to see and delight in the ever-present, all-consuming Creator, Sustainer, and Redeemer.

Like the prisoner freed from Plato's Cave, Christians must be set free from the cultural captivity of disenchantment. As theologian Hans Boersma says, we must "relearn to see the world with sacramental eyes."[77] It is our "only faithful way forward."[78] Once freed of disenchantment, we can call others to see and delight in the world as we do, in such a way that *unbelief*, and not belief in God, becomes more difficult. As Charles Taylor has said, "Going against God is not an option in the enchanted world."[79]

An enchanted world is infused with the divine. In an enchanted world, humanity is vulnerable, and "the prospect for rejecting God does not involve retiring to the safe redoubt of the buffered self, but rather chancing ourselves in the field of forces without him."[80] We must not be beholden to the lie that all is well in the world and the church. This is not a time for business as usual. Eternal destinies are at stake. The future of the church is at stake.

In the chapters that follow I invite you to journey with me as we unpack our model of cultural apologetics, beginning in "our Athens" with the universal longings for beauty, truth, and goodness and utilizing our God-given guides: imagination, reason, and conscience.

---

77. Boersma, *Heavenly Participation: The Weaving of a Sacramental Tapestry* (Grand Rapids: Eerdmans, 2011), 99.

78. Boersma, *Heavenly Participation*, 189.

79. Taylor, *A Secular Age* (Cambridge, MA: Belknap, 2007), 41.

80. Taylor, *A Secular Age*, 41.

INTERLUDE

Looking at and Looking Along

C. S. Lewis describes a time when he was standing in a dark toolshed. A single beam of light penetrated the darkness through a crack at the top of the shed door. *Looking at* the beam, all Lewis could see was the light and the dust particles floating within the light.

Then, Lewis shifted his position so he was *looking along* the beam of light.

He saw green leaves swishing in the wind on the tree outside. Further along, ninety-six million miles away, he saw the sun. His conclusion? "Looking along the beam, and looking at the beam are very different experiences."[1] In *looking at* the beam, Lewis contemplated the nature of light itself. In *looking along* the beam, Lewis was led to its source: the sun.

The distinction between looking at and looking along will be helpful as we consider the plausibility and desirability of Jesus and the gospel in a disenchanted culture. In the chapters that follow, as we build our bridge from "Athens" to Jesus and the gospel, we will spend time *looking at* each plank— imagination, reason, and conscience—examining its nature and exploring the cause of its existence. We will also look at some underappreciated reasons for the existence of God: the connection between the human imagination and a divine artist, the argument from human reason to a divine mind, and the argument from objective morality to a divine goodness.

---

1. C. S. Lewis, "Meditation in a Toolshed," *God in the Dock: Essays on Theology and Ethics*, ed. Walter Hooper (Grand Rapids: Eerdmans, 1970), 212.

We will also *look along* our newly constructed bridge, testing each plank's strength, walking their length, enjoying the experiences of imagining, reasoning, and willing on our quest for beauty, truth, and goodness. Once the objects of our quest are found, we shall look beyond them to their source, finding Christ as the Beauty of all beautiful things, the Truth to which all truths point, and the Good of all good things. In Christ, the objects of our contemplation and enjoyment come together. Reason and romance, head and heart, are part of a single, integrated path, which leads to Christ if faithfully followed.

Annie Dillard said this about light: "I cannot cause light; the most I can do is try to put myself in the path of its beam."[2] In what follows, we will attempt just that with respect to beauty, truth, and goodness. We shall put ourselves in the path of these "lights," following the crumbs, clues, and signs along the way, until we pass through them to Christ himself. And we will learn how to invite others on the journey as cultural apologists.

2. Annie Dillard, *Pilgrim at Tinker Creek* (New York: Harper Perennial, 2007), 35.

CHAPTER 4

IMAGINATION

> To see the beauty of the world is to put your hands on the
> lines that run uninterrupted through life and through death.
> Touching them is an act of hope, for perhaps someone on
> the other side, if there is another side, is touching them, too.[1]
>
> *Mark Helprin*

> Being then God's offspring, we ought not to think that the
> divine being is like gold or silver or stone, an image formed
> by the art and imagination of man.
>
> *Acts 17:29 ESV*

In the movie *La La Land,* Emma Stone's character Mia is coaxed into one final audition before abandoning her dream of becoming an actress. Having been passed over too often for better looking or more dynamic actresses, she has lost hope that she is good enough to make it in the entertainment business. Urged on by her boyfriend Sebastian, an aspiring Jazz artist, and with a sense of reckless abandonment sprinkled with a dose of hope, she walks into the room where two casting agents are waiting for her. They ask her to tell them a story. A smile curls on her lips. Mia sings about her aunt, a dreamer in Paris who inspired her to become an actress. As Mia stands before the casting agents,

---

1. The quote is from a fictional character, and Italian professor of aesthetics, in the novel *A Soldier of the Great War* by Mark Helprin, as quoted in Gregory Wolfe, *Beauty Will Save the World: Recovering the Human in an Ideological Age* (Wilmington, DE: ISI Books, 2011), 8.

all the years of toil, waiting, hope, and longing find expression. She sings of "fools who dream," "hearts that ache," and "ripples from pebbles." When I first heard these words, watching the film in a theater, the words, emotion, and melody conspired together to lay my heart bare.

It's a raw, intense, and beautiful scene, one that touched my wife and I profoundly, and we found ourselves weeping. But to understand why, I need to share the rest of the story of our date that night. Earlier that evening at dinner, my wife, Ethel, and I had talked about our own dreams. Ethel had always longed to follow in the footsteps of Wendell Berry, Marilynne Robinson, and Flannery O'Connor and write fiction that evokes beauty, truth, and goodness without being sentimental, preachy, or crass. Yet the demands of raising four children, serving in ministry, and supporting a husband pursuing higher education had kept her from those dreams—until recently. Now that I'm done pursuing my academic dreams, we've agreed that it's Ethel's time to explore her dreams. This past year Ethel took creative writing classes at Dallas Theological Seminary, the first tangible steps toward realizing her dream. This has affirmed her abilities, challenged her to hone her craft, and encouraged her to pursue writing as a vocation. But doubts linger. As we ate that evening, Ethel had shared her doubts: "What if I am not good enough? What if I get passed over because others are better, brighter, younger?"

We had also talked of my hopes. My paternal grandfather and grandmother were an actor and musician, respectively. After my grandfather passed away, I was looking through a collection of his papers and I stumbled upon his birth certificate. I had always known my grandfather as Val Gould, but the name on his birth certificate was Zelig Goldfader. Puzzled, I asked my dad why it was different. Pausing, my father shared that my grandfather was Jewish. His parents had emigrated to the United States from Russia, settling in Worcester, Massachusetts, shortly before his birth in 1912. When grandfather was sixteen, he left home to become an actor, but Hollywood in the 1920s and '30s was a hotbed of anti-Semitism. To blend in, Zelig Goldfader, my grandfather, changed his name to Val Gould.

Until that moment, I had never realized I was Jewish.

I also learned that he had been a vaudevillian actor, performing with stars such as Mae West in London and traveling the world speaking to American troops with Bob Hope during and after the Great War. As "Mr. Quaker Oats" my grandfather spoke on democracy and patriotism to almost one million high school students in the 1950s and '60s (in full eighteenth-century garb, of course). He had bit roles in television, radio, and several movies. Talking about my grandparents that night, I wondered, "Why had I never become an artist? Was there something in me lying dormant, a hidden talent waiting to be unleashed?"

And so, unexpectedly, our hearts were primed for that tearful moment watching *La La Land*. That scene connected with the deep longings, and fears, in my wife's heart. It connected with something in my heart as well—my desire to live a great life, to do something that matters. And so we wept.

Great art does that. Stories move the heart. Beauty awakens our longings, and the imagination paints pictures in our mind that help us see reality more clearly. As we talked about the movie on our drive home, we were especially aware of this powerful medium. Art has an ability to bypass our defenses and touch our identity in a way that nothing else does (see figure 4.1).

FIGURE 4.1: The Human Quest for Beauty

THE EXILE OF BEAUTY

While our culture recognizes and celebrates various expressions of art and recognizes our hunger for beauty, in many quarters, confusion abounds over its value. Some hold beauty *captive*, exploiting it as a commodity for awakening our base appetites and fleecing our bank accounts. Others exile beauty, viewing our longing for beauty with ambivalence or outright disdain. As cultural apologists we need to bring an appreciation for beauty back into the church, reclaiming it as an essential aspect of Christian formation and the proclamation of the gospel. Let's begin by considering the history of the church and its relationship with the arts. Our attitude toward art, music, and other human attempts to create and capture beauty have evolved and shifted over the last five hundred years. It's a complicated history, and today I believe many Christians confuse the nature and role of beauty for three reasons.

First, there is a strain of *anti-intellectualism* in today's church. Classically, beauty was thought to be an objective feature of the world, and judgments of taste were about beautiful objects, not simply a matter of personal, subjective opinion dependent on the subject's state of mind.[2] The Enlightenment era introduced a profound shift, relegating the values and judgments that were once considered objectively true to the realm of personal preference. Beauty became a matter of opinion and taste, and today we witness the full flowering of this trend toward the subjective. Personal preference reigns supreme and has been enshrined as the new authority in our disenchanted world: "You like brussels sprouts; I like Twinkies. You like Van Halen; I like van Gogh. You like Pablo Picasso; I like Paul Simon." Something is beautiful to me and repulsive to you. It seems beauty is simply "in the eye of the beholder." Yet while it may be true that we behold beauty with the eye (or ear or pallet), beauty is more than a matter of personal taste.

Beauty is an objective feature of reality, part of the furniture of the world God has made. But the contemporary subjectivism about beauty has caused confusion within the church. Like the culture at large, we have bought into the so-called fact-value split.[3] We lack a theology of beauty. Failing to understand *what* beauty is, we don't understand its purpose or where it comes from.

---

2. Roger Scruton, *Beauty: A Very Short Introduction* (Oxford: Oxford University Press, 2011), 5.

3. For more on the devastating consequences of the fact-value split, see Nancy Pearcey, *Saving Leonardo: A Call to Resist the Secular Assault on Mind, Morals, and Meaning* (Nashville: B&H, 2010).

Second, the Western church is captive to *pragmatism*. As products of our culture, our minds have been trained to prefer the pragmatic over the beautiful. We seek programs, strategies, and policies that produce immediate results. We focus (rightly) on truth and argue for our position. We focus (rightly) on morality and goodness and argue for our way of living. But we forget that truth and goodness are related to beauty. It is possible to communicate the truth in an ugly way. Someone can do what is morally right without a corresponding love for the beauty and glory of God. Some in our churches today deride art as a utilitarian practice—something done rather than something curated. But the Bible, in presenting God as Creator, encourages us to associate beauty with creativity and imagination. Others might see beauty as irrelevant to Christian discipleship and evangelism, disconnected from presenting the truth about God. Yet we neglect the role of beauty to our detriment, as beauty plays a key role in awakening and sustaining our longing for what is good, our longing to return home in our spiritual journey.

A third reason for the neglect of beauty in the church might be called *philistinism*.[4] While our contemporary culture acknowledges the place of beauty, a consideration of today's art—whether music, painting, sculpture, dance, literature, or film—leaves many of us in the church cringing at its glorification of gore, sexuality, and the perverse. Rightly wanting to pursue purity, Christians shun certain forms of art to avoid the corrosive and ugly. Yet this can have negative side effects as the quest for beauty is abandoned. The imagination atrophies, and ironically in the name of piety and purity, our perception of reality grows mundane and ordinary, lacking an appreciation for the mysterious, the holy, and the beautiful.

Anti-intellectualism, pragmatism, and philistinism are traps we must avoid. The Bible calls us to love God with all of our being, and this means connecting our whole life to the lordship of Jesus and the beauty of the gospel. A key task of cultural apologetics is cultivating and creating beauty. We must learn to utilize art, the imagination, and our innate longing for beauty to draw others to the beauty of Jesus and the gospel.

To begin, we will need to develop a biblical theology of beauty. We begin with God's commandment to Moses to build the tabernacle.

---

4. Wolfe, *Beauty Will Save the World*, 5.

BEAUTY'S CALL

In Exodus, the Israelites "go out" from the land of Egypt as God delivers Israel from slavery and establishes them as his chosen nation. They are blessed to be a blessing to all (Gen. 12:1–3). In Exodus 31:1–11, God commands Moses to build the tabernacle and its furnishings, physical objects that will house his manifest presence among his people:

> Then the LORD said to Moses, "See, I have chosen Bezalel son of Uri, the son of Hur, of the tribe of Judah, and I have filled him with the Spirit of God, with wisdom, with understanding, with knowledge and with all kinds of skills—to make artistic designs for work in gold, silver and bronze, to cut and set stones, to work in wood, and to engage in all kinds of crafts. Moreover, I have appointed Oholiab son of Ahisamak, of the tribe of Dan, to help him. Also I have given ability to all the skilled workers to make everything I have commanded you: the tent of meeting, the ark of the covenant law with the atonement cover on it, and all the other furnishings of the tent—the table and its articles, the pure gold lampstand and all its accessories, the altar of incense, the altar of burnt offering and all its utensils, the basin with its stand—and also the woven garments, both the sacred garments for Aaron the priest and the garments for his sons when they serve as priests, and the anointing oil and fragrant incense for the Holy Place. They are to make them just as I commanded you."

We can make several observations about God's instructions regarding the objects that accommodate his holy presence.

First, *notice that there are artists within the community of Israel*. This may be obvious, but it is worth noting. We read of Bezalel (v. 2), Oholiab (v. 6), and a community of artists (v. 6).[5] This is quite striking because the Israelites have just escaped from Egypt where they were enslaved for hundreds of years, performing manual labor for Pharaoh's and Egypt's glory. We might expect these artistic endeavors to be lost during that time. Surely there are needs to be met. Who has time to create or appreciate art while living in slavery? Yet here we

---

5. This community of artists included both men and woman, as we learn in Exodus 35:25–26.

find a community of artists among the former slaves. While the word *artist* is not specifically mentioned, we find words, depending on the translation used, such as "craftsmanship," various "kinds of skills," the role of a "craftsman," the creation of "artistic designs," and an acknowledgment of "skilled workers." Culturally, we tend to separate the disciplines of art and craft, but prior to the industrial revolution these two disciplines were more closely related as craftsmanship—the expression of creativity in making things and objects. Craftsmanship can be understood as the "skilled manipulation of materials in object making," and the best craftsman had the ability to "transfigure matter" and "reveal beauty."[6]

Second, notice that *God calls the artists by name and fills them with his Spirit to accomplish their task.* God is involved in the creative process. He knows who the best artists are. He knows their abilities and their heart. God calls Bezalel and Oholiab by name. Not only does God call the artist by name, we read in verse 3 that God filled Bezalel with his Spirit, which is the first mention in Scripture of someone being filled with the Spirit of God. This filling of the Spirit is not identical to the New Covenant indwelling of the Holy Spirit; instead, it should be understood as a God-given ability to accomplish a task God wants that person to do. Bezalel (and Oholiab) are called by God to lead the tabernacle construction project, and they are filled with God's Spirit to carry out his command (Ex. 31:2–5).

Finally, notice that *God calls the artists in Israel to make things: art and artistic designs, the tabernacle, and its furnishings.* According to Francis Schaeffer, God's command to Moses to make the tabernacle and its furnishings encompasses "every form of representational art that men have ever known."[7] This command to make and create things raises several important questions. First, why the tabernacle? God had rescued his people from the hands of Egypt. He had given them a cloud by day and a fire by night to lead them. He had given them the law, a moral code to live by, but still they needed something else. They needed God's presence, and this is what led to the creation of the tabernacle. As God says in Exodus 25:8, "Then have them make a sanctuary for me, and I

---

6. Mary McCleary, "The Work of Our Hands," in *It Was Good: Making Art to the Glory of God*, ed. Ned Bustard (Baltimore: Square Halo, 2006), 127.

7. Francis Schaeffer, *Art and the Bible* (Downers Grove, IL: InterVarsity Press, 2006), 20.

will dwell among them." What the Israelites needed most—and this is a theme from Genesis to Revelation—is God's presence.

But why the specific materials mentioned? Fourteen specific materials are called for in the construction of the tabernacle and its furnishings, including gold, silver, and bronze (Ex. 25:3; 31:4); onyx stones (Ex. 25:7; 31:5); acacia wood (Ex. 25:5; 31:5); woven garments of blue, purple, and scarlet materials, fine linen, and goat hair (Ex. 25:4; 31:10); oils, fragrant incense (Ex. 31:11), and more.[8] If God's goal was pragmatic and utilitarian, many of these materials would not have been used. Iron is a more practical building material than gold, silver, or bronze. Onyx stones are scarce and rarely mentioned, but they appear in the description of the garden of Eden (Gen. 2:12). Colored wool was expensive and difficult to obtain. And why the specific dimensions? In Exodus 25:9, God commands Moses, "Make this tabernacle and all its furnishings exactly like the pattern I will show you," and we see the detailed pattern in Exodus 25–30.

My purpose in asking these questions is to draw your attention to a deeper, more fundamental question: Where else in Scripture do we see God delineating and defining, separating and specifying boundaries, filling a place with abundance, order, and beauty? We see this clearly in the creation account of Genesis. The central joy of the garden of Eden—a place of deep order, abundance, and beauty—was the unmediated presence of God himself. And just as he had done in Eden, God gives his people the tabernacle as a place of order, abundance, and beauty. God himself dwells in the tabernacle, which he created to remind his people of their *home*.[9] The tabernacle was a divinely crafted model that pointed to a greater reality, when all was as it should be and humanity experienced the unmediated presence of God.

What does this suggest about the role of art in attuning our hearts and desires to God? Does God care about art? Does he utilize beauty? Does he seek to engage our imagination? Scripture answers with a resounding yes! Art is not meant to be an *object* of worship; it is an *aid* to worship.[10] We can go a step

---

8. McCleary, "The Work of Our Hands," 126.

9. I first heard the connection between the tabernacle and the garden of Eden in an excellent sermon on Exodus 25 by JT English, "Finding Your Way Home," the Village Church, Flower Mound, Texas, March 26, 2017, http://www.tvcresources.net/resource-library/sermons/finding-our-way-home.

10. Thus, the command in Ex. 20:4 against graven images is not to be understood, as some do, as a prohibition by God against art itself. As Schaeffer notes, "Scripture does not forbid the making of representational art but rather the worship of it," *Art and the Bible*, 20.

further, however. God is the master artist: it is *his* pattern for the tabernacle, and it is *our* home he creates and cultivates in the opening chapters of Genesis. As Andy Crouch notes, the creation account of Genesis reveals God as an artist and a gardener.[11] As God's image bearers, we are called to be artists and gardeners after his image. We should be creators and cultivators of goodness, truth, and beauty in what we make and how we attribute meaning.

In an essay on art, beauty, and the imagination, pastor Timothy Keller asks several important questions that assist us in drawing several conclusions about the place of beauty and the arts in the church. As we've already noted, there was a community of artists in Israel. The same is needed today. Many artists exist outside the church, often in isolation or silenced within the church.[12] According to Keller, we need artists because they "reveal something about the greater reality in an indefinable but inescapable way."[13] Artists curate beauty, aiding us in seeing reality as it is, painting the world in its proper light and helping us to see it as enchanted, mysterious, and sacred. Artists help us *see* and *understand* truth. In seeing and understanding truth, reality as it is, we *enjoy* it. In seeing and understanding *and* enjoying reality as it is, we are moved to *worship* God, who is the source of all things. "The Church needs artists to assist the body in understanding truth, but just as importantly the Church needs artists to equip the Church to praise God. We cannot praise God without art."[14] Keller provocatively presses his point even further: "Without art we cannot reach the world. . . . The simple fact is the imagination 'gets you,' even when your reason is completely against the idea of God."[15] Art and imagination help us see the meaning of the world, our lives, and the things we make. We know, even in this disenchanted world, that life has meaning. Art helps us apprehend meaning, and in apprehending meaning, we are moved to find its source. As Keller puts it, "There is a sort of schizophrenia that occurs if you are listening to Bach and you hear the glory of God and yet your mind says there is no God and there is no meaning."[16]

---

11. Andy Crouch, *Culture Making: Recovering Our Creative Calling* (Downers Grove, IL: InterVarsity Press, 2008), chs. 1, 5.

12. Although there are encouraging signs of life within the church. For an excellent discussion of how art and beauty can figure into the normal rhythm of church life, see David O. Taylor, ed. *For the Beauty of the Church: Casting a Vision for the Arts* (Grand Rapids: Baker, 2010).

13. Timothy Keller, "Why We Need Artists," in Bustard, *It Was Good*, 120.

14. Keller, "Why We Need Artists," 122.

15. Keller, "Why We Need Artists," 123.

16. Keller, "Why We Need Artists," 123.

Beauty calls us home. It *awakens* and *transports* us. Beauty—in nature, in art, in humans, in the divine—awakens a longing within us for a world where everything is as it should be, where everything fits together in the right way. This longing, once aroused, compels us. Beauty also transports us out of the mundane. Consider, for example, a scene from the siege of Leningrad in World War II. During a German bombing raid, as people crouched in a bunker, a diarist wrote of an old man who started to play upon his violin. As the old man played, the diarist reported, "There are explosions all around us, and he is playing the violin as if he is leading us to safety. . . . The terror was somehow less powerful—it had lost its grip on us. It was outside us now; and inside we had our music, and everyone felt its power."[17] In the bunker, they were confronted with bombs, blood, and corpses. The music transported them to another place. It reminded them how things should be, and they experienced a measure of peace, happiness, and rest. The beauty of the music reminded them of their humanity, and it sustained them through the darkest of times. As Roger Scruton insightfully observes,

> Art, as we have known it, stands on the threshold of the transcenden-
> tal. It points beyond this world of accidental and disconnected things to
> another realm, in which human life is endowed with an emotional logic
> that makes suffering noble and love worthwhile. Nobody who is alert to
> beauty, therefore, is without the concept of redemption—of a final tran-
> scendence of moral disorder into a "kingdom of ends."[18]

Beauty is a divine megaphone to rouse a disenchanted world.[19]

Keller also notes that Christians express their artistic identity in a certain way—in community with others. Christian artists should pursue their art with others (both artists and nonartists).[20]

Let me clarify that not all followers of Christ are called to be professional artists. I know this because the apex of my painting career still hangs on my

---

17. M. T. Anderson, *Symphony for the City of the Dead* (Somerville, MA: Candlewick, 2015), 239.

18. Scruton, *Beauty*, 156.

19. C. S. Lewis famously states that pain is God's "megaphone to rouse a deaf world." C. S. Lewis, *The Problem of Pain* (San Francisco: HarperCollins, 1996), 91. I am suggesting something similar with respect to beauty.

20. Keller, "Why We Need Artists," 123–24.

bedroom wall in my parents' house, where all third-grade art belongs. The apex of my dancing abilities was my brief stint as a break-dance teacher for the neighborhood kids. As an eighth-grader, I managed to swindle thirty dollars from twenty kids while teaching break dancing in my basement. I could do a smooth moonwalk, a bumpy worm, and channel an electric wave throughout my body. Break dancing, like dancing in general, is a gift, and when we dance we participate in that eternal Trinitarian dance of Father, Son, and Holy Spirit, which bubbled over into the gift of creating a world full of wonder and delight. Still, my dancing abilities, and unfortunately the newly acquired abilities of my students that year, did not evoke thoughts of order, abundance, and beauty. Still we tried, and in trying we found delight even in our poorest attempts.

Regardless of our own artistic ability (or lack thereof), Christians are called to be creators and cultivators of the good, true, and beautiful. Andy Crouch says that we express our God-given humanity as creative cultivators through the *things* and *meaning* we make of the world.[21] As artists and gardeners, we do this by *bringing beauty back into our lives and into the church*. The things we make—omelets, outfits, sermons, bridges, buildings, cars, movies, stories, blog posts, tweets, paintings, PowerPoint presentations, photos, research papers, movie reviews, furniture, landscapes—we should make with beauty in mind. Resist the temptation to value utility over beauty in what you make. In addition, realize that *the most beautiful thing you can do is locate your life in God's story*. Find your meaning in the true story, a story that is alive and inviting. One of the most powerful yet often overlooked apologetics is the attractiveness of the Christian life. A life of self-denial and service to God and neighbor is beautiful. It's also startling. Christ-followers will "shine among them like stars in the sky" (Phil. 2:15) in this disenchanted age, helping others see and understand the meaning of holiness. If we seek beauty, along with goodness and truth in the things and the meaning we make in the world, and if we support those who are called to be artists as a vocation, then we will grow in our ability to see, understand, and praise God. Moreover, we will help the nonbeliever see that meaning and beauty find its source in Jesus and the gospel.

Listen to beauty's call. Do you hear it? It beckons us home.

---

21. Crouch, *Culture Making*, 22–25.

LOOKING AT IMAGINATION

If beauty is what calls us, drawing forth our longings, it is the imagination that guides us in perceiving and creating beauty. But what is the *imagination*? Philosophers, theologians, and artists offer different definitions, but there is broad consensus on what imagination is *not*. It is not our memory, perception, or beliefs. Yet it is similar in some ways to memory, perception, and belief. Most notably imagining is "a representational state"—there is intentionality or "aboutness" to our imagination.[22] Most who study the nature of imagination agree that it is crucial to our lives, playing a significant role in perceiving, creating, dreaming, meaning, judging, learning, and moralizing. As the philosopher Colin McGinn provocatively suggests, man is *"Homo imaginans"*—the one who imagines.[23]

Historical and contemporary accounts of the nature and role of the imagination help us better understand this pervasive yet elusive aspect of our human nature. According to Aristotle, the imagination is an intermediary between the sense organ and the intellect "that in virtue of which we say an image arises in us."[24] Immanuel Kant argued that "the power of imagination, as a faculty of intuition without the presence of the object, is either *productive . . .* or *reproductive*."[25] The nineteenth-century Romantic poet Samuel Taylor Coleridge, in *Biographia Literaria*, viewed the imagination as a bridge between the human mind and the supernatural:

> The Imagination, then, I consider either as primary or secondary. The primary Imagination I hold to be the living Power and prime Agent of all human Perception, and as a repetition in the finite mind of the eternal act of creation in the infinite I AM. The secondary [Imagination] I consider as an echo of the former, co-existing with the conscious will, yet still as

22. Amy Kind, "Introduction: Exploring Imagination," in *The Routledge Handbook of Philosophy of Imagination*, ed. Amy Kind (New York: Routledge, 2016), 3.

23. Colin McGinn, *Mindsight: Image, Dream, Meaning* (Cambridge, MA: Harvard University Press, 2004), 5. I say we are more than *Homo imaginans*, but not less.

24. Aristotle, *De Anima* III.3, 427b–249a, quote at 428a1–2, cited in Deborah K. W. Modrak, "Aristotle on Phantasia," in Kind, *The Routledge Handbook of Philosophy of Imagination*, 15.

25. Immanuel Kant, *Anthropology from a Pragmatic Point of View*, trans. Robert B. Louden (Cambridge: Cambridge University Press, 2006), cited in Samantha Matherne, "Kant's Theory of the Imagination," in Kind, *The Routledge Handbook of Philosophy of Imagination*, 56.

identical with the primary in the *kind* of its agency, and differing only in *degree*, and in the *mode* of its operation. It dissolves, diffuses, dissipates, in order to re-create. [26]

Picking up this Romantic thread, C. S. Lewis argues in the twentieth century that while reason is "the natural organ of truth," it is the imagination that is "the organ of meaning."[27] Lewis's friend J. R. R. Tolkien focused on the creative capacities of the imagination in his essay "On Fairy-Stories," writing that the imagination is a power to form "mental images of things not actually present . . . but [in its highest use] which are indeed not to be found in our primary world at all, or are generally believed not to be found there."[28] And in an important work on the nature of worship, contemporary philosopher James K. A. Smith emphasizes the passive and responsive character of the imagination (without denying the active and creative powers of the imagination) when he describes the imagination as "a kind of faculty by which we navigate and make sense of our world, but in ways and on a register that flies below the radar of conscious reflection, and specifically in ways that are fundamentally aesthetic in nature."[29]

Piecing together these various strands of thought, we can conclude the following about the human imagination. The imagination is (1) a faculty of the mind (2) that mediates between sense and intellect (i.e., perception and reason) and the human mind and the divine mind (i.e., finite creatures and the infinite Creator) (3) for meaning and inventing. Each part of this working definition requires unpacking.

A faculty is a group or set of powers or capacities. Thus a faculty of the mind is a grouping of mental powers or capacities. In addition to the faculty of imagination, the mind has sensory, emotional, and intellectual faculties. These faculties possess powers to do the work of perceiving, feeling, thinking, and imagining. While they are distinct, the mental states (e.g., mental events, activities, and processes) characteristic of each faculty of the mind possess intentional content. The mental state is *of* or *about* some object or situation. We say, "I see

---

26. Samuel T. Coleridge, *Biographia Literaria* (New York: Leavitt, Lord & Co., 1834), 172.

27. C. S. Lewis, "Bluspels and Flalansferes: A Semantic Nightmare," in *Selected Literary Essays*, ed. Walter Hooper (Cambridge: Cambridge University Press, 1969), 265.

28. J. R. R. Tolkien, "On Fairy-Stories," *The Tolkien Reader* (New York: Ballantine, 1966), 68–69.

29. James K. A. Smith, *Imagining the Kingdom: How Worship Works* (Grand Rapids: Baker, 2013), 19.

the chair in front of me," or "I'm angry at my child." We state, "I think about the Eiffel Tower," or "I imagine that the Cyclops is after Odysseus."

As embodied creatures, we interact with the world through a complex interplay of body and mind, habit and story, imagination, intellect and will. Consider the question my tenderhearted son Travis (at age four) once asked me: "When you say God works in someone's heart, does he use hammers and screwdrivers?" Travis was trying to understand how an immaterial being— namely God—could work in a person's life. "When Dad works around the house, he uses hammers and screwdrivers, so perhaps God does the same in a person's life." Through his imaginative powers, fueled by the raw material of his experience as an embodied creature, Travis sought understanding and knowledge. In this example we see how the imagination mediates between our sense organ and the intellect. The primary world of experience is the bank from which we draw our checks as we seek through metaphor, story, language, and image to make sense of God, our lives, and the world.[30] As Michael Ward puts it in his discussion of C. S. Lewis's view of the imagination, "Reason depends not only on what we might call the ground floor (imagination) but also on the basement (physical sensation) in order to be supplied with its raw materials."[31] Imagination helps us understand our experience (from nonsense to meaning) and in turn delivers to reason meanings that can be judged as true or false.

The raw material of physical sensation, James K. A. Smith notes, does not come to us unmediated either. The story in which we narrate our lives shapes how we perceive. As "narrative animals" stories seep into our bones and become "the orienting background of our being-in-the-world."[32] The stories that narrate our lives, according to Smith, "capture our imagination precisely because narrative trains our emotions, and those emotions actually condition our perception of the world."[33] The imagination is crucial, even central, to how we experience, understand, and thus act in the world.

---

30. The bank metaphor is from C. S. Lewis, who when describing poetry notes, "Always the real world is the bank on which the poet draws his cheques; and though a metaphysical lyric may be a fine and private place, all the meanings embraced within it are but passengers who come there from the public, eternal, objective world of reality and haste thither again." Lewis, "Image and Imagination," in *Image and Imagination: Essays and Reviews*, ed. Walter Hooper (Cambridge: Cambridge University Press, 2013), 49.

31. Michael Ward, "The Good Serves the Better and Both the Best: C. S. Lewis on Imagination and Reason in Apologetics," in *Imaginative Apologetics*, ed., Andrew Davison (Grand Rapids: Baker, 2012), 75.

32. Smith, *Imagining the Kingdom*, 14–15.

33. Smith, *Imagining the Kingdom*, 32.

The imagination is the organ of creativity. More recently, my son Travis (now fifteen years old) worked on a science project to design a device that kept an egg from cracking after falling from a height of thirty feet. The only stipulation was that the egg must be visible. I watched with mild amusement as Travis gathered together cardboard boxes, yarn, pipe cleaners, rubber bands, old rags, and scotch tape. After an hour of cutting, taping, piecing together, and stuffing a box-like contraption with a parachute attachment, Travis was ready for the maiden voyage of his egg-protector. He tossed it from his second-story window, and the eighteen-foot test drop was a success. So was the thirty-foot drop in class.

The creative work my son did on this project illustrates two important characteristics of creative activity: *novelty* and *value*.[34] A creative act must be, to some degree, novel; something new is brought into being through this creative work. The thing brought into being must also have some value. Travis's contraption brought into being *ex materia* through his imaginative capacities was novel and it had some value—in this case it gained him a good science grade.

Through the process of inventing, our imagination playfully and spontaneously pulls together ideas and images to make something new. But how do we explain the process of inventing? How did it arise? What purpose does it serve? Evolutionary accounts of man's creative capacities don't provide adequate justification for the imagination and our inventive faculties. Evolution subjects every motive to our need to survive, but this motive fails to ring true in our experience. Human beings often create at times and in ways that seem at odds with the will to survive. Ask yourself why the Russian composer Dmitri Shostakovich would continue to compose music during the siege of Leningrad, even as German bombs fell around him,[35] or why a community of artists would exist among Hebrew slaves in Egypt. Survival is not a comprehensive paradigm to explain humanity's imaginative and creative impulse.

As cultural apologists, our task is to demonstrate that the best explanation for why we make architecture and jokes, sculptures and gardens, stories and mythical creatures is because we bear the image of a God who is the master creator, comedian, and storyteller. In the imaginative act of inventing,

---

34. Dustin Stokes, "Imagination and Creativity," in Kind, *The Routledge Handbook of Philosophy of Imagination*, 247.

35. Anderson, *Symphony for the City of the Dead*, 223.

for example, we see the connection between our finite minds and the divine mind. The divine imagination is rich and exuberant, bursting forth with joy, playfulness, and delight.[36] So too is the human imagination in the act of inventing or subcreating. As Tolkien puts it, "We make in our measure and in our derivative mode, because we are made: and not only made, but made in the image and likeness of a Maker."[37] In invention the human imagination partakes of the divine. It engages in the serious business of heaven: creating and cultivating beauty and meaning in order to spread God's joy, delight, and glory.

LOOKING ALONG THE IMAGINATION

In Mary Shelley's masterpiece, *Frankenstein*, we learn of a young scientist, Victor Frankenstein, consumed with the desire to unlock the mystery of life. After many nights in his laboratory, he manages to bring to life a horrendous looking creature cobbled together from human body parts. Yet instead of experiencing the exhilaration of having created new life, Frankenstein is filled with horror. Listen to how Shelley describes the fateful moment:

> It was already one in the morning; the rain pattered dismally against the panes, and my candle was nearly burnt out, when, by the glimmer of the half-extinguished light, I saw the dull yellow eye of the creature open; it breathed hard, and a convulsive motion agitated its limbs.[38]

At that moment, looking into the dull yellow eyes of the creature he brought to life, Frankenstein learns something of the sacredness of life. This is the moment of his greatest triumph. He had succeeded where others had failed. Yet in that moment he knew that he was playing with a power he could not control:

> How can I describe my emotions at this catastrophe, or how delineate the wretch whom with such infinite pains and care I had endeavoured

---

36. No, God is not a sober and serious-minded curmudgeon. He is playful, bringing into being armadillos and ostriches and platypuses and myriads of other fantastical creatures.

37. Tolkien, "On Fairy-Stories," 75.

38. Mary Shelley, *Frankenstein* (London: Penguin, 1985), 105.

to form? His limbs were in proportion, and I had selected his features as beautiful. Beautiful! Great God! His yellow skin scarcely covered the work of muscles and arteries beneath; his hair was of a lustrous black, and flowing; his teeth of pearly whiteness; but these luxuriances only formed a more horrid contrast with his watery eyes, that seemed almost of the same colour as the dun-white sockets in which they were set.[39]

Shelley paints a vivid picture of the dangers of unchecked, sinful human creativity. The unnamed creature seeks affirmation and love from his creator, but his longing is met instead with horror and disgust. The creature searches the eyes of his creator, wondering why he has been made. For what purpose did my creator make me? But no answer is forthcoming. Frankenstein flees. The creature follows him to his bedchamber, mutters some incoherent sounds, and reaches an arm toward his creator only to have Frankenstein evade him and run out of the building. From the moment of his creation, the creature is intimately connected to his creator. And though Frankenstein wants to deny it, or perhaps forget it, he and his creation are inescapably bound together. The creature he has made seeks to find favor with members of the human race, but because he had no purpose in life, he must find his own purpose. In the end, he seeks to destroy his creator. As the creature tells Frankenstein, "Yet you, my creator, detest and spurn me, thy creature, to whom thou art bound by ties only dissoluble by the annihilation of one of us."[40]

Mary Shelley's tale transports us *into* the story itself and we experience horror and fright as the tale unfolds. But the story—like all good art—speaks to our primary experience as well. It leads us to reflect on the sacredness of life as a gift to be received and enjoyed in humble creaturely response. Reading the story, I also grasped anew the deep love of the Father, who, unlike the creator Frankenstein, looks upon his creation with joy and delight, proclaiming it "very good" (Gen. 1:31). I marveled at the Father's pursuing love as I contemplated how we, like *Frankenstein* in reverse, ran away from our Creator only to have him pursue us, even becoming like us, so that we might be brought home. My response was one of joy and praise.

Art activates the imagination to awaken longing in our hearts and minds.

---

39. Shelley, *Frankenstein*, 105.
40. Shelley, *Frankenstein*, 145.

And the imagination helps us narrate our lives, serving as a guide to explore the various facets and dimensions of our longings, aiding us in drawing connections between the art and our lives. In my brief encounter with *Frankenstein*, I looked *along* the imagination to see how, through story, my imagination could help me better understand reality.

Stories, especially *good* stories, can provide us, Tolkien argues, a means of escape, recovery, and consolation.[41] Good stories command what Tolkien calls "secondary belief."[42] We escape from our primary world and enter a secondary world through the imagination. While we are "in" the secondary world, we experience joy and sorrow, hope and fear, as if we were part of the story. When we put the book down or leave the theater, if the story has done its job, we should see reality afresh. Stories help "clean our windows"[43] so that we see the familiar in its proper light as beautiful, mysterious, and sacred.

This is all part of the process of recovery, the journey of return from disenchantment to reenchantment. Many stories, especially fairy stories, provide this sense of consolation as a happy ending. We experience joy as the story resolves and all is made right in the universe—at least for a moment. Through stories, the imagination helps us see and delight in reality as Jesus does. They help us understand and discern the meaning behind our observation of the world.

Consider the stories that have been most impactful in your life. What is it about these stories that has captivated you, holding your attention? How do these stories imaginatively help you understand the world? In my own reading journey, I've experienced the power of story through Joseph Conrad's *Heart of Darkness*, which shocked me with the absurdity of evil. Victor Hugo's *Les Misérables* showed me the high cost of redemption, while J. R. R. Tolkien's *Leaf by Niggle* freed me to pursue the one "leaf" God called me to paint in life. C. S. Lewis offered rich portraits of spiritual realities through his Narnian tales. These stories, and many others like them, have been rich sources of imaginative soul food, feeding the hunger of my desire and activating my imaginative faculties to better grasp the deep beauty of Jesus, the gospel, and the world God has made. We are too small to apprehend and understand all of reality from our singular point of view. As Lewis eloquently states, "But in reading great

---

41. Tolkien, "On Fairy-Stories," 75–87.
42. Tolkien, "On Fairy-Stories," 61.
43. Tolkien, "On Fairy-Stories," 77.

literature I become a thousand men and yet remain myself. Like the night sky in the Greek poem, I see with a myriad eyes, but it is still I who see. Here, as in worship, in love, in moral action, and in knowing, I transcend myself; and am never more myself than when I do."[44] Stories—whether found in literature, film, painting, music, theater—enlarge us by helping us understand our place in the world.

At this point, one might object that these fictional stories I mention are not factually true. How can myths like these engage our desires and better help us see and understand reality? In his reflection on fairy stories, Tolkien offers a provocative answer. He argues that we long for fairy stories because they point us to an underlying reality, one that is *more real* than the primary world of our experience. "The peculiar quality of the 'joy' in successful Fantasy can thus be explained as a sudden glimpse of the underlying reality or truth."[45] Tolkien, Lewis, and many others would argue that this underlying reality is the gospel story. It is a story that is alive and inviting—a true story that underlies fairy stories.

For the task of cultural apologetics, we can generalize this point even further. Many, if not all, good stories are good *precisely because* they point to the one true story of the world: the gospel. In the gospel, as in the very best fairy stories, we find what we long for: a magical world, life eternal, love unbounded, the defeat of evil, and a happy ending. And all good stories point us to Jesus, even if they do so indirectly. We are drawn to some stories over others because we intuit that they reflect reality, that they are somehow connected to another, ongoing story. Fictional stories prepare us to recognize the true story when we see it. They are windows to another world, beckoning us to look through for the One who offers us joy unending.

ART AND THE KINGDOM

How, then, as cultural apologists, can we unlock the innate power of human desire through the longing for beauty and the faculty of the imagination? Can we use the power of beauty and creative art—especially the power of story—to

44. C. S. Lewis, *An Experiment in Criticism* (Cambridge: Cambridge University Press, 1961), 141.
45. Tolkien, "On Fairy-Stories," 88.

build bridges from "our Athens" of contemporary culture to the timeless beauty of Jesus and the gospel? Recall from chapter 1 that a cultural apologetic will have both local and global concerns. Locally, we want our family members, friends, colleagues, and neighbors to give the gospel a fair hearing. We want them to understand the message of Christ and respond in faith. Globally, we want to see Christians exert leadership within the culture-shaping institutions that mold our collective mind-set, conscience, and imagination so that Jesus and the gospel will be seen as reasonable and desirable. In light of these local and global concerns, how can art, beauty, and the imagination help us point others to Jesus? Let me offer three practical suggestions.

First, our evangelism, apologetics, teaching, and preaching must cultivate "imaginative reasoning."[46] Jesus used metaphor, story, analogy, hyperbole, and a variety of creative methods to engage his listeners and assist them in understanding his message.[47] We should do likewise when we share the gospel, engage in apologetic discussions, preach, and relate with others. As our culture grows increasingly biblically illiterate, concepts such as sin, soul, and forgiveness become difficult to understand when they are disconnected from biblical narratives. Our disenchanted age teaches that human beings are just bodies and that morality is relative, so why would my soul (whatever that is) need forgiveness (whatever that is)? We must love those we seek to reach by engaging their intellect and their imagination: speaking in their language, borrowing illustrations, motifs, stories, and metaphors from the aesthetic currency of the culture so that they can understand us when we speak of Jesus.

Imaginative reasoning is not easy. We must study theology, *and* we must study culture. Then we must learn to make thoughtful connections between the two. This requires energy, insight, and the development of intellectual virtue. We must daily pick up our crosses and follow Jesus and his call to be salt and light in a world of decay and darkness.

Second, we can support and encourage art and artists within the church. The church needs artists because they help us see reality as beautiful, meaningful, and mysterious. Writing music, creating images, designing liturgy,

---

46. For an excellent discussion of how to cultivate imaginative reason, see Holly Ordway, *Apologetics and the Christian Imagination* (Steubenville, OH: Emmaus Road, 2017).

47. Steve Turner, *Imagine: A Vision for Christians in the Arts*, 2nd ed. (Downers Grove, IL: InterVarsity Press, 2017), 88–89.

and filling the spaces we inhabit with beauty—all of these are necessary for a holistic worship experience. And the reverse is equally true. Artists need the church. Many Christian artists, frustrated at the exile of beauty from the local church, will choose to work and create alone, but we must encourage artists to resist this temptation. Without the benefit of a like-minded community of faith, the artist will eventually become unmoored spiritually, and the effectiveness of his or her witness will be muted. Churches should encourage communities of artists to meet for prayer, discipleship, and collaboration. They could consider sponsoring an arts festival where artists display *and* sell their works. Church building committees should resist the temptation to value utility alone, including artistic voices in discussions of facilities. Churches should also provide regular teaching on the connections between art and the kingdom. Like the Israel of old, we pray for a revival of gifted artists and the return of beauty from exile.

Third, we must encourage artists' faithfulness. Every Christian is called to be a faithful witness for Christ, but in calling artists to faithfulness I want to highlight the crucial yet often neglected truth that art is a worthy vocation unto the Lord. Not only can Christians be active in the arts, they ought to be. God, as we've seen, is the master artist, and as his image bearers, he calls us also to create and cultivate. There are several crucial factors for those who are considering what it means to be a faithful artist, but two I will concentrate on are technical excellence and faithful presence.

Those pursuing artistic endeavors should strive for technical excellence. This may require years of honing one's craft.[48] It is not enough to catch a vision for "Christian art" and settle for poor quality or shabby work accompanied by a request for God's blessing.[49] Being a Christian and an artist means respecting both the form of art and the content of Christianity.[50] Artists who are Christians need not limit their art to that which is explicitly religious. Art "infused with godly perception"[51] is intrinsically valuable and worthy, offering a glimpse of the divine that baptizes the imagination and functions to "prepare the way for the LORD" (Isa. 40:3).

---

48. McCleary, "The Work of Our Hands," 135–39.

49. Turner, *Imagine*, 129.

50. According to journalist and poet Steve Turner, Bono and the band U2 are a good model for artists who are Christians in this regard (Turner, *Imagine*, 134).

51. Turner, *Imagine*, 28.

In addition to the church community, artists should be "faithfully present within" the art community.[52] Some need to be actively involved in the key culture-shaping institutions for the arts including Hollywood, Broadway, the National Endowment for the Arts, art museums (such as the Louvre in Paris, the Smithsonian in Washington, DC, and the Metropolitan Museum of Art in New York), and publishing houses (such as Hachette, Random House, HarperCollins, and Simon & Schuster). Recall from chapter 1 Hunter's claim that cultural influence is largely top-down.[53] For example, consider how a small number of elites working in Hollywood exert an incredible amount of control over the collective imagination and mind-set of culture through the stories they tell. As a movie director in Hollywood has said: "L.A. is the town that controls world storytelling for both children and adults."[54] Hollywood and other elite institutions that produce and cultivate art have an inordinate influence on the narratives that shape our world, and if we want Christianity to be viewed as reasonable and desirable, Christian artists and leaders should be sitting at the table of these key culture-shaping institutions, offering our voice, conscience, and imagination as a subversive narrative that contrasts with the dominant spirit of the age. This will require long-term strategic thinking and a rejection of pragmatism, but the fate of future generations hangs on how much we care for culture and the artists who nurture it.[55]

BEAUTY WILL SAVE THE WORLD

In Dostoevsky's novel *The Idiot*, one of the characters provocatively states that "beauty will save the world."[56] It's a startling statement, but what does he mean? The more common saviors people turn to are money, machines, knowledge,

---

52. Recall from chapter 1 that the term "faithfully present within" is from James Davison Hunter, *To Change the World: The Irony, Tragedy, and Possibility of Christianity in the Late Modern World* (Oxford: Oxford University Press, 2010).

53. See especially Hunter, *To Change the World*, 32–47.

54. Turner, *Imagine*, 152.

55. For an excellent discussion of how art and the curating of beauty can nourish culture, see Makoto Fujimura, *Culture Care: Reconnecting with Beauty for Our Common Life* (Downers Grove, IL: InterVarsity Press, 2017).

56. The translation of *The Idiot* I possess renders the oft-quoted phrase as follows: "With beauty like that one might turn the world upside down" (Fyodor Dostoevsky, *The Idiot* [Hertfordshire: Wordsworth, 1996], 73). I first came across this provocative statement in Gregory Wolfe's, *Beauty Will Save the World*, 1.

or political power, not beauty. We may appreciate beauty, but we treat it as superfluous or impractical, something we can do without.

To this point, I've argued for the centrality of beauty to life and the necessity of Christian engagement with the arts as a component of a robust cultural apologetic. When we neglect or denigrate the human longing for beauty, we cut ourselves off from a source of blessing and shalom. We also miss out on one of God's powerful reminders of his purposes, our longing for home. In cultures where traditional missionary efforts have been ineffective, appeals to the universal longing for beauty have proven to be effective in evangelism. In Japan the music of Johann Sebastian Bach now plays a role in evangelizing the country.[57] The renowned organist Masaaki Suzuki calls Bach's music "the fifth Gospel" because many Japanese are considering or even converting to Christianity after hearing his music. Why? Because listening to Bach has cultivated hope in the hearts of these individuals and provided a stepping stone for them to understand the meaning of God's love. In Japan, beauty and the imagination play a key role in a cultural apologetic that makes Christianity plausible and desirable. The beauty of Christian art has prompted the Japanese to ask: How can Bach exist in a world full of despair and loneliness? Answering that question has set several Japanese people on the path to Jesus, who is the source of Bach's inspiration and the source of beauty itself.

This is what we mean when we affirm that beauty will save the world. In cultures resistant to traditional means of evangelism, where direct verbal appeals are rejected, a cultural apologetic must analyze the cultural longings, hopes, and dreams. In a world of increasing loneliness, angst and darkness, authentic beauty calls and invites people to consider something beyond this fallen and broken world. Pope Benedict XVI once said, "Art and the saints are the greatest apologetic for our faith."[58] The human longing for beauty and goodness are both powerful yet often neglected starting points for building bridges to Jesus and the gospel. In a world immune to rational arguments, beauty and goodness are the filters through which the gospel message is first considered.

---

57. Uwe Siemon-Netto, "J. S. Bach in Japan," *First Things*, June 2000, https://www.firstthings.com/article/2000/06/j-s-bach-in-japan. See also Nancy Pearcey's discussion of Bach and Japan in *Saving Leonardo*, 267–68.

58. Quoted in Rod Dreher, *The Benedict Option: A Strategy for Christians in a Post-Christian Nation* (New York: Sentinel, 2017), 117.

In the *Confessions*, Augustine refers to God as the "beauty of all things beautiful."[59] Christians believe that Jesus is both beautiful and the source of all beauty. So when we say that *beauty can save the world*, there is a deeper truth that underlies our hope, because beauty is found in a person, Jesus Christ, the savior of the world. Jesus took on our sin and the ugliness, horror, and pain of this world so we can find forgiveness, hope, healing, and wholeness. The creativity of God-infused art calls to our longings. The imagination guides us forward. Beauty will save the world.

---

59. Augustine, *Confessions*, trans. Henry Chadwick (Oxford: Oxford University Press, 1998), 3.6.10 (p. 41).

CHAPTER 5

REASON

> You will not find the warrior, the poet, the philosopher or the
> Christian by staring in his eyes as if he were your mistress:
> better fight beside him, read with him, argue with him,
> pray with him.
>
> *C. S. Lewis[1]*

> Desire without knowledge is not good—
> how much more will hasty feet miss the way!
>
> *Proverbs 19:2*

An economics professor stands before his class ready to take attendance.
"Adams?" Here.
"Adamly?" Here.
"Adamousky?"
Finally, an apathetic student mindlessly raises her hand. The teacher continues, "Adamson? Here. Adler? Here. Anderson? Anderson? Here!" And then, my favorite line, a line I've often repeated while teaching in my own classroom. "Bueller? Bueller? Bueller? Bueller?"

The movie, of course, is the 1986 classic *Ferris Bueller's Day Off.* Chronicling the adventures of three friends who skip school for a day, the movie accurately captured my own perspective on life and learning as a freshman in high school.

---

1. C. S. Lewis, *The Four Loves* (New York: Harcourt Brace Jovanovich, 1960), 104.

I found my classes boring, my teachers uninspiring, and the adult world erected to support and enforce my education confining. Like Ferris, I longed to escape to the greener pastures of self-expression and personal freedom.

Time and experience have changed my perspective. Thirty years later, watching *Ferris Bueller's Day Off* with my high-school age children, I'm not impressed. Learning can be uninspiring, and doing whatever you want without a care for the consequences can be exhilarating in the moment. But a cavalier perspective like that of Ferris Bueller is more often than not a recipe for disaster. It is also an overused trope. It captures the imagination and frustration of youth but fails to reflect the wisdom of real life.

More specifically, it is imbued with a spirit of anti-intellectualism, a common trend in American culture. Over the past several decades we've witnessed the dumbing down of the Western mind. With the advent of the information age and the ubiquity of image, video, and the internet, our brains themselves are changing, and not for the better. Studies have demonstrated that we are *losing* our minds. Nicholas Carr, in his book *The Shallows*, says it simply: "Whether I'm online or not, my mind now expects to take in information the way the Net distributes it: in a swiftly moving stream of particles. Once I was a scuba diver in the sea of words. Now I zip along the surface like a guy on a Jet Ski."[2]

In this "swiftly moving stream of particles," we lose our ability to sustain linear thought. Again, Carr summarizes: "Calm, focused, undistracted, the linear mind is being pushed aside by a new kind of mind that wants and needs to take in and dole out information in short, disjointed, often overlapping bursts—the faster, the better."[3] Contemplation and the cultivation of intellectual virtue, long viewed as marks of maturity and the highest human ideal, are no longer viewed as essential to happiness and human flourishing. There is a shift in "society's attitude toward intellectual achievement,"[4] as Carr argues, from "being cultivators of personal knowledge to being hunters and gatherers in the electronic data forest."[5] Auguste Rodin's 1902 sculpture *The Thinker* once embodied this high human ideal of the contemplative life.[6] Today that

---

2. Nicholas Carr, *The Shallows: What the Internet Is Doing to Our Brains* (New York: Norton, 2010), 6–7.
3. Carr, *The Shallows*, 10.
4. Carr, *The Shallows*, 112.
5. Carr, *The Shallows*, 138.
6. Teddy Wayne, "The End of Reflection," *New York Times*, June 11, 2016, https://www.nytimes.com/2016/06/12/fashion/internet-technology-phones-introspection.html?_r=0.

sculpture could be recast as *The Tweeter*, a familiar image of a person sitting with their head down staring at a phone while dispensing words of wisdom in 280-character bursts. The short, pithy and quickly forgotten statement now embodies the spirit of our individualistic, consumer-focused age. Some might say we are losing our humanity.

Things are not business as usual. With the advent of the internet age, we are seeing the loss of the contemplative mind. Our longing for truth has grown muted. Worse still, since the Enlightenment, the modern intelligentsia have been telling us that belief in God is unreasonable. As the "Age of Reason" matured in the eighteenth century, thinkers such as David Hume (1711–76) and Voltaire (1694–1778) began to openly ridicule Christianity. Hume, in his famous essay "Of Miracles," sarcastically concludes his investigation with this slight: "So that, upon the whole, we may conclude, that the *Christian Religion* not only was at first attended with miracles, but even at this day cannot be believed by any reasonable person without one."[7] Voltaire, in a letter to Frederick the Great, stated, "Christianity is the most ridiculous, the most absurd, and bloody religion that has ever infected the world."[8] In the nineteenth century, Karl Marx (1818–83) proclaimed religion "the opium of the people."[9] Friedrich Nietzsche (1844–1900) called Christianity "the most fatal kind of self-presumption ever."[10] Charles Darwin (1809–82), in his 1859 *On the Origin of Species*, argued that biological complexity can be explained without appeal to God. The noted Oxford biologist Richard Dawkins thinks Darwin dealt "biology's deadliest blow to supernaturalism"[11] making it "possible to be an intellectually fulfilled atheist."[12]

More recently, the so-called New Atheists loudly argue that faith in God is delusive and destructive. While there is nothing new or interesting about their arguments for atheism, their rhetoric is noteworthy.[13] Faith in God is a delusion,

---

7. David Hume, *An Enquiry Concerning Human Understanding* (Indianapolis: Hackett, 1993), 90.

8. As quoted in Albrecht Classen, *Handbook of Medieval Studies: Terms—Methods—Trends*, vol. 1 (Berlin: De Gruyter, 2010), 382. Voltaire was also known to end his letters to friends with *"Ecrasez l'infame"* ("crush the infamy," that is, the Christian religion).

9. Karl Marx, "Toward a Critique of Hegel's *Philosophy of Right*," in *Karl Marx: Selected Writings*, ed. David McLellan (New York: Oxford University Press, 1977), 64.

10. Friedrich Nietzsche, *Beyond Good and Evil*, trans. R. J. Hollingdale (London: Penguin, 2003), 89.

11. Richard Dawkins, afterword to *A Universe from Nothing: Why There Is Something Rather Than Nothing*, by Lawrence M. Krauss (New York: Atria, 2012), 191.

12. Richard Dawkins, *The Blind Watchmaker: Why the Evidence of Evolution Reveals a Universe without Design* (New York: Norton, 1986), 6.

13. The "Four Horsemen" of New Atheism are Richard Dawkins, Sam Harris, Christopher Hitchens,

decries Dawkins, and "an evil precisely because it requires no justification and brooks no argument."[14] Monotheistic religion "is grounded on wish-thinking," according to the late Christopher Hitchens, and "a plagiarism of a plagiarism of a hearsay of a hearsay, of an illusion of an illusion, extending all the way back to a fabrication of a few nonevents."[15] Sam Harris pulls no punches when he claims "there is no more evidence to justify a belief in the literal existence of Yahweh and Satan than there is to keep Zeus perched upon his mountain throne or Poseidon churning the seas."[16] The point should be clear: atheists today are bold and confident in their unbelief. They assert there is no evidence for God. Faith is blind, a jump into the abyss of irrationality and incoherency.

We are told it is time to move on from the God question because science has settled this issue. "*Is there a God?*" asks Duke philosopher Alex Rosenberg. "We already know the correct answer to that one."[17] Instead, we need to "take the best reason for atheism—science—and show what else it commits us atheists to believing."[18] Yet the answers atheism provides for life's perennial questions are depressing: there is no purpose, no meaning, no freedom, no objective morality, no life after death.

We are left with a quasi-religious commitment to scientism and, if that is not enough, a healthy dose of antidepressants.[19]

Combining the cultural loss of a contemplative mind and the outspoken voices declaring the victory of science and atheism, many people have felt pressure to believe Christianity is unreasonable. Internet atheists proclaim the absence of evidence and ridicule the blindness of faith. Christians who aren't mindful may contribute to this view, seeing their own faith in experiential or emotional categories. Those believers who try to mount a defense of the faith are viewed with suspicion or ignored. The love of learning, the quest

---

and Daniel Dennett. From 2004 to 2007, each wrote a scathing attack on religion in general and Christianity in particular.

14. Richard Dawkins, *The God Delusion* (New York: Mariner Books, 2008), 347.

15. Christopher Hitchens, *God Is Not Great: How Religion Poisons Everything* (New York: Twelve Publishers, 2007), 4, 280.

16. Sam Harris, *The End of Faith: Religion, Terror, and the Future of Reason* (New York: Norton, 2004), 16.

17. Alex Rosenberg, *The Atheist's Guide to Reality: Enjoying Life without Illusion* (New York: Norton, 2011), 3, italics in original.

18. Rosenberg, *The Atheist's Guide to Reality*, 3.

19. Rosenberg is wrong about science too. Science actually confirms God's existence. See ch. 7 and the discussion "Does Science Disprove God?" on pp. 182–86.

for understanding, and the cultivation of the desire to know is fading as the rise of entertainment media—films, games, websites, social media posts, and other forms of mind-numbing distractions—multiply and become ever more pervasive. What hope does the Christian faith have to be taken seriously and viewed as reasonable today? A cultural apologetic approach would encourage us to reconsider the roots of the human quest for truth (see figure 5.1).

FIGURE 5.1: The Human Quest for Truth

THE QUEST FOR TRUTH

It was my freshman year of college. Two upperclassmen were knocking on my dorm room, asking if I had a minute to talk with them about "spiritual things." I didn't really have the time. My calculus class was coming up and I had to prepare. But I reluctantly invited them in. They proceeded to share the gospel message and asked me the ultimate question: "What do you make of Jesus Christ?"

Honestly, I didn't know what to say or think. I'd grown up in church. Jesus was fine and dandy, and I thought he felt the same about me. But they pressed deeper: "Have you invited Jesus into your life?" Well, no, not really. "Would you like to invite Jesus into your heart?" I panicked. No, I wouldn't, but maybe if I did, they'd go away. "Sure," I feebly mumbled. They led me in the sinner's prayer and welcomed me like the prodigal son as they drove me, now late, to class.

When they called the next week, I politely asked them to leave me alone. No, I wasn't ready for Jesus. Obviously, my "prayer" was not sincere.

But that episode stuck with me. There were two things that nagged me, like a stubborn pebble in my shoe. First, why were these guys so excited about something I had always thought irrelevant? Second, what if Christianity was *true*? I knew that something had shifted in my thoughts. I wasn't yet a Christian, but I was considering things I had never considered before. I was awakened to a new reality. For the first time, I wanted to know if what they said about Jesus and the gospel was true to the way things are. If so, I realized, I'd be a fool to reject Christianity.

So, naturally, I started attending an apologetics class at a local church. I now realize that my response is far from the norm. My friend Mike, who had shared he was a Christian, invited me along and I went. It was the first time someone had presented the evidence for the Christian faith, and I was shocked at the cumulative case for Christianity. Week after week, I learned about the evidence for God's existence, the deity of Christ, and the historicity of the resurrection. I marveled as the teacher dropped a stack of books on the table each class, inviting us to dig in for ourselves. Knowing that I was a seeker, the class pressed me: "What do you think about the evidence for God?" I told them it was strong. "At some point, you need to make a decision." They were right. Eventually, I would need to bend my knee to what my mind was coming to believe as true. The summer after my freshman year I prayed the same "sinner's prayer," but this time I did it with a sincerity of heart and a conviction of mind. I had found the truth, and the truth had set me free (John 8:32).

Many have walked the plank of reason on the journey toward Christ. As an eighteen-year-old, Augustine's (354–430) mind was stirred to seek truth as he read philosophy.[20] Josh McDowell, the bestselling author of *Evidence That*

---

20. Augustine, *Confessions*, trans. Henry Chadwick (Oxford: Oxford University Press, 1998), 38–39.

Demands a Verdict, was challenged as a university student to intellectually examine the claims of Christianity.[21] When he couldn't refute the evidence, especially for the resurrection, he became a Christian.[22] Lee Strobel, an award-winning investigative journalist at the *Chicago Tribune* began his journey toward Christ when his wife became a Christian. He was intrigued with the new—and pleasant—changes in her life, yet he had always assumed belief in God was irrational and unpleasant. To better understand his wife's transformation, Strobel "launched an all-out investigation into the facts surrounding the case for Christianity."[23] Applying his seasoned investigative skills, Strobel concluded that the evidence for Christianity is overwhelming. Walking the plank of reason, examining the evidence from history, science, philosophy, psychology, and more, many have found their way to Jesus.

This longing for truth is a universal human desire. As we noted in chapter 1, Aristotle famously claimed in *Metaphysics*, "All men by nature desire to know."[24] It is a distinctive feature of our human condition. As C. S. Lewis wrote, "One of the things that distinguishes man from other animals is that he wants to know things, wants to find out what reality is like, simply for the sake of knowing. When that desire is completely quenched in anyone, I think he has become something less than human."[25] This innate desire for truth and understanding is most evident in children. As any parent will attest, as soon as they are able, children begin to try and understand their world.

"What are you doing, Daddy?"

"I'm fixing the faucet."

"Why are you doing that?"

"So we can drink water."

"Why do we drink water?"

"So we can live."

"Why do we live?"

21. Josh McDowell and Sean McDowell, *Evidence That Demands a Verdict: Life-Changing Truth for a Skeptical World* (Nashville: Nelson, 2017).

22. Josh McDowell, *The Resurrection Factor: Compelling Evidence Which Proves the Resurrection of Jesus Christ* (San Bernardino, CA: Here's Life, 1989), 1–8.

23. Lee Strobel, *The Case for Christ: A Journalist's Personal Investigation of the Evidence for Jesus* (Grand Rapids: Zondervan, 1998), 14.

24. Aristotle, *Metaphysics* 980ª21, in *The Complete Works of Aristotle*, vol. 2, ed. Jonathan Barnes (Princeton, NJ: Princeton University Press, 1984), 1552.

25. C. S. Lewis, "Man or Rabbit?" in *God in the Dock*, ed. Walter Hooper (Grand Rapids: Eerdmans, 1970), 108.

"So we can love God."

"Why does God want us to love him?"

"So we can be happy."[26]

"Why do we want to be happy?"

And on and on we go until patience runs out.

Our rational musings all begin with a sense of wonder. Socrates claims that philosophy begins here: "This is an experience which is characteristic of a philosopher, this wondering: this is where philosophy begins and nowhere else."[27] Aristotle argues likewise:

For it is owing to their wonder that men both now begin and at first began to philosophize; they wondered originally at the obvious difficulties, then advanced little by little and stated difficulties about the greater matters, e.g. about the phenomena of the moon and those of the sun and the stars, and about the genesis of the universe.[28]

Anyone who asks questions and seeks answers is a philosopher. The question is not *if* we will engage in philosophy but whether we will be a good philosopher or a bad one. Many of us are poor philosophers because our thinking lacks breadth and depth; we've ceased asking questions and have become content with daily doses of mindless entertainment. As Neil Postman once quipped, we are amusing ourselves to death.[29] We allow Google's search engine to think for us. We have been lulled to sleep, and the innate and God-given longing for truth and knowledge has been muted.

Part of our task as cultural apologists is to awaken in others this innate longing for truth and knowledge. We do this by arguing for the intrinsic worth of knowledge, that the pursuit of knowledge is valuable, pleasurable, and that every truth discovered, every piece of knowledge gained, illuminates the divine. Christians believe that all truth points to its source in Christ, the creator of all

---

26. Happy in the rich, classical sense: flourishing in light of our nature as moral, rational, relational, imaginative, desiring, free creatures.

27. Plato, *Theaetetus* 155d, trans. M. J. Levett and Rev. Myles Burnyeat, in *Plato: The Complete Works*, ed. John M. Cooper (Indianapolis, IN: Hackett, 1997), 173.

28. Aristotle, *Metaphyiscs* 982^{b}12–17 (p. 1554).

29. Neil Postman, *Amusing Ourselves to Death: Public Discourse in the Age of Show Business* (New York: Penguin, 1985).

things. Contrary to cultural trends, truth is not "whatever works" or "whatever coheres with other beliefs"; rather, we find truth when our thoughts, beliefs, or statements correspond to reality, when we are rightly related to the way the world is. God has given us reason as a guide on this journey to help us discover truth and its source. As cultural apologists, we want to help others see and understand the value of reason and then look *along* the path of reason on our quest for Jesus and the gospel.

LOOKING AT REASON

The great Christian minister Isaac Watts (1674–1748) is best known for his theologically rich and moving hymns such as *Joy to the World* and *When I Survey the Wondrous Cross*. Less known is Watts's work writing a textbook on logic and reason, originally published in London in 1724.[30] The book was subtitled *The Right Use of Reason in the Inquiry after Truth with a Variety of Rules to Guard against Error in the Affairs of Religion and Human Life, as Well as in the Sciences*, and it became the standard text on logic for over one hundred years. It was used in schools such as Oxford, Cambridge, Harvard, and Yale. Watts's life serves as an example for us today as cultural apologists, showing us how the head and the heart must unite to create and cultivate in a way that embodies goodness, truth, and beauty for the glory of God and the benefit of man.

"Logic," according to Watts, "is the art of using Reason well in our inquiries after truth, and the communication of it to others."[31] Cultivating reason, which is "the glory of human nature," helps us "distinguish good from evil, as well as truth from falsehood."[32] In the pursuit of truth, "We become acquainted with the name of things both in heaven and earth, and their various relations to each other."[33] Pursuing truth and engaging the mind must be central in a well-lived life: "Our wisdom, prudence, and piety, our present conduct and our future hope, are all influenced by the use of our rational powers in the search after truth."[34]

---

30. Isaac Watts, *Logic: The Right Use of Reason in the Inquiry after Truth* (Grand Rapids: Soli Deo Gloria, 2013).
31. Watts, *Logic*, 1.
32. Watts, *Logic*, 1–2.
33. Watts, *Logic*, 2.
34. Watts, *Logic*, 2.

Scripture affirms the importance of reason in the pursuit of truth, in our spiritual formation unto Christ, and in our evangelism and apologetic interactions with others. God reveals himself through Scripture and through what he has made. As Francis Bacon said, God has given us two books as sources of truth: the book of God's *works* (creation) and the book of God's *word* (the Bible).[35] Scripture implores us to study both books: "Do your best to present yourself to God as one approved, a worker who does not need to be ashamed and who correctly handles the word of truth" (2 Tim. 2:15); "Go to the ant, you sluggard; consider its ways and be wise!" (Prov. 6:6).

In Romans 12:2, the apostle Paul connects the use of reason and the mind in spiritual formation: "Do not conform to the pattern of this world, but be transformed by the renewing of your mind. Then you will be able to test and approve what God's will is—his good, pleasing and perfect will." And in writing about how we engage others in conversations about Jesus and the gospel, Peter implores believers to "always be prepared to give an answer to everyone who asks you to give the reason for the hope that you have" (1 Peter 3:15). Faithfulness to Christ requires the diligent cultivation of intellectual virtues conducive to the pursuit of truth and love of God and neighbor. This also means that we seek to root out false, accidental, and irrational beliefs. Since our beliefs "are the rails upon which our lives run,"[36] our beliefs must be rational and justified. These justified true beliefs will help us live *and* help us love, because we love best what we know best. The greatest commandment includes loving God with our minds: "Love the Lord your God with all your heart and with all your soul and with all your *mind*" (Matt. 22:37, emphasis added). The proper use of reason is essential to human flourishing, as it is essential in making a case for Jesus and the gospel.

But how do we know that something is "true"? By what process do we utilize our reason to arrive at the truth? The reasoning process involves several components, including (1) the reception of facts from sensation, reports of others (i.e., testimony), memory, introspection, or the imagination; (2) the perception of self-evident truths (including the laws of logical inference); and (3) the arrangement of the facts to arrive at new truths that are not self-evident.[37]

---

35. Francis Bacon, *The Advancement of Learning* (Oxford: Clarendon, 1891), 10.
36. J. P. Moreland, *Love Your God with All Your Mind*, 3rd ed. (Colorado Springs: NavPress, 2012), 86.
37. Michael Ward, "The Good Serves the Better and Both the Best: C. S. Lewis on Imagination and

Many of our beliefs are what philosophers call *basic* beliefs. These are beliefs that are justified (and rational) in virtue of experience. For example, in looking out my window I am justified in my belief that it is raining. I can say this because I see that it is raining and then come to believe, on the basis of my perceptual experience, the proposition *it is raining*. Some self-evident beliefs, such as my belief in the law of noncontradiction, are also considered basic beliefs because they are grounded in a kind of rational seeming or experience. In addition to these basic beliefs, several of our beliefs are *nonbasic* or inferential beliefs. I infer from the propositions *it is raining* and *if it is raining, I will get wet when walking outside without an umbrella* (a further fact I have come to believe on the basis of the evidence from experience) the proposition that *I will get wet when walking outside without an umbrella*. This third proposition is a piece of inferential knowledge, an example of a common logical inference pattern (called *modus ponens*) that we use every day. In science, mathematics, and in everyday life we regularly make rational inferences and gain inferential knowledge from them.

For Christians living in an age of disenchantment, there is a pressing question we must answer: *Does the Christian faith measure up to the standards of reason?* In short, is the Christian faith reasonable? It would go beyond the subject of this book to fully answer that question, but I believe the answer is clearly *yes*. There is plenty of evidence to justify belief in God.[38] The same is true of our beliefs in the trustworthiness of the Gospels, the deity of Christ, the historicity of the resurrection, and the exclusivity of the Christian faith. We can freely examine the evidence presented by both theists and atheists and conclude that unbelief need not be due to a failure of evidence.[39] In truth, the Christian suffers from an embarrassment of riches, as evidenced by the works of Christian

---

Reason in Apologetics," in *Imaginative Apologetics*, ed. Andrew Davison (Grand Rapids: Baker, 2011), 74. See also Victor Reppert, "The Argument from Reason," in *The Blackwell Companion to Natural Theology*, ed. William Lane Craig and J. P. Moreland (Malden, MA: Wiley-Blackwell, 2012), 362–63.

38. There are several competing views in epistemology on the nature of justification. *Evidentialism* is the view that a belief is justified for a person if the person has sufficient evidence for it. Another popular view among Christian philosophers is a version of *reliabilism* called *Reformed Epistemology*. According to Alvin Plantinga, one of the view's leading defenders, belief in God is rational as long as the belief was formed by properly functioning cognitive faculties. If theism is true, then belief in God is rational, reliably produced by cognitive faculties functioning as God designed. Hence, for the Reformed Epistemologist, belief in God is rational too. For more on Evidentialism, see Trent Dougherty, ed., *Evidentialism and Its Discontents* (New York: Oxford University Press, 2011). For more on Reformed Epistemology, see Alvin Plantinga, *Warranted Christian Belief* (Oxford: Oxford University Press, 2000).

39. Recall from chapter 2 that the evidence for God is both widely available and easily resistible.

philosophers, scientists, and historians such as J. P. Moreland, William Lane Craig, Stephen C. Meyer, Douglas Axe, Craig S. Keener, and N. T. Wright.[40]

Whether or not Christianity is reasonable, we must first consider at least two additional questions: Given the claims of naturalism, how can reason itself be justified? And how can we *show or persuade* others that Christianity is true and reasonable? It is one thing to assert Christianity's reasonableness or to point them to a book that makes a rational argument, but it is another to persuasively show that Christianity is true. In the remainder of this section, we will consider the first question and in the following section turn our attention to the second.

The Argument from Reason to God

Recall that naturalism is the view that there are no supernatural beings. The natural world is causally closed, so there is nothing "outside the box," nothing transcendent, nothing that impinges on the material world from beyond. As Graham Oppy summarizes, the naturalist is committed to the following three claims:

> (1) There are none but natural causes involving none by natural entities;
> (2) the distribution of minds in the universe is late and local: only recently evolved creatures have minds and mental properties, and those minds and mental properties are tied to relatively complex biological structures of the evolved creatures in question; and (3) there is nothing that is divine, or sacred, or worthy of worship.[41]

This implies that the basic level of analysis is physics: all reality, at rock bottom, is captured by tiny bits of matter (quarks or strings) that are properly understood by the discipline of physics.[42] But if this is true, a deep puzzle arises:

---

40. J. P. Moreland, *Scaling the Secular City: A Defense of Christianity* (Grand Rapids: Baker, 1987); William Lane Craig, *Reasonable Faith: Christian Truth and Apologetics*, 3rd ed. (Wheaton, IL: Crossway, 2008); Stephen C. Meyer, *Signature in the Cell: DNA and the Evidence for Intelligent Design* (New York: HarperOne, 2010); Douglas Axe, *Undeniable: How Biology Confirms Our Intuition That Life Is Designed* (San Francisco: HarperOne, 2016); Craig S. Keener, *Miracles: The Credibility of the New Testament Accounts*, 2 vols. (Grand Rapids: Baker, 2011); N. T. Wright, *The Resurrection of the Son of God* (Minneapolis: Fortress, 2003). To these texts I humbly add my own work on apologetics: Paul M. Gould, Travis Dickinson, and R. Keith Loftin, *Stand Firm: Apologetics and the Brilliance of the Gospel* (Nashville: B&H, 2018).

41. Graham Oppy, "Conflict Model," in *Four Views on Christianity and Philosophy*, ed. Paul M. Gould and Richard Brian Davis (Grand Rapids: Zondervan, 2016), 29–30.

42. See also Reppert, "The Argument from Reason," 345.

How is our world *intelligible* if humanity is only the result of tiny bits of matter bumping into each other over time? Where does our capacity for reason arise?

C. S. Lewis saw a deep conflict between the claims of naturalism and reason itself. As he states in *Miracles*,

> Thus a strict materialism refutes itself for the reason given long ago by Professor Haldane: "If my mental processes are determined wholly by the motions of atoms in my brain, I have no reason to suppose that my beliefs are true . . . and hence I have no reason for supposing my brain to be composed of atoms" (*Possible Worlds*, p. 209). . . . [Naturalism] discredits our processes of reasoning or at least reduces their credit to such a humble level that it can no longer support Naturalism itself.[43]

To say this another way, if our mental lives are governed by immutable physical laws, then our thoughts, beliefs, and inferences are—by definition—nonrational. My thoughts are not guided by a mind or genuine mental causes, but by purely material causes. But if this assumption is true, the belief that naturalism is true isn't rational either. Naturalism conflicts with reason, according to Lewis. By removing all nonmaterial causes from the equation, naturalism negates the existence of reason itself.

Let's suppose that Lewis is wrong and that there is no contradiction between the precepts of naturalism and the reality of minds. The naturalist still has a huge problem. Naturalism tells us that minds evolve from nonrational, blind, mechanistic processes. As Graham Oppy said, minds emerge "late and local," and the fact that minds occur at all is enormously surprising under the assumptions of naturalism. On the other hand, if we assume theism is true, the existence of minds is unsurprising. We would expect a perfectly rational and good personal being to spread his joy and delight by creating a world full of epistemic, moral, and aesthetic value. For in such a world it is possible to love, know, act, and create. It is easy to see how such features could be exhibited in a world created by a personal God.

We can formulate an argument from the existence of reason (minds) to the existence of God as follows:

---

43. C. S. Lewis, *Miracles* (New York: Touchstone, 1996), 24.

1. The existence of minds is not surprising under theism.
2. The existence of minds is enormously surprising under naturalism.
3. Therefore, the existence of minds strongly supports theism over naturalism.[44]

What can we say in defense of premises (1) and (2)? Again, Lewis is helpful in noting four features of the act of thinking, all of which are unsurprising under theism but are enormously surprising under naturalism.[45]

In the chapter in *Miracles* on "The Cardinal Difficulty of Naturalism," Lewis begins by noting the *intentionality* and *alethicity* of the act of thinking: "Acts of thinking are no doubt events; but they are a very special sort of events. They are 'about' something other than themselves and can be true or false. Events in general are not 'about' anything and cannot be true or false."[46] Intentionality, as noted earlier, refers to the object-directedness of something. My thought is *of* my wife or *about* the nature of rain. Yet the phenomenon of intentionality is at odds with naturalism. Physical entities, states, and events are not intrinsically *of* or *about* anything. Consider the words and sentences on this page. While these physical markings exhibit intentionality, their intentionality is not intrinsic; it is derived, dependent on how we use words and sentences and the meaning we assign to them. This point can be generalized to all physical things, including human brain processes. Chemical events and neuron firings in the brain, according to Edward Feser, are "composed as they are of meaningless chemical components" and thus "seem as inherently devoid of intentionality as soundwaves or ink marks."[47] So the first problem for

44. This argument is a modification of the fine-tuning argument as formulated by Robin Collins. See e.g., Robin Collins, "The Anthropic Teleological Argument," in *Philosophy of Religion: Selected Readings*, ed. Michael Peterson, William Hasker, Bruce Reichenbach, and David Basinger, 5th ed. (New York: Oxford University Press, 2014), 191. The inference that justifies the conclusion in the argument is called "the likelihood principle." The principle states that "an event or state of affairs E counts as evidence in favor of a hypothesis H_1 over a hypothesis H_2 if E is more probable under H_1 than H_2 with the degree of support proportional to the ratio of probabilities under the two respective hypotheses" (191).

45. These four features of acts of thought are nicely summarized in Reppert, "The Argument from Reason," 357–58. In his explication of the argument from reason, Reppert specifies nine features of rational inference, all of which create a cumulative case argument from reason to God (356). See also Reppert, *C. S. Lewis's Dangerous Idea: A Philosophical Defense of Lewis's Argument from Reason* (Downers Grove, IL: InterVarsity Press, 2003).

46. Lewis, *Miracles*, 27.

47. Edward Feser, *Philosophy of Mind: A Short Introduction* (Oxford: Oneworld, 2006), 172, cited in Reppert, "The Argument from Reason," 365.

the naturalist is to explain how the intrinsic intentionality of acts of thinking has evolved from purely physical objects and processes that do not themselves possess intrinsic intentionality. While there are several reductive attempts to account for this intentionality in a materialistic world, none are promising.[48] Some naturalists, such as Alex Rosenberg, recognize that physical objects do not exhibit intrinsic intentionality and bite the bullet, admitting that words and sentences are meaningless.[49] This is a steep price to pay, however, for then there is no reason to think that the arguments for naturalism given by eliminativists such as Rosenberg are meaningful or true. By eliminating the validity of statements, Rosenberg has jettisoned the capacity for rational dialogue. With theism, alternatively, the ground floor of reality is mental, not material. Reason, as C. S. Lewis puts it, is "older than Nature."[50] The reality of intrinsic intentionality, which is arguably the "mark of the mental,"[51] provides justification for premises (1) and (2) of the argument from reason.

The second feature of the act of thinking is alethicity (from the Greek *aletheia*, meaning "truth"), which pertains to the fact that our thoughts can be true or false. A corollary of the intentional nature of thoughts is that they are capable of *representing* something as being a certain way. My thoughts that "the Willis Tower (formerly the Sears Tower) is in Chicago" and that "the Eiffel Tower is in London" correctly (for the first thought) and incorrectly (for the second thought) represent something to be the case. Thus, my first thought is true, and my second false. The fact that our mental lives can accurately or inaccurately represent the world is enormously surprising given naturalism. If minds are just brains, and mental processes are just complicated physical processes, it is hard to make sense of how our thoughts are about anything at all. C. S. Lewis bluntly states the problem: "To talk about one bit of matter being

---

48. An account of intentionality is reductive if it explains macroproperties (such as mental states) in terms of the microproperties of physical objects and states (such as brain states). For a survey and critical commentary on four prominent naturalistic theories of intentionality—causal, biological, instrumental, and conceptual role theories—see Feser, *Philosophy of Mind*, 174–93.

49. "Introspection certainly produces the illusion of *about*ness. But it's got to be an illusion, since nothing physical can be *about* anything. . . . The real problem is to explain away this illusion." Rosenberg, *The Atheist's Guide to Reality*, 193.

50. Lewis, *Miracles*, 34.

51. This idea was pressed forcefully by the philosopher Franz Brentano's 1874 work *Psychologie vom empirischen Standpunkte*. English translation: Brentano, *Psychology from an Empirical Standpoint*, ed. Oskar Kraus and Linda L. McAlister, trans. Antos C. Rancurello, D. B. Terrell, and Linda L. McAlister (New York: Routledge, 1995).

true of another seems to me to be nonsense."[52] In theism, however, the human mind's ability to discern truth and falsehood is grounded in the fact that God has created human beings with the ability to reason.

Lewis notes a third feature of ability to reason in *Miracles*: "Hence, acts of inference can, and must be considered in two different lights. On the one hand they are subjective events, items in somebody's psychological history. On the other hand, they are insights into, or knowings of, something other than themselves."[53] Here Lewis notes the reality of *mental causation* in acts of thinking: "The fact that one mental state can cause another mental state in virtue of its propositional content."[54] In our earlier syllogism about getting wet in rain, for example, we reasoned to a new bit of knowledge by entertaining and accepting other bits of knowledge. This is the phenomenon of mental causation at work in rational inference.

The reality of mental causation is enormously difficult to reconcile with naturalism. Naturalistic attempts to account for mental causation by *identifying* the mental with brain states, or alternatively as *supervening* on brain states, effectively renders the mental superfluous. The physical processes and states do all the causal work.[55] As J. P. Moreland notes, if the universe is causally closed (i.e., there are only physical or material causes), then the "sequence of mental events running through a person's consciousness is like a series of causally impotent shadows."[56] Moreover, as Feser argues, if "the electrochemical properties of the neural processes with which the thoughts are associated are entirely sufficient to bring about whatever effects they do bring about," then "the meanings or contents of the thoughts is irrelevant."[57] The ability to rationally deliberate over the propositional content of our mental lives is hard to explain given the paltry resources available to the

---

52. C. S. Lewis, *Christian Reflections* (Grand Rapids: Eerdmans, 1967), 64, quoted in Reppert, *C. S. Lewis's Dangerous Idea*, 74.

53. Lewis, *Miracles*, 34.

54. Reppert, *C. S. Lewis's Dangerous Idea*, 78.

55. Feser, *Philosophy of Mind*, 152. The causal powers of mental states "drain away" since it is the causal powers of corresponding brain states that do all the work. See Jaegwon Kim, *Mind in a Physical World: An Essay on the Mind-Body Problem and Mental Causation* (Cambridge, MA: MIT Press, 1998); Kim, *Physicalism, or Something Near Enough* (Princeton: Princeton University Press, 2005); Ned Block, "Do Causal Powers Drain Away?" *Philosophy and Phenomenal Research* 67 (2003): 133–50; and Brandon Rickabaugh and Todd Buras, "The Argument from Reason, and Mental Causal Drainage: A Reply to van Inwagen," *Philosophia Christi* 19, no. 2 (2017): 381–98.

56. J. P. Moreland, *The Recalcitrant Imago Dei: Human Persons and the Failure of Naturalism* (London: SCM, 2009), 51.

57. Feser, *Philosophy of Mind*, 152.

naturalist. If theism is true, however, mind is both prior to matter and the cause of matter. Mental causation fits nicely within a theistic framework.

Finally, Lewis notes a fourth characteristic of rational thought.

> What from the first point of view is the psychological transition from thought A to thought B, at some particular moment in some particular mind, is, from the thinker's point of view a perception of an implication (if A, then B). When we are adopting the psychological point of view we may use the past tense. "B *followed* A in my thoughts." But when we assert the implication we always use the present—"B *follows* from A." If it ever "follows from" in the logical sense, it does so always. And we cannot possibly reject the second point of view as a subjective illusion without discrediting all human knowledge.[58]

Lewis is observing that acts of inference are governed by *logical laws*, laws that specify the truth-preserving relationships among propositions. Our earlier syllogism was an instance of the logical inference law *modus ponens*, which states, "Whenever *If P, then Q* and *P*, it follows that *Q*." Logical laws are intrinsically intentional, meaning they are *about* relationships among propositions. Moreover, logical laws are necessary truths. A statement or proposition is necessarily true if it could not be false. The statement "The Union won the Civil War" is a contingent truth; it could have been false since it is possible for the Union to have lost the war. Logical laws possess a much firmer grip on reality; they cannot possibly be false.

That logical laws are necessary is self-evident. As soon as we understand, for example, what the law of noncontradiction expresses (i.e., that two mutually exclusive statements cannot both be true at the same time and in the same sense), we see, or rationally intuit, its necessity. One might claim that logical laws are contingent. But in response, we should ask: Can you plausibly imagine a world where the law of noncontradiction fails to hold? Arguably such a world is impossible to imagine.

Herein lies a further problem for the naturalist, for the *only* ingredients available in a purely material cosmos for making sense of intrinsically necessary logical laws are *physical entities, events, and laws*. But physical entities, events,

---

58. Lewis, *Miracles*, 27.

and laws are contingent, grounding contingent truths alone. If God exists, however, we find a fitting explanation for the existence of these logical laws. Logical laws are grounded in and expressions of a perfectly rational (necessarily existing) God. Some Christian philosophers, such as James N. Anderson and Greg Welty, have even argued logical laws *are* divine thoughts about how propositions essentially relate.[59] If so, then "every logical argument," including every argument for atheism, "presupposes the existence of God."[60]

These four features of rational inference—*intentionality, alethicity, mental causation*, and the existence of *logical laws*—provide powerful reasons for believing that the existence of rational minds is not surprising in a theistic framework (premise 1). On the other hand, given the empty world of naturalism and the restriction to "none but natural causes involving none but natural entities," it is not clear that naturalism has the sufficient resources to account for the existence of minds, whether they be late and local or existing at all. The existence of minds is quite surprising in a naturalistic account of reality (premise 2).

But what about Oppy's claim that evolution explains the origin and development of minds in a naturalistic world? If evolution can provide a plausible account of the origin and development of minds, then it could be argued that premise (2) is false, rendering the argument from reason uncogent. But arguing that premise (2) is false on the grounds that we can give an evolutionary account of the origin and development of minds won't help for at least two reasons. First, it is evident that we understand far more about the world than what is required for survival. As John Polkinghorne said, "It seems incredible that, say, Einstein's ability to conceive of the General Theory of Relativity was just a spin-off from the struggle for survival. What survival value does such an ability possess?"[61] The answer is "none." As Polkinghorne claims, the human capacity for the kind of abstract reasoning employed in pure mathematics has little practical value for humankind's struggle for survival. It is difficult to see how such complex reasoning abilities could evolve from nonrational, nonpurposeful, blind forces.[62]

59. James N. Anderson and Greg Welty, "The Lord of Noncontradiction: An Argument for God from Logic," *Philosophia Christi* 13, no. 2 (2011): 321–38.

60. Anderson and Welty, "The Lord of Noncontradiction," 337.

61. John Polkinghorne, *Science and Creation: The Search for Understanding* (West Conshohocken, PA: Templeton Press, 2006), 29–30.

62. Erik J. Wielenberg admits this in claiming that on naturalism plus evolution, we would not expect to understand how intentionality arises via natural selection. "Understanding how evolutionary processes could produce intentional states is (at least in part) a philosophical problem, just the sort of problem evolutionary

Further, if naturalism and neo-Darwinian evolution are granted, then as Lewis and more recently Alvin Plantinga argue, we have no reason to think evolution or naturalism are true.[63] Evolution holds that the principal function of our cognitive faculties is to select beliefs that contribute to our survival, *not* beliefs that are true. If we are the product of blind evolution in a naturalistic universe, we are not *justified* in thinking evolution, naturalism, or any of our beliefs—like those produced by cognitive faculties such as introspection, perception, memory, and so on—are true. Naturalism conjoined with evolution is self-defeating.

Reason itself, and the deliberative processes that govern rationality, point to a reality "outside the box," a world governed by truth and not mere survival instincts. The world is ontologically haunted by a self-existent, immaterial, cosmic mind. As Lewis has said, "To admit [a] cosmic mind is to admit a God outside Nature, a transcendent and supernatural God."[64] This is the argument from reason to God.

LOOKING ALONG REASON

"That is interesting but can you stop and listen for a moment?"

Adam's plea came on the heels of my lengthy twenty-minute spiel. I'd caught myself an atheist. And he was willing to talk. I didn't want to waste the opportunity, so I immediately launched into my best arguments for God and the Christian faith as we sat across from each other in his freshman dorm dining hall. I pulled out a napkin and walked through an airtight argument for God's existence, accompanied by a chart showing mutually exclusive options: the universe either began or it didn't begin (it began); the beginning of the universe was either caused or uncaused (it was caused); the cause of the

---

theory predicts our brains will be bad at solving." Wielenberg, *God and the Reach of Reason* (New York: Cambridge University Press, 2008), 107. But the fact that we can, and often do, solve philosophical problems and make substantial advances in understanding our world suggests that appeals to mystery are *ad hoc* attempts to save a dying theory (i.e., naturalism). Moreover, intentionality is a problem for the naturalist because of what we do know about mental and physical states and their incompatibility, not because of what we don't know. See Reppert, "The Argument from Reason," 374–75; and Thomas Nagel, *Mind and Cosmos* (Oxford: Oxford University Press, 2012).

63. Lewis, *Miracles*, 28–9; Alvin Plantinga, *Where the Conflict Really Lies: Science, Religion, and Naturalism* (Oxford: Oxford University Press, 2011), ch. 10.

64. Lewis, *Miracles*, 43.

beginning of the universe was either personal or nonpersonal (it was personal). See? The napkin proves it. God exists!

I looked up after presenting my airtight case, fully expecting Adam to admit defeat. Instead, I saw exasperation in his eyes. I was not *listening* to him. My arguments had failed to scratch where he itched. Seeing my mistake, I set down my pen and napkin, sat back in my chair and apologized. "Tell me why you don't believe in God?"

Adam poured out his heart. His unbelief had little to do with the evidence. It had everything to do with his poor relationship with his father. I learned a lesson that night. Making the case for Christianity is about far more than delivering true content. We must not neglect the relational aspect. We are called to speak the truth *in love* (Eph. 4:15). When we present a case for Jesus and the gospel, Peter implores us to do so "with gentleness and respect" (1 Peter 3:15).

Communication theorists distinguish between the content and the relational aspects of communication. According to Tim Muehlhoff and Richard Langer, "The content level is the literal meanings of the words we are using that convey our message. The relational level expresses the amount of affection, respect, and compassion between people."[65] That night I had shown Adam little respect or compassion, so my initial attempts at persuasion were unsuccessful. Thankfully, he was gracious and allowed me another chance.

But we don't always get a second chance. Many today are convinced that Christianity is irrelevant. Ineffectual attempts to communicate the Christian message that assume, as I did, that people are open to the gospel if evidence and reason are employed will only reinforce this irrelevancy. Some are openly hostile toward Christianity, fueled by a cultural script that encourages confrontation. This argumentative script "urges us to approach the world—and the people in it—in an adversarial frame of mind."[66] In this cultural milieu, it is difficult for the message of the gospel to get a fair hearing. What is needed, according to Os Guinness, is a recovery of the "lost art" of Christian persuasion: "Many of us today lack a vital part of a way of communicating that is prominent in the Gospels and throughout the Scriptures, but largely absent in the church

---

65. Tim Muehlhoff and Richard Langer, *Winsome Persuasion: Christian Influence in a Post-Christian World* (Downers Grove, IL: InterVarsity Press, 2017), 63.

66. Deborah Tannen, *The Argument Culture: Moving from Debate to Dialogue* (New York: Random House, 1998), 3, quoted in Muehlhoff and Langer, *Winsome Persuasion*, 54.

today—persuasion, the art of speaking to people who, for whatever reason, are indifferent or resistant to what we have to say."[67] How do we persuade others of the reasonableness of Christianity? There is no one-size-fits-all approach to persuasion, but there are principles, rooted in Scripture, that can help us show others the reasonableness of Jesus and the gospel. Let's consider a few basic tools that can help us utilize persuasion effectively as cultural apologists.

Starting Posture

The adversarial, argumentative script followed by so many in culture today has led to incivility and gridlock.[68] We scream at each other, even as we talk past each other. Whatever the topic—politics, religion, or the best taco joint in town—our arguments rarely convince others. How we argue matters too, and in this lies the opportunity for a counterscript, one where others are treated with love, compassion, and care.[69] This is Jesus's way, and it must be the way of his followers too if we are to persuade others. As Aristotle noted long ago, the credibility of our message (*logos*) is influenced by who we are (*ethos*).[70] Any argument, no matter how tightly made, can be (and often is) undermined by a vicious posture toward those we seek to persuade. God brings us truth through his love and compassion, and we must do the same with others.

Starting Points

Recall from chapter 1 our look at Paul's engagement with the Greek philosophers at Mars Hill. He began his speech to the Athenians by identifying a shared starting point—their worship of the unknown God—and building a bridge from their accepted beliefs to Jesus and the gospel. I've argued that we should identify similar starting points within "our Athens"—the cultural context in which we find ourselves. We've explored several of these starting points already, including the universal longings for truth, goodness, and beauty.

As we identify starting points, it is necessary to consider the *plausibility structure* and *sacred core* of others, especially when we are making a case for Jesus and the

67. Os Guinness, *Fool's Talk: Recovering the Art of Christian Persuasion* (Downers Grove, IL: InterVarsity Press, 2015), 18.

68. Muehlhoff and Langer, *Winsome Persuasion*, 58–59.

69. Muehlhoff and Langer, *Winsome Persuasion*, 58–59.

70. Muehlhoff and Langer, *Winsome Persuasion*, 68.

gospel.[71] Originally coined by sociologist Peter Berger, a plausibility structure is a set of ideas or beliefs that an individual or group of individuals is or is not willing to consider as plausibly true. For example, setting aside a few notable exceptions, most people think the idea of a flat earth is just not plausible today. If someone says the earth is flat, they are not taken seriously. "Surely they must be joking," we think to ourselves. Or perhaps they are using a metaphor. For many people, the belief in the divinity of Jesus is implausible too. So how can we help others see the reasonableness of belief in the divinity of Jesus? One approach is to begin with an idea that is generally considered plausible. For example, I could begin by noting widely accepted criteria for establishing the trustworthiness of historical documents. From this plausible starting point, an effective case can be made for the trustworthiness of the biographies of Christ, then the historicity of the resurrection, and finally the validity of Jesus's claims to stand in the very place of God. As Muehlhoff and Langer note, "The key to crafting a successful message is to find starting points consisting of beliefs that the strong public already finds plausible."[72]

In addition to plausibility structures, I also mentioned having an awareness of the sacred core of an individual (or community). This sacred core is "the set of values or beliefs cherished by [an individual or] members of a particular community."[73] When crafting an argument, it is important to be aware of and respectful toward the sacred core—those cherished and beloved beliefs—lest you fall into a "rhetorical minefield" that derails your discussion or presentation.[74] I was once sharing the gospel with a student named Chris, who held as part of his sacred core the belief that people are born gay or straight. When he found out that the Christian organization I was associated with held a campus outreach event the prior year with speakers advertised as "ex-gays," he was livid. He threw every explicative in the book at me and stormed out of the room. Because it contradicted his sacred core, this new information derailed my case for Jesus and the gospel. Thankfully it was only temporary. Chris came back, apologized, and reengaged in our conversation. Not only did we have an honest and constructive talk about homosexuality, we eventually returned to the original discussion (an argument for God). If I hadn't demonstrated a long-term

---

71. Muehlhoff and Langer, *Winsome Persuasion*, 102–6.
72. Muehlhoff and Langer, *Winsome Persuasion*, 103.
73. Muehlhoff and Langer, *Winsome Persuasion*, 104.
74. Muehlhoff and Langer, *Winsome Persuasion*, 105.

awareness of and respect for his sacred core beliefs, our conversation would likely have ended, and with it, my opportunity to build a case for Jesus and the gospel. We must value the sacred cores of the individuals and communities we seek to persuade with generosity, charity, and respect.

Making the Case

Sharing the truth, goodness, and beauty of Christianity with others is a process. Sometimes you'll need to engage false beliefs that stand as a hindrance to the gospel. At other times, you'll simply need to present a positive case for Christianity. The process can be messy, full of give and take, starts and stops. We depend on the Holy Spirit for guidance, but learning how to craft an argument is still necessary for effective persuasion, so we must understand the basic forms of an effective argument.

An argument is one or more statements (called premises) strung together in support of another statement (called the conclusion). There are two basic argument forms: *deductive* and *inductive*. In a deductive argument, if the premises are true, the conclusion inescapably follows. For example, from "All men are mortals" and "Socrates is a man," it inescapably follows that "Socrates is a mortal." The argument from desire presented in chapter 3 and the moral argument presented in chapter 6 are both examples of deductive arguments. In an inductive argument, if the premises are true, the conclusion probably follows, but not inescapably. For example, from "It has rained all week" and "The forecast calls for more rain today," it probably but not inevitably follows that "It will rain today." The argument from reason presented earlier in this chapter is an example of an inductive argument.[75] You can study a quality logic text in order to familiarize yourself with various deductive argument forms (such as *modus ponens*, *modus tollens*, and disjunctive syllogism) and inductive argument forms (such as inference to the best explanation, inductive inference, and the argument from analogy).[76] I recommend that you practice formulating arguments or analyzing the arguments of others to learn how to defend your premises and undercut the premises of others. Master common formal and informal

---

75. Exercise for the reader: How might you reformulate the argument from reason as a deductive argument? How might you reformulate the arguments from desire and morality as inductive arguments?

76. A good introductory text is T. Ryan Byerly, *Introducing Logic and Critical Thinking* (Grand Rapids: Baker, 2017).

fallacies. (Formal fallacies include affirming the consequent and denying the antecedent; informal fallacies include the genetic fallacy and begging the question.)[77] And then make your case, creatively using reason in dialogue with others, through blog posts, tweets, videos, songs, artwork, essays, and stories. Becoming an effective case-maker takes time, study, and practice, but it is part of what it means to follow in the footsteps of Jesus and the disciples, all of whom gave arguments, reasons, and evidence for their positions.

As you study and prepare, remember that the goal in effective persuasion is to be a *faithful witness*. The goal isn't to win the argument or shame a community or individual for holding false beliefs. God stands accused by sin and the devil, but as Os Guinness says well, "God is his own lead counsel, his own best apologist."[78] The Holy Spirit, the Spirit of truth (John 16:13), is the defense attorney making God's defense by opening the eyes of the blind and convicting the hearts of sinners. Our job as cultural apologists is to understand those we seek to reach and to present our case in truth and with love. The gift of reason, creatively engaged in partnership with the Holy Spirit, will help guide the lost to the truth of Christ.

REASON AND THE KINGDOM

Whenever the apostle Paul arrived in a new city, one of his first stops was the local synagogue. As the hub of Jewish religious life in the first century, the synagogue exerted substantial cultural influence. If you could reach the synagogue, you could reach the city. Paul was strategic in his apologetic approach to engaging the culture, and in a similar manner we should ask ourselves: What today functions as a center of power for the discovery of truth and the advancement of knowledge? I believe one of the best answers to that question is the modern university.

Consider these facts.[79] In America, a majority of the most highly educated people in society are located within a single institution, the university. In addition,

77. For an accessible book on how to spot fallacies and make your case in dialogue with others, See Greg Koukl, *Tactics: A Game Plan for Discussing Your Christian Convictions* (Grand Rapids: Zondervan, 2009).

78. Guinness, *Fool's Talk*, 28.

79. For more details regarding the facts discussed in this paragraph, see Paul M. Gould, *The Outrageous Idea of the Missional Professor* (Eugene, OR: Wipf & Stock, 2014), 40–51.

the ideas propagated on the university campus shape the mind of our culture through books, op-eds, and public lectures. The university defines the terms of debate and the issues to be discussed for years to come.[80] Virtually all current and future leaders of culture—in education, the arts, politics, and the church—pass through the doors of the university. The great statesman and scholar Charles Malik does not exaggerate in his claims that "this great Western institution, the university, dominates the world today more than any other institution: more than the church, more than the government, more than all other institutions."[81] If we are to be strategic in our cultural apologetic, we must work to cultivate Christian leadership and a Christian presence within the halls of the academy. The perceived reasonableness and desirability of Christianity depends upon how effectively we accomplish this task. Allow me to suggest three practical ideas for reaching three different audiences associated with the modern, American university.

The first idea applies to Christian professors and students who are considering a career as a teacher or professor. *Be missional.* As a university professor, God has strategically placed you within at least two mission fields: the local campus setting and your specific academic discipline. In your local setting, being missional includes coming together with like-minded believers for prayer and study, a commitment to excellence in teaching and service, and engaging in apologetics, evangelism, and discipleship when the opportunity arises. Within the context of your academic discipline, being missional includes seeking to integrate faith with excellent scholarship, addressing the sub- or anti-Christian biases within a discipline, and selecting research projects that contribute to the plausibility or desirability of Christianity.[82] A missional life within a secular university will turn heads and cause people to sit up and take notice, and it will be challenged. But this is the call of Christ for those whom God has placed within the university.

For those who are future professors (i.e., graduates and undergraduates who have identified God's call to academia), I would further advise you to *be intentional in cultivating your craft, your walk with God, and your vision for ministry.* As those who are now professors will attest, the road to academia is anything but easy. It is potted with dangers, dissolutions, and doubts. There is

---

80. Mark A. Noll, *The Scandal of the Evangelical Mind* (Grand Rapids: Eerdmans, 1994), 51.

81. Charles Malik, *A Christian Critique of the University* (Waterloo, ON: North Waterloo Academic Press, 1987), 19–20.

82. Much more could be said on this topic, of course. I've tried to say more in my book *The Outrageous Idea of the Missional Professor.*

a high cost to your soul, your bank account, and even your physical health in pursuing and attaining a PhD and a university post. It takes chutzpah, perseverance, diligence, intelligence, the grace of God, and the support of others. Some of you reading this book are called to serve academia in your future. My encouragement to you is to seek first God's kingdom and his righteousness (Matt. 6:33) and to resist the temptation to fall into the meritorious mind-set so pervasive in the academy, where one's worth is measured by their publications. Find godly mentors within your discipline. Read and study the work of Christian scholars in your field who have gone before you. Know that the call to be a professor is a noble one, worthy of your time, energy, and intellect. May God use, guide, and provide for you as you seek to serve him in the academy.

Finally, I believe there is a call for the broader church community to *be supportive of current and future professors as well as those called to work with them.* I long for the day when churches will call professors up to the front of the sanctuary and pray for them at the start of a school year, sending them as missionaries to their mission field. Christian academics may feel out of place within the walls of the church, and this is a tragedy. Christian professors are a vital part of God's missionary endeavor, as strategically placed ambassadors for Christ in a key center of cultural influence. You might consider financially supporting Christian graduate students as well as ministries such as Faculty Commons, Ratio Christi, InterVarsity, Grad Resources, Global Scholars, and the Consortium of Christian Study Centers, all of whom have active and thriving ministries to professors and graduate students.[83] We are one body with many parts—we need each other.

Truth calls. Reason guides. A cultural apologetic of return will not shy away from demonstrating the truth of Christianity. Neither will it surrender the university to the barbarians. Rather, Christians must seek to be faithfully present both upstream in the academy and downstream in the lives of individuals and communities that are shaped by the academy. Such faithful presence will demonstrate to a watching world the truth of Christianity and the power of the cross.

---

83. See https://www.facultycommons.com; https://ratiochristi.org/prof/; https://gfm.intervarsity.org; http://gradresources.org; https://studycentersonline.org; https://www.global-scholars.org. Global Scholars has recently launched an ambitious and God-sized ministry to support, encourage, and mobilize current and future Christian professors from all over the world called the *Society of Christian Scholars*. For more, see http://societyofchristianscholars.org.

CHAPTER 6

CONSCIENCE

> When the light in most people's faces comes from the glow
> of the laptop, the smartphone, or the television screen,
> we are living in a Dark Age.
>
> *Father Martin Bernhard, of the Monastery of St. Benedict[1]*

> Live such good lives among the pagans that, though they
> accuse you of doing wrong, they may see your good deeds
> and glorify God on the day he visits us.
>
> *1 Peter 2:12*

Picture an old hag cloaked in darkness. Lurching about, her cold eyes dripping with judgment, her stomach growling, seeking a victim to devour. A bony finger protrudes, disembodied, summoned from the depths of her garment. She points, condemning from a distance. The stench of garlic lingers in the empty space.

The old hag pictured here symbolizes the face of evil in some of our most beloved fairy stories. She is the Evil Queen in *Snow White*, the Wicked Stepmother in *Cinderella*, the oven roasting witch in *Hansel and Gretel*. Today, the witch has spun her magic again, stepping out of the pages of fairy stories and into reality. Where is the witch found today?

For many people today, the witch lives among us as the church. The

---

1. Quoted in Rod Dreher, *The Benedict Option: A Strategy for Christians in a Post-Christian Nation* (New York: Sentinel, 2017), 71.

judgmental, controlling, condemning hag of the past has been transferred to Christianity in the popular imagination. The church is seen by many as an intolerant and judgmental community. Yet while the church is unpopular, it's different for Jesus. Everyone wants to claim him as their own. He is white, black, yellow, brown, a Republican and a Democrat, progay and antigay, prodemocracy and procommunism, for guns and against. Name a cause and there is a Jesus waiting in the wings to support it and validate it. Jesus is the ever-loving, ever-ready friend—a genie in the background of our lives ready to help whenever he's called upon.

There are gaps between appearance and reality here: the gap between the Jesus we want and the Jesus we need and the gap between the church as perceived (the old hag) and the church as it *should* be and one day will be (the beautiful and alluring bride of Christ). For Christianity to be desirable, we must narrow the gaps between how things are and how things ought to be.

Even though the crowds want a piece of Jesus, many are not willing to drink the living water Jesus offers (John 7:37). This is partly because the path of self-denial is hard and costly, but some of the blame falls on the church. According to Barna Research Group, the most common complaint of those outside the faith, as summarized by David Kinnaman and Gabe Lyons, is that "Christians no longer represent what Jesus had in mind, that Christianity in our society is not what it was meant to be."[2] Christians today are known primarily by what they stand against instead of what they stand for. For the majority of people aged sixteen to twenty-nine, Christians are anti-homosexual, judgmental, hypocritical, too political, old-fashioned, insensitive, boring, unaccepting of other faiths, and confusing.[3]

In the flattened world of our disenchanted age, self-expression and the unfettered satisfaction of desires are the highest goods. The chief sins are a failure to be true to oneself (i.e., hypocrisy) and a failure to be tolerant (i.e., judgmentalism). Christians exhibit both sins in spades. We are accused of hypocrisy when our beliefs and lifestyle fail to match, and sadly, Christians all too often publicly condemn activities in which they privately participate. Studies reveal

---

2. David Kinnaman and Gabe Lyons, *Unchristian: What a New Generation Really Thinks about Christianity . . . and Why It Matters* (Grand Rapids: Baker, 2007), 15. My original first sentence to this chapter was "Christianity has an image problem." Then I opened Kinnaman and Lyons's book only to find that exact sentence on the first page. My opening paragraphs are an attempt to say the same thing in a more concrete way.

3. Kinnaman and Lyons, *Unchristian*, 26–28. While the study by Kinnaman and Lyons is now over a decade old, the negative perception of present-day Christianity continues, perhaps even worsening, as Christians are divided amongst themselves and from the majority culture over politics, sexuality, race, immigration, and religious freedom.

that there is little difference in the lifestyle of believers and nonbelievers (setting aside a few extra religious activities for the practicing Christian).[4] The lives of some Christians make a great argument for atheism, or as Os Guinness bluntly observes, "The church is a leading spawning ground for atheists."[5]

It is no secret that Christianity has a public relations problem. The fix is not to hire a new marketing firm. The problem runs deeper than a surface level solution. It is a matter of our hearts and souls. Fragmentation, selfishness, and small-minded thoughts and loves infect the church. Even though Christians no longer stand under the penalty of sin, the desires of the flesh still have power.

If the church is compromised and nominal, how might Christianity be seen as good to those outside the church? Is it possible for our culture to transition from seeing the church as an evil witch to an alluring bride of the King? I believe the answer is yes, but the transformation begins by reconsidering the human quest for goodness (see figure 6.1).

FIGURE 6.1: The Human Quest for Goodness

4. Kinnaman and Lyons, *Unchristian*, 46–48.

5. Os Guinness, *Fool's Talk: Recovering the Art of Christian Persuasion* (Downers Grove, IL: InterVarsity Press, 2015), 205.

LONGING FOR GOODNESS

Picture a fleet of ships. C. S. Lewis tells us there are three ingredients needed for the fleet to make a successful voyage.[6] First, each ship must be individually seaworthy. The hull must not leak, the mast and boom should be in working order, and the sails ready to catch the wind. Second, each ship must be rightly related to the others. The ships must be far enough apart to avoid collision, yet close enough to help each other in times of need. Finally, the ships must be rightly related to their end, their destination. They must follow a course that will lead them where they wish to go.

Lewis introduces the image of a fleet of ships as a metaphor to help us understand the nature of the moral life. He equates living the good life with the successful voyage of the fleet, and he argues that it, too, has three components. To experience the good life, we first must be rightly related within ourselves such that our imagination, reason, and conscience work in concert to promote right behavior and, over time, the excellence of character. A life well lived is a life of intellectual and moral *virtue*. But human flourishing also means being rightly related to others. Any injustices perpetrated between human beings—lying, murder, theft, abuse, disrespect—are violations of shalom, of peace and order. We were created to live in harmony with others. Even in the garden of Eden, it was not good for Adam to be alone (Gen. 2:18). The good life is a life lived with others, one filled with deep and abiding relationships. We were created to be known and to know, to be loved and to love.

Finally, human flourishing requires us to be rightly related to our end— our purpose. We were created to love and serve God according to the nature he gave us, and we thrive when we live this way. If we locate our lives in the gospel story and live under God's rule and reign, we will find our identity, meaning, and purpose. The good life is a flourishing life, a life rightly ordered with respect to self, others, and our end.

This threefold conception of the good life also illuminates the anatomy of our universal longing for goodness. The quest for goodness finds expression in our longing for *wholeness* (the individual component to human flourishing), *justice* (the social component), and a life of *significance* (kingdom-directed component). Let's examine each of the three aspects of the human quest for goodness in more detail.

---

6. C. S. Lewis, *Mere Christianity* (New York: HarperCollins, 2001), 69–75.

The Longing for Wholeness

Dr. Jekyll was a respected and wealthy physician and scientist living in nineteenth-century London. By his own admission, his worst fault as a young man was "a certain impatient gaiety of disposition" that was hard to reconcile with the "imperious desire to carry my head high, and wear a more than commonly grave countenance before the public."[7] Jekyll wanted to have fun, but he didn't want others to see him as a lightweight. This innocent fault eventually led him to lead a duplicitous life, and soon Dr. Jekyll was a profound "double dealer."[8] His warring desires led to a split in his identity, yet both sides of his nature were genuine and earnest. He was himself when he laid aside restraint and plunged into shame as the evil Mr. Hyde. He was also himself when he advanced knowledge and provided relief from sorrow and suffering as the good Dr. Jekyll. But these two selves, one guided by knowledge, virtue, chivalry, and concern for people and the other guided by unrestraint, greed, and lust, could not coexist for long. As Robert Louis Stevenson illustrates through his fictional story, the base nature, once it has been unmoored from constraint, will eventually overtake our better selves.

Stevenson's classic novel about the *Strange Case of Dr. Jekyll and Mr. Hyde* evokes within me two responses. The first is fear. The story scares me because it offers a chilling and all too familiar portrait of my own interior life. I long for holiness and purity, but I fear the revolt of my baser nature. This struggle with sin and the flesh is real, and the temptation we feel toward the base appetites is strong. We all have the potential to become a full-fledged "double dealer." In times of struggle, I cry out with the apostle Paul: "Who will rescue me from this body that is subject to death? Thanks be to God, who delivers me through Jesus Christ our Lord!" (Rom. 7:24–25).

Second, Stevenson's book awakens within me the longing to be whole. I long for my thoughts and emotions, my actions and character, to be united and working together for the same goal. All too often one dimension of my life is at cross-purposes with another. Chaos results. People are hurt. Peace remains elusive. I'm not alone in longing to be whole. Like Humpty Dumpty after his fall, we are fragmented people. All the king's men—whether doctors, counselors, or entertainers—can apply all the king's tools—medicine, self-help programs, and worldly pleasures—in

---

7. Robert Louis Stevenson, *The Strange Case of Dr. Jekyll and Mr. Hyde* (Mineola, NY: Dover, 1991), 42.
8. Stevenson, *The Strange Case of Dr. Jekyll and Mr. Hyde*, 42.

an attempt to put us together, but they make little progress. At best, we experience temporary amnesia and forget our brokenness for a moment.

We all long for unity and wholeness in life.

We long for unity because we've been created for wholeness by the perfectly united triune God. And this divine unity serves as the pattern for every other form of unity:

> The Christian doctrine of God thus contains an assertion about the nature of unity. It asserts that all the actual unities of our earthly experience, from the unity of the hydrogen atom to the unity of a work of art, of the human self, or of a human society, are imperfect instances of what unity truly is. We may find in them analogies to that true unity, and learn from them something of what perfect unity must be. But perfect unity itself is to be found only in God, and it is through the revelation of God in Christ that we find the unity of God to be of such a kind as to cast light upon all lesser unities.[9]

Man can only attain wholeness when God, the perfect triunity, heals us. Our options are few: either we experience wholeness of body and spirit, or we suffer disintegration. As I've wrote elsewhere, "A life directed toward wholeness is a life filled with flourishing, delight, and integrity. A life bent toward compartmentalization or disintegration is one of misery, emptiness, and the loss of self."[10]

But where can we find the wholeness we long for? By looking to Jesus as our greatest joy, hope, love, and happiness.[11] And as we experience wholeness, a watching world will take note, as they seek a cup of living water for their restless souls.

The Longing for Justice

Why does God allow pain and suffering? This is one of the most common questions people ask to express their doubts about God. It is a question driven by an intuition that something has gone terribly wrong with the world.

9. Leonard Hodgson, *The Doctrine of the Trinity* (London: Nisbet, 1955), 96.
10. Paul M. Gould, *The Outrageous Idea of the Missional Professor* (Eugene, OR: Wipf & Stock, 2014), 28.
11. "Look to yourself, and you will find in the long run only hatred, loneliness, despair, rage, ruin, and decay. But look for Christ and you will find Him, and with Him everything else thrown in." Lewis, *Mere Christianity*, 227.

Things are not the way they are supposed to be.[12] It doesn't take much to convince others that the world isn't right. Daily we read of wars, famine, human trafficking, racism, murder, and bribery.[13] Turning our gaze inward, we see our own brokenness and evil. Lust, angst, hatred, jealousy, and discord lurk in every crack and crevice of the human heart. The question of why God allows evil reveals a deep human longing for a world made right. And this longing for justice, if traced to its source, leads us to Jesus. As Bethany Hanke Hoang and Kristen Deede Johnson write, "God's very character is one of justice, and he has given us Jesus as the manifestation of his justice both now and for eternity."[14] Seeing Jesus, we know tragedy doesn't get the last word. Despair is not inevitable. This hope, once kindled, can lead us home.

It was the fall of 1939, and the English poet W. H. Auden,[15] having drifted away from the Christianity of his youth, was now a convinced atheist. War had recently broken out in Europe, so one evening Auden went to a theater in the German-speaking section of Manhattan to see a documentary of the Nazi invasion of Poland. What he saw sickened him. He watched the atrocities carried out by Germans on the screen, then listened to the cheers of Germans watching in the theater. His belief in natural human goodness conflicted with the evil he saw and experienced that day, and he found himself in a state of turmoil. As an atheist, he had rejected the notion of moral absolutes, yet this belief was inconsistent with his strong desire to condemn Hitler as an evil man leading others into great evil. The injustices perpetrated by the Nazis stirred something deep within Auden's soul. He recognized the innate call of justice and began to reconsider his rejection of the Christian faith: "I thought I had done with Christianity for good."[16] As he sought an absolute source of goodness from which to condemn evil and a power to make things right again, Auden began a journey that eventually led him to convert to Christianity.

12. Cornelius Plantinga Jr., *Not the Way It's Supposed to Be: A Breviary of Sin* (Grand Rapids: Eerdmans, 1995).

13. Consider the scorn of modern day slavery. As of 2016 there are 45.8 million people from 167 countries in some form of slavery (See the Global Slavery Index 2016, https://www.globalslaveryindex.org/findings/). The slave industry worldwide nets over $150 billion a year, two-thirds from sex trafficking alone. See Bethany Hanke Hoang and Kristen Deede Johnson, *The Justice Calling: Where Passion Meets Perseverance* (Grand Rapids: Brazos, 2016), 2.

14. Hanke Hoang and Deede Johnson, *The Justice Calling*, 3.

15. The story of W. H. Auden as summarized in this paragraph is from Guinness, *Fool's Talk*, 131–36.

16. Arthur Kirsch, *Auden and Christianity* (New Haven, CT: Yale University Press, 2005), 13, quoted in Guinness, *Fool's Talk*, 133.

Sometimes the journey to Christ begins when someone encounters horrendous evil. At other times the journey to Christ starts as the nonbeliever joins with believers to promote justice. Sek Saroeun was a Buddhist and a law student.[17] Working as a DJ at a bar in Phnom Penh, Cambodia, Sek knew liquor was not the only item on the menu. Girls, often young girls, were sold for sex. Disgusted by this evil, Sek began to work as an undercover informant for the International Justice Mission (IJM), a Christian human rights group. While spinning music and scanning the bar for suspects, Sek also skimmed the pages of a Bible someone had loaned him. The words of Scripture brought him comfort and alleviated his mounting fear of being exposed as an informant. Sek found his heart changing as he worked alongside Christians to protect these vulnerable young girls. As he later shared, his "fear led to longing; longing led to transformation that is unimaginable."[18] Not only did Sek eventually become a Christian, today he is the top lawyer for the International Justice Mission in Cambodia.

The human heart is stirred and awakened when confronted with horrendous evil and injustice. As C. S. Lewis famously wrote, pain is God's "megaphone to rouse a deaf world."[19] And once aroused, the world asks a question: Who will rescue us? Who or what will heal our brokenness? Will this hope flower into healing and wholeness, or will it be smashed against the rocks of a reality devoid of morals and meaning? One of the great mysteries about God is that he calls us, as the church, to join with him to bring hope and healing, justice and peace, to a watching world. How will we respond to his call to be agents of shalom?

Meeting the needs of the oppressed and vulnerable is good and right. But it is also good because it helps others see Christianity as desirable.[20] A cultural

---

17. The story of Sek Saroeun summarized in this paragraph is from Kate Shellnut, "Cambodia Rising," *Christianity Today* (June 2017): 27–32.

18. Shellnutt, "Cambodia Rising," 27.

19. C. S. Lewis, *The Problem of Pain* (San Francisco: HarperCollins, 1996), 91.

20. Plato distinguished three kinds of goods: things that are good themselves, things that are good for the benefits they bring, and things that are both good themselves and for the benefits they bring (Plato, *Republic*, bk. 2, 357b–d). I suggest that justice is in the third category. Thus, I disagree with my friend Tim Muehlhoff when he and Richard Langer say, "We do neighbor love because we want to be good neighbors and love people. Period. While open doors to the gospel or improved *ethos* may be a side benefit, it is not the goal." Muehlhoff and Langer, *Winsome Persuasion: Christian Influence in a Post-Christian World* (Downers Grove, IL: InterVarsity Press, 2017), 186. While I agree that we want to be good neighbors and love people simply because it is the good and right thing to do, I think we also ought to be good neighbors because it helps Christianity's image. Paying attention to how Christianity is perceived is important—eternal destinies

apologetic of return helps others perceive the good of Christianity by showing them how it makes the world more inviting, just, and whole.

Longing for Significance

After graduating from college, I worked as a certified public accountant. Naturally, when my wife and I got married, I immediately applied my skills as an accounting wizard to our finances. My wife, Ethel, who had rarely reconciled a checkbook or kept a budget, was in awe (let's just say) as I allocated funds each week to pay our bills and save money for the future. I remember one evening when Ethel told our Bible study group of newly marrieds that my hobby was playing with my calculator. From that moment, I was known as "the bean counter." It has taken several years (and a PhD in philosophy) to live down that label.

I excelled at crunching the numbers and was quickly promoted at my job, yet I sensed that God had something else for me. Ethel and I had both become Christians in college, and we shared a desire to see other college students come to faith in Christ, so after a couple years working in business, we joined a parachurch ministry and began full-time ministry to college students.

It was exhilarating to share the gospel each day. God used us to disciple students, and it was such a privilege to see them growing in their faith. As we settled into the rhythm of campus ministry, my heart began to stir yet again. I engaged students who had differing ideas about God and the world, and I grew hungry to learn about apologetics, theology, and philosophy.[21] I sensed God's call for me to pursue further education so I could more effectively reach the university community. After four years of campus ministry at Miami University in Ohio, with a two-year-old and a baby on the way, we sold our house, packed our bags, and moved to Los Angeles so I could attend seminary.

Over the next decade, we moved from Ohio to California and then from California to Indiana. We had three additional children and I spent thousands of dollars and thousands of hours devoting myself to books, classes, and research. We met new friends and settled into new church communities,

---

hang in the balance—and therefore it is good and right to want the benefit just actions bring in terms of the progress of the gospel too.

21. For a more detailed telling of my journey into academia, see my *The Outrageous Idea of the Missional Professor*, 70–76.

and said goodbye to those friends and beloved church communities. Every few years we left the familiar to pursue the next step on the journey, following God's leading. At first, it was a Master's degree, then a PhD, then a promotion in ministry and another move.

We did all of this because we knew that God had a work, a mission, for us. I was spurred on by Paul's words in Ephesians 2:10: "For we are God's handiwork, created in Christ Jesus to do good works, which God prepared in advance for us to do." With my PhD in hand, I felt I could begin that work in earnest, so in North Carolina I began serving on the executive committee of a national ministry to university faculty. I felt ready to change the world, but the job wasn't a good fit for me. I had been promoted out of my sweet spot, and I felt insignificant. Over the next few months, my sense of excitement faded. Depression and despair set in. I wrestled with God. *Is this it? Is this the good work you've created me for?*

Looking back at this time in my life, I see that God first wanted to do a work *in* me. Somewhere in the process of pursuing my education, I had ceased putting Jesus and his kingdom first. My journey had become all about me: building up *my* name and *my* kingdom. God knew I needed to relearn how to love Jesus as my first love, and North Carolina was another stopping point on the journey.

During those three years in North Carolina, the truth of Ephesians 2:10 sustained me. I knew that what God wanted most from me was my heart, and I was determined, aligning with the words of David, to look to God for help:

> My eyes are ever on the LORD,
> for only he will release my feet from the snare. (Ps. 25:15)

Today, as I teach, write, and speak, I sense that I have found the work God has called me to do. I find my heart singing in the classroom. I am deeply satisfied by the thrill of seeing an essay or book published and read—especially *this* book, which has developed and come to life over twenty years of ministry. As I travel and speak to university students, sharing the brilliance and beauty of Jesus and the gospel, I see God's loving care in my life. I've learned through failure, trial, temptation, and defeat that a life lived for someone greater than self is the only path to meaning and significance. I don't think I'm alone in wanting my life to matter. I believe that we all long for significance. We all want our lives to count for something bigger than ourselves.

This truth is beautifully illustrated by observing some of the world's most wealthy individuals, many of whom do not claim to be Christians yet have committed to giving away their wealth for the benefit of others. In 2010 Bill and Melinda Gates joined Warren Buffett in committing to give away over half of their wealth. They launched "The Giving Pledge" and invited other billionaires to also take the pledge.[22] As of 2017, there have been over 170 signers who have pledged to give away billions to alleviate suffering and inequality in the world. In their original statement, the Gates write, "We have been blessed with good fortune beyond our wildest expectations, and we are profoundly grateful. But just as these gifts are great, so we feel a great responsibility to use them well."[23] Facebook founder Mark Zuckerberg and his wife, Priscilla Chan, wrote in their 2015 commitment, "We've had so much opportunity in our lives, and we feel a deep responsibility to make the world a better place for future generations."[24] There is something interesting here, something that should make us sit up and take notice. Do you sense the obligation these billionaires feel toward others, including future generations? Do you wonder why they feel this way? After all, if naturalism is true and there is no transcendent reality, then there is no objective justice or actual obligation to others. It's just an illusion created by chemicals, a self-imposed obligation.

But what if that obligation is rooted in something deeper, something real. I believe this sense of obligation is rooted in our fundamental desire to live for something greater than ourselves, a desire given to us by our Creator. We long for a story that matters, a story of significance in which we can locate our lives and find meaning. The stories spun in our disenchanted age feel empty and boring. They point our focus inward. They do not capture our hearts but leave us depressed and discouraged. Yet even these stories betray themselves. Consider the 1993 comedy *Groundhog Day*, where Phil Connors, played by comedian Bill Murray, finds himself stuck in the same, endlessly repeating day. At first, he uses the knowledge gained each day to pursue pleasure and

22. See https://givingpledge.org/Home.aspx.

23. "Bill and Melinda Gates," The Giving Pledge, https://givingpledge.org/Pledger.aspx?id=199.

24. "Mark Zuckerberg and Priscilla Chan," The Giving Pledge, https://givingpledge.org/Pledger.aspx?id=314.

self-indulgence without regard for others. When these efforts prove fruitless, he turns to suicide, seeking escape, but to no avail. Only when Connors seeks the good of others does he escape the time loop. After coming to the end of himself in his attempts to find escape, he finds an impulse lies latent within his heart, and it turns out to be the means of his redemption.[25] This latent impulse may also be the means of redemption for those who find the dominant stories of this age hollow and boring.

The longings for wholeness, justice, and significance are three aspects of a universal longing for goodness found within the human heart. As cultural apologists, part of our task is to partner with the Holy Spirit in awakening this longing for goodness. We do this by pursuing the one who is perfectly whole, the source of justice, and the fount of meaning. We invite others to locate their lives in the gospel story as together we pursue wholeness, justice, and significance.

LOOKING AT MORALITY

In the conclusion of the *Critique of Practical Reason*, Kant said, "Two things fill the mind with ever new and increasing admiration and reverence . . . *the starry heavens above me and the moral law within me*."[26] Years later, C. S. Lewis picked up this Kantian insight and formulated an argument for God based on the reality of a moral law. Lewis thought the evidence from morality was a better indicator of God than the evidence from the universe since "you find out more about God from the Moral Law than from the universe in general just as you find out more about a man by listening to his conversation than by looking at a house he has built."[27] Lewis's argument for God from morality is found in the first five chapters of *Mere Christianity*. It can be summarized as follows:

1. There is a universal moral law.
2. If there is a universal moral law, there is a moral lawgiver.

---

25. David W. Henderson, *Tranquility: Cultivating a Quiet Soul in a Busy World* (Grand Rapids: Baker, 2015), 86.

26. Immanuel Kant, *Critique of Practical Reason*, trans. Mary Gregor (Cambridge: Cambridge University Press, 1997), 133.

27. Lewis, *Mere Christianity*, 29.

3. If there is a moral lawgiver, it must be something beyond the material cosmos.

4. Therefore, there is something beyond the material cosmos.

His conclusion is striking. As we saw with his arguments from desire and reason, it points us to a transcendent reality, but not directly to the God of Christianity. As Lewis himself admitted, we are "not yet within a hundred miles of the God of Christian theology."[28] Still, this argument gives us a starting point because the power behind the moral law is "more like a mind than it is anything else we know," directing the universe and urging us to do right and be good.[29]

But how do we move from an admission of a transcendent reality to the Christian understanding of God? Why should we think the mind behind the moral law is personal, let alone the personal God of Christianity? Lewis continued his argument, saying that a personal God was the best explanation for our present predicament: "It is after you have realized that there is a real Moral Law, and a Power behind the law, and that you have broken that law and put yourself wrong with that Power—it is after all this, and not a moment sooner, that Christianity begins to talk."[30]

Let's complete the argument from morality to God by adding an additional statement.

5. This object beyond the material cosmos is God.

From which it follows straight away that

6. God exists.

While simpler constructions of the moral argument exist, Lewis's will work just fine.[31] The moral argument is another key component of a cumulative case argument for God; it fills in important details about the nature of the

28. Lewis, *Mere Christianity*, 25.
29. Lewis, *Mere Christianity*, 25.
30. Lewis, *Mere Christianity*, 31.
31. William Lane Craig's formulation comes to mind as simpler: "(1) If God does not exist, objective moral values and duties do not exist. (2) Objective moral values and duties do exist. (3) Therefore, God exists." Craig, *Reasonable Faith*, 3rd ed. (Wheaton, IL: Crossway, 2008), 172.

transcendent cosmic mind (the argument from reason) that is the object of man's deepest desire (the argument from desire). Let's take a closer look at the support for and objections to each of its key premises.

In support of premise (1), the claim that there is a universal moral law, Lewis argued that we all have within us a sense of how we ought to behave and the kind of person we ought to be. This sense of "oughtness" presses upon us. He writes, "Human beings, all over the earth, have this curious idea that they ought to behave in a certain way, and cannot really get rid of it."[32] Lewis called this law of right behavior the moral law, and the evidence for this objective moral order is arguably a prephilosophical commitment. We intuitively know there is an objective moral order, and this knowledge is part and parcel of our shared human experience. As the apostle Paul said in Romans 2, the moral law is written on the human heart. Still, beyond this assertion, there are several positive arguments we can give for an objective moral law. For example, we can point to the reality of moral progress (the fact human civilizations can and have made moral progress suggests we can and have approached an objective moral ideal), the existence of deliberatively indispensable moral norms (when we deliberate on what we should do, we seem to be seeking an objective moral reason for action, not simply expressing our preferences), and the fact that moral objectivism allows for the ascription of unqualified evil to actions, such as the holocaust, sex trafficking, and genocide.[33]

While we may not have airtight proof, we have good reasons to think we live in a moral universe. Another way of stating this is to say that in addition to physical facts ("This chair is brown," "Gold is atomic number 79"), there are also moral facts ("Lying is wrong," "Bravery is a virtue"). As we observe the world, we find in the universe "a real law," and given its objectivity, it is a law "which none of us made."[34] Consequently, if there is an objective moral law, and none of us has made it, then there must be something else that explains the moral law, a moral lawgiver. This leads us to premise (2).

Why can we not argue that moral facts are brute or inexplicable? The philosopher Erik Wielenberg argues for this, what he calls "non-natural

---

32. Lewis, *Mere Christianity*, 8.

33. Angus Ritchie, *From Morality to Metaphysics: The Theistic Implications of Our Ethical Commitments* (Oxford: Oxford University Press, 2012), 11–39.

34. Lewis, *Mere Christianity*, 20.

non-theistic moral realism."[35] Wielenberg's theory is a version of moral realism because it endorses objective moral values and duties. So he would accept premise (1). It is nonnatural in that it endorses the view that brute ethical facts and properties are *sui generis*, meaning they are not reducible to purely natural facts and properties. But it is nontheistic because he argues that objective moral values and duties *do not require* a theistic foundation. Given nonnatural nontheistic moral realism, according to Wielenberg, "from valuelessness, value sometimes comes."[36] Let's call Wielenberg's view *Platonic atheism*.

How might a Christian respond to Wielenberg? We can start by arguing that it is more plausible to think values and duties attach to persons rather than things, and in this, theism is rationally preferable to Platonic atheism. As I type I'm sitting on a chair. I don't have any obligations to the chair. I don't owe it to the chair to weigh less than five-hundred pounds or to refrain from standing on it (although, given its wheels, I might not want to stand on it). I do, however, owe obligations to people. I am obliged to be honest when I share with students, to refrain from stealing someone's wallet, and to respect my elders. Plausibly, obligations (and values) attach to persons and not things. I am not obligated to a Platonic Form of *goodness* or some brute moral fact such as "Thou shall not lie." Theism accommodates this intuition whereas Platonic atheism does not. Thus, premise (2) is more reasonable than its denial.

Still, the "moral lawgiver" could just be something within the material cosmos—maybe moral facts supervene on physical facts about society or on purely material human nature. If so, then the moral lawgiver (e.g., "society" or "natural selection") would not be something beyond the material cosmos, and the theological conclusion (4) could be avoided. So why should we think premise (3) is true? We should think (3) is true because naturalistic (reductionistic) strategies for grounding morality fail to either secure the objectivity of morality or explain how our moral reasoning and beliefs have the ability to track truth. If morality is based on the individual or a society, morality becomes subjective: whatever an individual or group of individuals believes is right (or good) is right (or good) *for them*. If on the other hand, morality is grounded in evolutionary

---

35. See Erik J. Wielenberg, "In Defense of Non-Natural Non-Theistic Moral Realism," *Faith and Philosophy* 26, no. 1 (2009): 23–41, italics removed. See also Wielenberg's most recent work, *Robust Ethics: The Metaphysics and Epistemology of Godless Normative Realism* (Oxford: Oxford University Press, 2014).

36. Wielenberg, "In Defense of Non-Natural Non-Theistic Moral Realism," 40n68.

biology, it becomes difficult to explain how our moral intuitions and commitments (e.g., our commitment to protect the weak and vulnerable) can be explained in terms of human pleasure, survival, and replication.[37]

With respect to premise (5), we may ask what are the candidate transcendent objects that best explain the reality of the moral law? Our options boil down to either a *personal* or *impersonal* mind. It's not clear, however, that it is coherent to think of a pure impersonal mind legislating morality. To see why, we might ask what distinguishes a personal mind from an impersonal mind? Typically, a person is understood to be the kind of being that has (or is) an intellect and will. On the other hand, an impersonal mind, we might suppose, is a type of being with an intellect but not a will. If this is the correct way to think about persons and minds, then it is difficult to see how a pure mind could be the source of morality. Lewis argued that this absolute goodness *governs* the universe and is the *power* behind the moral law, but of course, only a person has the requisite power to govern and legislate in this way. A purely impersonal mind could (i) *know* what states of affairs are objectively valuable, (ii) *have good reasons* to bring those states of affairs about, and (iii) *want* to bring about those states of affairs, but importantly, (iv) lack the needed *power* to bring about those states of affairs.[38] A personal mind—an intellect and will—can act in such a way to bring about objectively valuable states of affairs, satisfying conditions (i)–(iv). Thus, only a personal mind can be the power behind the moral law, legislating how humans ought to behave.

Lewis was correct in his assertion that a personal mind best explains the reality of the moral law. To see how, let's recall that there are, in addition to physical facts, moral facts. Two such widely held moral facts are the intrinsic value of human persons and the duty to neighbor love. But what best explains

---

37. Granted, a fuller discussion would spell this out in greater detail and more slowly. For more on how evolutionary biology cannot explain our belief-generating and belief-evaluating capacities to track moral truth, see Ritchie, *From Morality to Metaphysics*, 40–66. As C. S. Lewis put it, if morality is a product of natural selection, then it is "an illusion," and our "transcendental pretensions" become "exposed for a sham." Lewis, *Miracles* (New York: Touchstone, 1996), 50, 53. See also the atheist philosopher Michael Ruse who argues that evolutionary naturalism renders morality subjective and illusory: "Darwinian theory shows that, in fact, morality is a function of (subjective) feelings; but it shows also that we have (and must have) the illusion of objectivity." Ruse, *Taking Darwin Seriously: A Naturalistic Approach to Philosophy* (Amherst, NY: Prometheus, 1998), 253, quoted in Mark D. Linville, "The Moral Argument," in *The Blackwell Companion to Natural Theology*, ed. William Lane Craig and J. P. Moreland (Malden, MA: Wiley-Blackwell, 2012), 393.

38. For an account of how (i)–(iv) are necessary conditions for a fully satisfying explanation of intentional action of a person, see Ritchie, *From Morality to Metaphysics*, 48–50.

these moral facts? Arguably, they are best explained by the existence of a personal God. As Mark Linville writes, "The *value* of persons is . . . grounded in the personhood of God."[39] Moreover, on the Christian story,

> Persons *qua* persons are created in the image of God in that God himself is a person. . . . The value of human persons is found in the fact that, as bearers of the *imago dei*, they bear a significant resemblance to God in their very personhood. God and human persons share an overlap of kind membership in personhood itself, and human dignity is found precisely in membership of that kind.[40]

But if the moral lawgiver is an impersonal mind, we are left wondering why human persons are intrinsically valuable and why we ought to love our neighbor. I conclude that premise (5) is true, and therefore God exists. This is at least one version of the argument from morality to God.

Notice how reflection on the nature of morality also sets us on a journey toward Christ, if we faithfully follow the path. The reality of a power behind the moral law, a power that presses upon us and hates most of what we do, is at once awe-inspiring and tragic. It is awe-inspiring to think that there is an absolute goodness, a power beyond the universe that presses itself within the universe. But it is equally tragic, for we fall woefully short of the moral law every day. This is the beginning of the gospel story. We start with man's tragedy—that we are part chicken, slob, and devil—before we can understand the divine comedy of God becoming man and the fairy-story ending with humanity becoming truly happy. Lewis's point is that we cannot understand the gospel until we understand we have transgressed the moral law. As Lewis concluded his discussion in *Mere Christianity*: "The Christian religion is, in the long run, a thing of unspeakable comfort. But it does not begin in comfort; it begins in . . . dismay. . . . If you look for truth, you may find comfort in the end: if you look for comfort you will not get either comfort or truth—only soft soap and wishful thinking to begin with and, in the end, despair."[41]

---

39. Linville, "The Moral Argument," 444.
40. Linville, "The Moral Argument," 444–45.
41. Lewis, *Mere Christianity*, 32.

LOOKING ALONG MORALITY

Years ago, the Cru ministry at Ball State University in Indiana invited me to give the final talk of a week-long evangelistic project with students. Their outreach was centered on one question: Is Christianity good for the world? To generate buzz they set up two, ten-foot-tall wooden boards at high traffic locations on campus. The main question was written across the top of the board, and students were invited to record their own answers, and each night, students explored a different part of the question. On the first night, students read poetry and sang songs at a coffeehouse, to investigate the connection between Jesus and beauty. On the second night, the campus ministry hosted a video debate between Christopher Hitchens ("Christianity is not good for the world") and Douglas Wilson ("Christianity is good for the world") exploring the connection between Jesus and ideas. On the third night, Cru leaders hosted a dinner for international students and investigated the connection between Jesus and the nations. Finally, on the last night, I spoke on the definitive answer to the main question that had vexed the campus that week.

As I walked into the auditorium and examined the two, ten-foot-tall signs, now graffitied and flanking the stage, the passion behind the student responses struck me. The question of Christianity's goodness had polarized the campus. Many had emphatically argued for Christianity's goodness, testifying to the hope and meaning Jesus provided. Others, equally as forceful, argued for Christianity's diabolical nature, testifying to the hurt Christians have caused. As I looked across the auditorium, preparing to speak, I realized we can no longer limit our focus to the reasonableness of Christianity. The dynamic of globalization, the digital revolution, and a cadre of vocal atheists have successfully called into question the *desirability* of Christianity. That night, I saw that a new, cultural apologetic was needed if Christianity was to get a fair hearing with the next generation.[42]

While I still agree with the answer I gave that night, upon reflection, I would push even further. I argued that Christianity is good for two reasons. First, because it is true, and being rightly related to reality is a good thing. Second, Christianity is good for the world because you get Jesus, and when

---

42. This conviction was further solidified a couple years later when I gave this same talk at Berkeley while the Occupy Movement protests were unfolding on the campus square.

you get Jesus you get everything. Because of Jesus, we are part of a story that gives our lives meaning, hope, forgiveness, and the possibility of wholeness. All of these, of course, are great goods. What I failed to explain, however, was that Christianity is good for *this* world, for the mundane realm of everyday life. How does Christianity make *this* world more inviting, more delightful, more flourishing than a world without it?

A cultural apologetic that walks along the plank of morality will *show* others how Christianity makes this world a better place. While there are New Atheists, internet atheists, and pundits who loudly decry the evil perpetrated in the name of God, the sober judgment of historians and sociologists is that Christianity has largely been a force of immense good in the world. The Baylor sociologist Rodney Stark (a Christian) summarizes the influence of Christianity on the West as follows: "The success of the West, including the rise of science, rested entirely on religious foundations, and the people who brought it about were devout Christians."[43] Bruce Sheiman (an atheist), in his book, *An Atheist Defends Religion*, agrees:

> A commitment to human dignity, personal liberty, and individual equal-
> ity did not previously appear in any other culture. Freedom in its myriad
> expression—of inquiry (science), government (democracy), and econom-
> ics (capitalism)—first emerged in the West and nowhere else. And to
> explain their development, one must look at what distinguishes the West
> culturally, namely, Christianity.[44]

For over 1,500 years the Christian imagination, mind, and conscience animated and shaped the West. As a result, many of its culture-shaping institutions have been formed by a Christian vision of reality, leading to the advancement of shalom and the good of all.

Beginning as a small sect within first-century Judaism, Christianity grew to become the official religion of the Roman Empire by the third century, and when Rome fell, it became the dominant religion embraced by barbarian

---

43. Rodney Stark, *The Victory of Reason: How Christianity Led to Freedom, Capitalism, and Western Success* (New York: Random House, 2005), xi.

44. Bruce Sheiman, *An Atheist Defends Religion: Why Humanity Is Better Off with Religion Than without It* (New York: Alpha, 2009), 99, quoted in Mark Coppenger, *Moral Apologetics* (Nashville: B&H, 2011), 174.

Europe. While the story of Christianity's growth is multifaceted, a central theme is the exemplary moral character of Christ-followers and their conviction that all humans are equally valuable.[45] Known as "promoters of ordinary goodness"[46] and "lovers of the poor,"[47] Christians followed their conscience as they outflanked the dominant pagan culture and instituted a new social order as the gospel took root.

Today the collective memory of our Christian heritage fades. Many students seem to think the era before smartphones was the age of the dinosaur. They possess little knowledge of the main contours of history, let alone their immediate past. As cultural apologists, we must remind others of Christianity's positive contribution to the world. Guided by the conviction that the world is rational, Christians have long championed education. They developed an elaborate library system within monasteries in the sixth and seventh centuries, advocated education for both sexes, and founded the first modern universities in Paris and Bologna in the twelfth century. A century later, Oxford, Cambridge, and a flood of other new institutions throughout Europe arose.[48] The cultural mandate to care for and cultivate God's creation (Gen. 1:28) led not only to the rise of science but to technological innovations that made the world a more inviting place in which to live.[49] Religious liberty, the freedom to worship according to one's conscience, was first defended by Christians in the sixteenth and seventeenth centuries, sowing the seeds for political liberalism and modern democracy.[50] Christians throughout history have been a large part of the efforts to abolish slavery, improve healthcare, meet the needs of the poor, establish equal rights for minorities and women, and champion the arts. The point should be clear: Christianity makes a positive difference in *this* world too.[51]

---

45. For a more detailed account of Christianity's growth from its inception to the Reformation, see James Davison Hunter, *To Change the World: The Irony, Tragedy, and Possibility of Christianity in the Late Modern World* (Oxford: Oxford University Press, 2010), 48–70.

46. Miroslav Volf, *Flourishing: Why We Need Religion in a Globalized World* (New Haven, CT: Yale University Press, 2015), 60.

47. Peter Brown, *Power and Persuasion in Late Antiquity: Towards a Christian Empire* (Madison: University of Wisconsin Press, 1992), 152, quoted in Hunter, *To Change the World*, 55.

48. Stark, *The Victory of Reason*, 52–53; Alvin J. Schmidt, *Under the Influence: How Christianity Transformed Civilization* (Grand Rapids: Zondervan, 2001), 170–93.

49. Stark, *The Victory of Reason*, 37–50.

50. Volf, *Flourishing*, 152–55.

51. What of the familiar claim that Christians have done much evil in the world? In reply, I say, indeed Christians have and do commit evils, sometimes in the name of God (the Crusades are often cited, but see Rodney Stark, *God's Battalions: The Case for the Crusades* [New York: HarperOne, 2009]). Two additional

GOODNESS AND THE KINGDOM

In the masterful book *After Virtue*, Alasdair MacIntyre argues that virtue, reason, and traditional notions of something's proper function no longer direct contemporary society.[52] Instead, *emotivism*, the idea that morality is guided by emotion, has become the dominant ethos. Unmoored from traditional norms of morality, human beings become barbarians, governed by their will to power without concern for the destruction. MacIntyre implored those who would still champion virtue to form alternate communities "within which the moral life could be sustained so that both morality and civility might survive the coming ages of barbarism and darkness."[53] We are waiting, MacIntyre asserts, "for another . . . St. Benedict."[54]

In 2017, Rod Dreher, the senior editor at *The American Conservative*, picked up this MacIntyrian thread and argued that we now are "living under barbarism" and that if the church is to survive, we must embrace *The Benedict Option*.[55] Benedict was a sixth-century monk who founded over a dozen monasteries in the countryside around Rome. He developed a list of rules as "a guide to living in Christian community" now known as the Rule of Saint Benedict.[56] As the Roman Empire was crumbling and moral chaos ensued in wider society, these monastic communities became centers of cultural activity and learning, missionary outposts, and places of provision and protection for those in need. The monasteries sustained Christian culture. They also played a key role in the conversion of barbarian Europe.[57]

Dreher's proposal in *The Benedict Option* is that if Christianity is to survive the current age of barbarism and darkness, we must adopt the example and

---

comments are relevant, however. First, the amount of evil done by Christians is much less than the evils perpetrated by atheists. Overall, as I've argued, Christianity is a source of good in *this* world (setting aside the infinite value of eternal life it offers through Christ). Second, when Christians do evil, they are acting in a manner inconsistent with the life and teachings of Jesus whereas atheists who do evil are not. On atheism, as I've argued, there is no objective ground for right and wrong, good and evil; anything goes as Dostoyevsky once wrote. For an eye-opening discussion of the oppressive nature of Islam and other non-Christian religions, see Coppenger, *Moral Apologetics*, 132–60. For an excellent discussion on how religions malfunction, see Volf, *Flourishing*, 76–79. For more on the objection that the God of Christianity is morally deviant in some way (which implies that his followers are too), see ch. 7.

52. Alasdair MacIntyre, *After Virtue*, 3rd ed. (Notre Dame: University of Notre Dame Press, 2007).

53. MacIntyre, *After Virtue*, 263.

54. MacIntyre, *After Virtue*, 263.

55. Dreher, *The Benedict Option*, 17–18.

56. Dreher, *The Benedict Option*, 14–15.

57. See Hunter, *To Change the World*, 56–61.

ancient practices of Saint Benedict, practices which draw on the wisdom of Scripture and the traditions of the ancient church. We must build new churches, schools, and institutions that foster a Christian identity. We are to "quit piling up sandbags," wasting time, energy, and resources as we fight political battles or try to reclaim thoroughly secularized institutions such as the University, Madison Avenue, Hollywood, or Wall Street. Instead, it is time "to build an ark in which to shelter until the water recedes and we can put our feet on dry land again."[58] By adopting the Benedict option, "Christian faith can survive and prosper through the flood."[59]

There is much to applaud about Dreher's proposal. He is right to sound the alarm. As we have already noted, things are not business as usual, and the age of disenchantment has changed cultural assumptions. Christians must be more than sincere; they must be wise.[60] I appreciate Dreher's call for Christians to take seriously the life of spiritual discipline as a means to spiritual maturity and identity formation. As a parent with teens, I value his discussion of the pervasive and destructive effects of sex and technology on the church today (he reserves a chapter for each topic that I've made required reading in my house). He adeptly and successfully argues that a sacramental view of sex is desperately needed once again in the church. He powerfully demonstrates how technology is not neutral, and carried within it are the seeds of our own destruction as our loves and longings are redirected toward the petty and perverse.

However, I have two reservations that keep me from fully embracing the Benedict option. First, Dreher's proposal is built on a faulty understanding of culture and how cultures change. Dreher adopts what James Davison Hunter calls a "bottom-up" view of culture and cultural change: change enough individual lives and local communities and eventually the world will change.[61] But Hunter has persuasively argued that cultures rarely change from the bottom up. Rather, cultural change is almost always top-down: *the culture-shaping institutions and its leaders are the real influencers.*[62] So while it is important and

---

58. Dreher, *The Benedict Option*, 12.

59. Dreher, *The Benedict Option*, 19.

60. As James Davison Hunter pleads: "God, save us from Christians who are well-intentioned, but not wise." Hunter, *To Change the World*, 276.

61. Granted, Dreher doesn't use the language of "change the world." Still, his proposal can be understood in these terms, for he thinks the best way to save Christian culture, and therefore, the culture at large, is to build arks to wait out the flood of this present dark age.

62. Hunter, *To Change the World*, 6–47.

necessary to preserve a robust Christian identity, it is not enough to simply build, as Dreher suggests, parallel institutions. We must attend to how Christianity is perceived by the culture-shaping institutions, or Christianity will continue to be viewed as implausible and undesirable. Eventually, these parallel institutions may themselves falter. Dreher's *Benedict Option* is a helpful proposal for how the church should function as a community, but it is not a viable proposal for how Christians ought to relate to culture.

In addition, the Benedict option is not sufficiently missional. Dreher rightly points out that we cannot give to others what we do not possess ourselves.[63] As Christians, we need to locate our lives in God's story, deny ourselves, and follow in the steps of Jesus. But large-scale withdrawal from cultural-shaping institutions is not a positive proposal for cultural engagement. It may have worked for the monastic communities of the past, but those communities operated in an "enchanted" age, a time when religion was naturally embraced and religious communities played a more central role in shaping culture. With the rise of globalization and the disenchantment accompanying the advent of our digital age, things are different. Religion exists as a powerful presence "downstream" at the level of individual lives but is largely absent "upstream" in key culture-shaping institutions.[64] If we abandon these culture-shaping institutions, religion will continue to be regarded as unreasonable and undesirable, making belief in God increasingly difficult, even for the faithful. As Hunter argues, the best strategy is to be "faithfully present within" all social structures and in all realms of social life.[65]

Think of it this way. The call of Jesus to "go into all the world" (Mark 16:15) is typically thought of as two dimensional: we go to every point—length and width—on a map.[66] But we must learn to think in three dimensions, not two. At every point on the map, we must also go *deep*, penetrating into the social and ideational structures of culture so that the gospel will be viewed as reasonable and desirable.[67] As Hunter puts it,

---

63. Dreher, *The Benedict Option*, 19.

64. Hunter, *To Change the World*, 91–92.

65. Hunter, *To Change the World*, 238–48.

66. Thanks to my friend Gregory E. Ganssle for the insight that the great commission should be thought of as three dimensional instead of two dimensional. Actually, Greg argues for a fourth dimension, time, which will be discussed in ch. 8.

67. Perhaps we ought to look to Saint Patrick, instead of Saint Benedict as our model for cultural engagement. Patrick (385–461) was captured as a teen and enslaved in Ireland for six years before escaping

The church is to go into all realms of social life: in volunteer and paid labor—skilled and unskilled labor, the crafts, engineering, commerce, art, law, architecture, teaching, health care, and service. Indeed, the church should be *sending people out* in these realms—not only discipling those in these fields by providing the theological resources to form them well, but in fact mentoring and providing financial support for young adults who are gifted and called into these vocations.[68]

How do we do this? By faithfully taking up the vocation to which God has called us *and* becoming the kinds of people God wants us to be (as Dreher's *Benedict Option* so helpfully sets forth), the conscience of those around us will be rekindled. Lord willing, we will set down a plank—the plank of conscience—as we build a bridge from "our Athens" to Jesus and the gospel.

---

home to Britain. Later he returned to the land of his captivity in order to bring the gospel to the lost. Patrick went to every point on the map in Ireland, establishing over 365 churches and monasteries (Hunter, *To Change the World*, 58). He also went deep at every point, first converting the leader of each clan, which led to the conversion of the clan members. Eventually known as a key center of European Christianity, Ireland has even been said to have saved civilization by one *New York Times* bestseller. See Thomas Cahill, *How the Irish Saved Civilization* (New York: Anchor, 1995).

68. Hunter, *To Change the World*, 257, emphasis in original.

CHAPTER 7

ADDRESSING BARRIERS

> False ideas are the greatest obstacles to the reception of
> the gospel.
>
> *J. Gresham Machen*[1]

> The one who states his case first seems right, until the other
> comes and examines him.
>
> *Proverbs 18:17 ESV*

D ying as she births her second child, Emily's life is tragically cut short. Now buried among her dead family and fellow townspeople on a peaceful hilltop in Grover's Corners, New Hampshire, Emily is not yet ready to let go of her earthly life. She asks for, and is granted, the opportunity to watch a day from her past. She picks her twelfth birthday, Tuesday, February 11, 1899. Her mom was young and beautiful. The house was full of levity and warmth, untouched by the pains yet to unfold. As she watched that day—her mom yelling up the stairs, her dad reading the paper, the smell of bacon in the air, a gift secretly placed on the doorstep with the milk by her then future husband, George—Emily witnesses the sacredness of the moment. But no one noticed at the time, including the young Emily. Gazing from the vantage of eternity, Emily laments, "Let's look at one another."[2] But the

---

1. J. Gresham Machen, *What Is Christianity?* (Grand Rapids: Eerdmans, 1951), 162, quoted in J. P. Moreland and William Lane Craig, *Philosophical Foundations for a Christian Worldview* (Downers Grove, IL: InterVarsity Press, 2003), 2.

2. Thornton Wilder, *Our Town* (New York: HarperCollins, 1998), 107.

moment passes, and with it, the opportunity to see the gift of togetherness. It is all too much for Emily: "I can't. I can't go on. It goes so fast. We don't have time to look at one another."[3] With one last glance, she asks to be taken back to her grave: "Good-by, Good-by, world. Good-by, Grover's Corners . . . Mama and Papa. Good-by to clocks ticking . . . and Mama's sunflowers. And food and coffee. And new-ironed dresses and hot baths . . . and sleeping and waking up. Oh, earth, you're too wonderful for anybody to realize you."[4]

On her way back to the grave, she asks her guide, "Do any human beings ever realize life while they live it?—every, every minute?" The answer: "No." But then, "The saints and poets, maybe—they do some."[5] This powerful moment, as described by Thornton Wilder in his Pulitzer Prize–winning play *Our Town*, helps us understand, through imagination and story, the meaning of the world. Life is like his three-act play: act 1, daily life; act 2, love and marriage; act 3, death. But all of it is a gift. All of it is sacred, if only we had eyes to see, like the saints and poets. If only we imagined ourselves as part of a divine story.

The play *Our Town* gives us a glimpse of the grand story of God, a story playing throughout the entire cosmos. The universe, writes John Calvin, is a "dazzling theatre" for God's glory.[6] On this grand stage, God is "reconciling the world to himself in Christ" (2 Cor. 5:19). While God has the primary part, he has dignified humanity with a supporting role. Kevin Vanhoozer assigns to theology the task of helping "the church understand the play and learn her part," and so "pastors and theologians are workers in dramatic fittingness, and their task is to help individuals and the local church understand . . . their place in the drama of redemption."[7]

Let's expand Vanhoozer's insight. In addition to pastors and theologians, it is the responsibility of the cultural apologist to help the church and those outside her walls to imagine a world infused with the divine and then to invite them to take their place within the unfolding divine drama. We must help

---

3. Wilder, *Our Town*, 108.
4. Wilder, *Our Town*, 108.
5. Wilder, *Our Town*, 108.
6. John Calvin, *Institutes of the Christian Religion*, ed. John T. McNeill, trans. Ford Lewis Battles, 2 vols. (Louisville: Westminster John Knox, 1960), 1:61.
7. Kevin J. Vanhoozer, *Pictures at a Theological Exhibition: Scenes of the Church's Worship, Witness, and Wisdom* (Downers Grove, IL: InterVarsity Press, 2016), 35–36.

others see the world from the perspective of eternity. Just as Emily needed a new vantage point to see the sacredness of life, so too many within culture need a new picture or a new "social imaginary," as Charles Taylor calls it, to see God and the world he has made.[8]

J. Gresham Machen's pithy statement, "False ideas are the greatest obstacles to the reception of the gospel," has served to galvanize a generation of apologists and culture warriors to boldly defend and proclaim the truth and rationality of Christianity. As we have seen, the obstacles to faith in a disenchanted age go beyond the intellectual. The metaphors we live by and the loves that drive us matter too. Echoing Machen, I would say that false ideas, disordered loves, and disenchanted imaginations are some of the greatest obstacles to the reception of the gospel.

Each culture has its own set of obstacles or barriers to Jesus and the gospel. In chapter 1, we saw two kinds of barriers, internal and external. Internal barriers pertain to us as the people of God, the church, and the content and character of our lives. External barriers are obstacles to faith found in the culture at large, barriers that must be overcome by those on the path to faith. In this chapter, we will explore some of the most pressing barriers to Jesus and the gospel in today's disenchanted world, beginning with several internal barriers.

INTERNAL BARRIERS

As Christians, we are often our own worst enemies. Our lives, words, and choices can undercut our efforts to share the love of Christ with others. No one on this side of heaven is perfect, yet the call to daily denial of self as apprentices of Jesus will, with the Lord's help, transform us over time. Our lives reek of self-interest and worldliness to the extent that we are uninformed by Scripture or unmotivated by the gospel call or unguided by the Holy Spirit. And the world will see us for what we are—hypocrites—and turn to run the other way.

In this section we will explore three internal barriers to Jesus and the gospel that are especially pressing in our disenchanted world: anti-intellectualism, fragmentation, and an unbaptized imagination (see figure 7.1).

---

8. Taylor describes a social imaginary as "the way ordinary people 'imagine' their social surroundings . . . carried in images, stories, legends, etc." Charles Taylor, *A Secular Age* (Cambridge, MA: Belknap, 2007), 171–72.

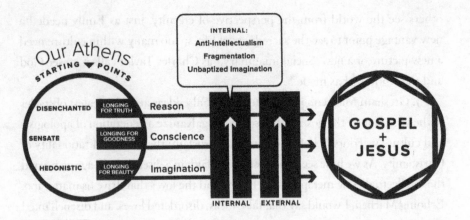

FIGURE 7.1: Internal Barriers to the Gospel

Anti-Intellectualism

"The scandal of the evangelical mind," Mark Noll begins, "is that there is not much of an evangelical mind."[9] This oft-quoted opening sentence to Noll's groundbreaking 1994 book, which explores the state of the Christian mind at the end of the twentieth century, is as true today as it was when it was first written. While there are some encouraging signs of growth, the Christian mind continues to atrophy from nonuse and misuse. Christians today no longer know how to make informed decisions. Guided by raw and untutored emotion instead of reason, image instead of argument, the church is vulnerable to the ever-changing whims of a culture charting a course through a disenchanted abyss.

The development of anti-intellectualism in the church has eroded the credibility of the gospel. Pastors and church leaders have neglected the centrality of the mind in the process of spiritual formation, and many Christians are spiritually deformed. Believers today tend to think about faith in subjective, noncognitive categories, and the idea that religious claims are knowledge claims has lost credibility. One result of this anti-intellectualism is that Christianity is viewed as irrelevant, a cultural relic of a bygone era.[10] Christians have a place in a secular society, suggests the New Atheist Daniel Dennett,

---

9. Mark Noll, *The Scandal of the Evangelical Mind* (Grand Rapids: Eerdmans, 1994), 3.

10. For more on the high cost of anti-intellectualism, see my *The Outrageous Idea of the Missional Professor* (Eugene, OR: Wipf & Stock, 2014), 52–58.

as long as we put them in zoos where their silly beliefs can be safely quarantined and silenced.[11]

It is tempting to blame anti-intellectualism's infection of the church on the broader culture. It is certainly more difficult to cultivate intellectual virtue when our friends, colleagues, and neighbors don't read, study, or express curiosity about deeper realities. Blaming culture, however, abdicates God's call for us to be light and salt in a world of darkness and disintegration. We must recognize our failure and acknowledge anti-intellectualism as a sin. Intellectual and theological laziness is a form of disobedience to the God who created us to know him, ourselves, and the world around us. God calls us to love him with our minds (Matt. 22:37), and this means we must resist the temptation to conform to the thought structures and emotional response patterns of the world (Rom. 12:2) by submitting every thought to the plumb line of Scripture (2 Cor. 10:5). God calls us to be men and women who cultivate intellectual virtue as part of our apprenticeship to Christ. But how can we throw off anti-intellectualism and become intellectually virtuous?

The first step in recovering the Christian intellect, as briefly discussed in chapter 1, is gaining an *accurate view of Jesus*.[12] Undoubtedly, many Christians will give Jesus moral and spiritual authority in their lives. But on matters of reality, beyond the privacy of our inner spiritual life, our actions betray us. If we truly believed Jesus had intellectual virtue, if we thought he held the keys to wisdom and knowledge (Col. 2:3), we would turn to Scripture for answers and guidance on the questions of life and existence. The sad truth is that we do not, turning instead to secular scientists or Hollywood for answers. Dallas Willard wonderfully reminded us to see Jesus as more than beautiful, loving, and kind; we need to recapture an understanding of him as brilliant, possessing wisdom and intellectual virtue, which makes him the authority on all matters of reality.[13]

The next step toward the recovery of the Christian mind is to *view study as part of our apprenticeship to Christ*. Many Christians today are largely ignorant of the historic teachings of the faith. Do you want to better understand the doctrines of divine providence, the Trinity, or the incarnation? Then grab your Bible in one

11. Daniel Dennett, *Darwin's Dangerous Idea: Evolution and the Meanings of Life* (New York: Touchstone, 1995), 515–20.

12. These two steps for cultivating intellectual virtue are further expanded in my *The Outrageous Idea of the Missional Professor*, 53–68.

13. Dallas Willard, *The Divine Conspiracy* (New York: HarperCollins, 1998), 93–95.

hand and a theology book in the other. Come alongside great thinkers from the history of the church such as Irenaeus, Augustine, Boethius, Anselm, Aquinas, Luther, Calvin, Wesley, or Edwards. Read their works and the works of those who help us understand them. Wrestle with their treatment of a passage in Scripture or their use of an ancient philosopher such as Plato or Aristotle. Don't stop with the Bible and theology or philosophy, study God's works too. Study the stars in the sky, the fish below the sea, and the interior of the human heart. Consider what you can learn about the God of the stars above and the fish below. What do the depths of the human heart reveal about the depth of God's love? Connecting the things you study and the God who lovingly creates and sustains all things leads to worship. It also helps those around us see the deep connection between knowledge and faith. The truths we discover and the knowledge we gain all point to the divine in one way or another. Our task as cultural apologists is to make these connections and share them with others.

As part of your apprenticeship to Christ, your study of God's Word and works will cultivate intellectual virtues, key among them the virtue of wisdom. J. P. Moreland notes the tight connection between a robust life of the mind and wisdom: "Wisdom is the application of knowledge gained from studying both God's written Word and His revealed truth in creation. If we are going to be wise, spiritual people prepared to meet the crisis of our age, we must be a studying, learning community that values the life of the mind."[14] Do you want to be wise? Do you want to cultivate intellectual virtues that lead to a flourishing life?[15] Then commit to studying God's Word and works. Doing so takes a small step toward reversing the cultural irrelevance of Christianity and helping others see Jesus as both beautiful *and* brilliant.

Fragmentation

"A specter is haunting the world," says theologian Miroslav Volf, "the specter of nihilism."[16] On the one hand, there is the world-denying "passive nihilism" of many followers of religion, who seek supernatural bliss even as

---

14. J. P. Moreland, *Love Your God with All Your Mind*, 3rd ed. (Colorado Springs: NavPress, 2012), 40.

15. For a helpful discussion of the intellectual virtues and the Christian life, see Philip E. Dow, *Virtuous Minds: Intellectual Character Development* (Downers Grove, IL: InterVarsity Press, 2013).

16. Miroslav Volf, *Flourishing: Why We Need Religion in a Globalized World* (New Haven, CT: Yale University Press, 2015), 197.

they pass over many of life's ordinary joys and pleasures.[17] On the other hand, there is the world-destroying "active nihilism" of the "free spirits," who "define their own values and live according to them."[18] Many in the West, according to Volf, are caught in the middle. Like Nietzsche's "last men," they adhere to a kind of "weary nihilism light," which is "tailored for creatures who desire comfort, grazing lazily in the valleys between the 'passive nihilism' of great religions and the 'active nihilism' of 'free spirits.'"[19]

Volf has put his finger on one of the problems we face as Christians living in a disenchanted age. Our world has been split into two realities, the mundane and the transcendent, and we no longer know how these separate worlds fit together.[20] Our innate longing for meaning compels us toward a transcendent, while our longing for pleasure draws us to the mundane. Many of us languish in the valley between the transcendent and the mundane, too distracted and lethargic to commit one way or the other. As we saw with the good Dr. Jekyll and his baser self, Mr. Hyde, we are a fragmented people. The countervailing pressures of our lives push and pull in different directions, and we are tempted to force a choice between meaning (the transcendent) and pleasure (the mundane). Yet as Volf points out, in placing meaning and pleasure in opposition "we always make the wrong choice. . . . Pleasure without meaning is vapid; meaning without pleasure is crushing. . . . Each is nihilistic without the other."[21] Volf argues we don't need to pit meaning and pleasure against each other. In the Christian story, there is unity between the two, offering the possibility of wholeness. But how can we find such wholeness and avoid the nihilisms that haunt our disenchanted age and much of the church?

The answer, not surprisingly, begins with our perception—how we see God and the world he made—which in turn spurs our acting in the world and, ultimately, the kind of person we become.[22] Recall that, in the Christian story, God is love, and he lovingly creates and sustains the world. Anything that

---

17. Volf, *Flourishing*, 198.

18. Volf, *Flourishing*, 200.

19. Volf, *Flourishing*, 199.

20. Volf, *Flourishing*, 71.

21. Volf, *Flourishing*, 201.

22. Crouch distinguishes between *postures* and *gestures*. While we shouldn't have the posture of a condemner, critic, consumer, or copier of culture, it is important at times to gesture (from a posture as creators and cultivators) in each of these directions, See Andy Crouch, *Culture Making: Recovering Our Creative Calling* (Downers Grove, IL: InterVarsity Press, 2008), 78–98.

exists and is not God—people, beasts, material objects—owes its existence to God. C. S. Lewis once quipped that there are no ordinary people.[23] We can go further: there are also no ordinary things. All things are "the Lover's gifts."[24]

As creatures, our meaning is found in our Creator. This means the transcendent realm is primary, but it does not diminish the value of the material cosmos. Far from it. The world was created by God as a gift to be enjoyed.[25] As Volf writes, "*Attachment to God amplifies and deepens enjoyment of the world.*"[26] Meaning and purpose are not pitted against each other; rather, they are united when properly ordered. Again, Volf puts it colorfully: "The right kind of love for the right kind of God bathes our world in the light of transcendent glory and turns it into a theatre of joy."[27]

The good news of the gospel runs deeper than the forgiveness of sins (and that is an inexhaustible well). God wants us to be whole. He wants us to flourish in *this* life and for eternity. But what does it look like to flourish in this life? Building on the work of philosopher Nicholas Wolterstorff, Volf identifies three aspects to human flourishing: an active dimension (life being led well), a passive dimension (life going well), and an affective dimension (life feeling good).[28]

The active dimension is the aspect most directly within our control. It points us to the necessity of looking to Jesus and following in his steps (1 Peter 2:21). Integrating our head (beliefs), heart (loves), and will (actions) requires intentionality and perseverance, and as any parent will testify, the maturation process is never easy. The road is full of potholes, hills and valleys, confusing signposts. The goal—Christ-likeness and a flourishing life—sustains us through the difficult times, even as the moments of difficulty spur us on. Nor are we meant to journey alone. God has provided a helper, the Holy Spirit (John 14:26), and a community, the church, to help us in the process of spiritual formation unto Christ.

Those who see and delight in the world as Jesus does become world celebrators instead of world deniers. This does not mean we affirm, consume, or copy everything our culture offers us; it means that our *posture* toward culture,

---

23. C. S. Lewis, *The Weight of Glory* (New York: HarperCollins, 2001), 46.

24. Volf, *Flourishing*, 205. What about things made by humans such as pornography or weapons of mass destruction? Are these too "the Lover's gifts"? The answer is surely no. Yet even in such evils we find aspects of "the Lover's gift" in the human ability to make things out of the material "stuff" created by God.

25. For more on how to cultivate a sacramental view of the world, see the next section.

26. Volf, *Flourishing*, 203, italics in original.

27. Volf, *Flourishing*, 206.

28. Volf, *Flourishing*, 75.

as Andy Crouch helpfully puts it, will not be inherently negative. As agents of shalom, we are cultivators and creators of what is good, true, and beautiful. We experience joy in the midst of suffering, hope in the face of affliction, and peace in the shelter of the Almighty.

Do you believe Jesus is worthy of your life, your passions, your energies, and your time? Do you want to find wholeness? As we explore these questions in the next section, pray that self-denial will become a natural part of your "second nature." Learning to deny oneself is the first step toward seeing, delighting, and living as Jesus did, and as John reminds us, "This is how we know we are in him: Whoever claims to live in him must live as Jesus did" (1 John 2:5–6).

Unbaptized Imagination

Whereas today we focus on barriers to belief, five hundred years ago in the age of enchantment there were several significant barriers to *unbelief*. As Charles Taylor highlights in his mammoth work *A Secular Age*, the medieval vision of reality included three beliefs that informed the collective imagination of European culture:

1. The natural world functioned as a signpost, pointing beyond itself to God.
2. Society was grounded in a heavenly reality; earthly kingdoms reflected the kingdom of God.
3. People lived in an *enchanted* world.[29]

By and large, people held to a sacramental view of reality in which everything was sacred and interconnected. All was a gift, and the Christian story shaped medieval human identity and informed their way of living and moving in the world. The disenchantment of reality changed everything, and today the individualism, reductionism, and hedonism that characterize our disenchanted age make unbelief possible and belief more difficult. These shifts have also, unfortunately, reshaped the Christian imagination.

Christians no longer hold a sacramental view of reality. We tend to view the world like everyone else does, as ordinary and mundane. The secular liturgies that shape culture shape Christians in the same ways.[30] The ideas and beliefs that

---

29. Taylor, *A Secular Age*, 25.
30. The term *secular liturgies* comes from James K. A. Smith. A liturgy, according to Smith, is a kind

fill our heart with wonder are largely the same things that fill the nonbeliever's heart with wonder: romantic comedies, political scandals, dystopian thrillers, sports, visits to the mall, a day at the amusement park, a trip to the beach. There is nothing unique or transcendent about contemporary Christianity, and fewer people view it as either reasonable or desirable. To reverse this and help unbelievers see Christianity as true and satisfying, Christians must again embrace a sacramental view of the world. I believe this begins by rebaptizing the Christian imagination.

We cannot force ourselves to see reality as sacred. This reversal takes more than a simple choice because the problem is metaphysical before it is epistemological. In other words, we don't see reality as it is *because we do not live in the right relationship to reality*. Not only are our beliefs wrong, our way of being in the world is wrong too. Believing true propositions is not enough to effect change, though it is a good start. This is because we are not merely believing animals. We are, as James K. A. Smith notes, *liturgical* animals too: "To say we are liturgical animals is simultaneously to emphasize that we are metaphorical animals, imaginative animals, poetic animals, storied animals. We act in the world more as characters in a drama than as soldiers dutifully following a command."[31] We don't "decide" to "see" the world as creation or nature; we imbibe a metaphorical inclination, almost unavoidably, by being immersed in liturgical environments.[32] "The Story becomes the background narrative and aesthetic orientation that habitually shapes how we constitute our world. We don't memorize the Story as told to us; we imbibe the Story as we perform it in a million little gestures."[33] Smith's point is one that we must take seriously. Many attempts to promote a Christian worldview or transform culture focus on changing beliefs and thoughts, which is a necessary starting point. But this alone is insufficient to bring the necessary change. The story we locate our lives in—the story we live by—forms and informs our loves and longings, our beliefs and emotions, and in turn, our way of being and acting in the world. Right beliefs are needed, but we also need practices and habits rooted in a larger narrative that can shape and renew our imagination.

---

of formative practice. See Smith, *Desiring the Kingdom: Worship, Worldview, and Cultural Formation* (Grand Rapids: Baker, 2009); Smith, *Imagining the Kingdom: How Worship Works* (Grand Rapids: Baker, 2013); and Smith, *Awaiting the King: Reforming Public Theology* (Grand Rapids: Baker, 2017).

   31. Smith, *Imagining the Kingdom*, 126–27.

   32. Smith, *Imagining the Kingdom*, 124.

   33. Smith, *Imagining the Kingdom*, 110.

To rebaptize our imagination, we must first find our identity, meaning, and purpose in the gospel story. This is more than understanding and communicating the story, it involves living it out through our daily, ordinary habits and actions. Christians are ones who are called out, set apart to be holy as followers of Christ (1 Peter 2:9), so the habits we form will be countercultural, requiring intentionality and awareness of the formative powers of liturgy, whether that liturgy is secular or sacred.

My suggestion here is twofold. We must first recognize that our lives are filled with all sorts of liturgies—practices and habits that shape who we are becoming. Many of these are secular, formed without God at the center, and with respect to these secular liturgies, we must realize that nothing, including the technology we use, is neutral. In our home, Ethel and I constantly battle with our teenage children over their smartphone usage. The phone, originally purposed as a tool, has quickly become a toy for mindless games and entertainment. It is a constant companion for our children (and for their parents, to be painfully honest)—a twenty-first-century paraclete![34] My daughter has shared that some kids, if given the choice between cutting off their pinky finger or giving up their phone, would rather lose the finger. At first, I assumed she was joking. She was not. Video streaming, now widely available on computers, tablets, and smartphones, has introduced new challenges to limiting screen time and monitoring the kinds of content watched. Teens regularly stay up until 4:00 a.m. on school nights to binge on the latest episodes of *Game of Thrones* or *House of Cards*. Why, our perplexed son asks, won't we let him do this? Everyone else does. What is easy to miss—setting aside the perversity of much of the content of these shows, games, and Snapchat conversations—is the formative power of these technologies. As Rod Dreher insightfully notes, "[Technology] is an ideology that conditions how we humans understand reality. . . . If we aren't mindful, [technology] trains us to accept the core truth claim of modernity: that the only meaning there is in the world is what we choose to assign it in our endless quest to master nature."[35] These secular liturgies form and shape our lives in ways that are contrary to the call of Christ. We are no longer all that different than the world around us.

---

34. In the Gospel of John, Jesus promises to send the Holy Spirit as a Helper (Paraclete) for the disciples after his ascension (John 14:26).

35. Rod Dreher, *The Benedict Option: A Strategy for Christians in a Post-Christian Nation* (New York: Sentinel, 2017), 219.

Instead, we must learn to embrace the call of Christ to self-denial and learn what it means to live a life of spiritual apprenticeship. As Jesus said to his disciples, "Whoever wants to be my disciple must deny themselves and take up their cross and follow me" (Matt. 16:24). Crucially, we must not neglect the bodily basis of our spiritual formation unto Christ. As Dallas Willard observes, *"Whatever is purely mental cannot transform the self."*[36] We must allow our beliefs, and the gospel story, to seep into our bones. More than reading and intellectual understanding, it is done through enacting the story of the gospel, through the daily bodily habits or liturgies that form and inform us:

> We need to learn the true story "by heart," at the gut level, and let it seep into our background in order to then shape our perception of the world. And that happens primarily and normatively in the practices of Christian worship—*provided that* the practices of Christian worship intentionally carry, embody, enact, and rehearse the normative shape of the Christian Story.[37]

This call to formative worship is profoundly countercultural. Our disenchanted culture seeks pleasure and the unbridled satisfaction of desire in a flattened world full, as Shakespeare's *Macbeth* said, "of sound and fury, signifying nothing."[38] Christ calls us to return to the sacred order of things, redirecting our loves and longings by finding our place within a cosmos permeated by the divine.

In our family, in addition to regular family worship at church, we seek to cultivate several classic spiritual disciplines including daily Scripture reading, Bible memorization, family prayer time, and serving others in our community.[39] Each of these activities pulls us outside of ourselves and turns our eyes toward heaven, training us to put God before ourselves. Repetition of these practices is vital, as Smith notes: "Quite simply, there is no formation without

---

36. Dallas Willard, *The Spirit of the Disciplines: Understanding How God Changes Lives* (San Francisco: HarperSanFrancisco, 1991), 152, italics in original.

37. Smith, *Imagining the Kingdom*, 163.

38. William Shakespeare, *Macbeth*, 5.5.26–28.

39. According to Dallas Willard, a spiritual discipline is "nothing but an activity undertaken to bring us into more effective cooperation with Christ and his Kingdom (Willard, *The Spirit of the Disciplines*, 156). Willard divides the spiritual disciplines into the "Disciplines of Abstinence" (solitude, silence, fasting, frugality, chastity, secrecy, and sacrifice) and the "Disciplines of Engagement" (study, worship, celebration, service, prayer, fellowship, confession, submission). For more on the spiritual disciplines, see also Richard J. Foster, *Celebration of the Disciplines: The Path to Spiritual Growth*, rev. ed. (San Francisco: HarperSanFrancisco, 1988).

repetition. . . . There will be no sanctification of our perception apart from the regular, repeated recentering of our imagination in the Story of the gospel as rehearsed and enacted in the 'practical logic' of Christian worship."[40] These daily, repeated encounters with God transform us and our imagination. They help us see clearly. For Christianity to be seen as reasonable and desirable in our culture, we who follow Christ must take a different path than the well-trodden road of self-centeredness. We must locate our lives in God's story and live for him moment by moment, picking up our crosses and following Jesus as we find our rhythm in the sacred order of the cosmos.

EXTERNAL BARRIERS

In the West, there are four firmly held beliefs that, if true, either refute Christianity or require Christians to significantly modify or jettison tradition. These barriers to belief are (1) the idea that science disproves God, (2) that belief in Jesus as the one and only God is intolerant, (3) that God is not good, and (4) that Christianity offers an archaic, repressive, and unloving ethic when it comes to human sexuality, marriage, the poor, race, and more (see figure 7.2). How does a cultural apologetic of reenchantment respond to these contemporary barriers to belief?

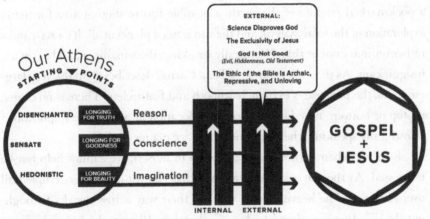

FIGURE 7.2: External Barriers to the Gospel

---

40. Smith, *Imagining the Kingdom*, 183.

Does Science Disprove God?

Modern human beings work hard to insulate themselves from nature. We live in houses powered by electricity, cooled by air-conditioning units, heated by furnaces, and enveloped by Wi-Fi. Our food is bought in stores and kept in stainless steel refrigerators. If we can afford it, we pay others to mow the lawn, scrub the toilets, and wash the car. When we are not frantically driving through a cement city on the way to work or through a manicured suburb carting kids to soccer or football, we enjoy the accoutrements of this great age: streamed television, graphically realistic video games, upscale restaurants, megastores, and endless sporting events.

But we live largely disconnected from the natural world around us. Throughout it all, the sun and the moon dutifully march across the sky unnoticed, familiar strangers marking the days before humanity turns once again into star dust. For a moment, on August 21, 2017, that changed. All eyes were on those familiar strangers as they danced across Middle America in a total eclipse. But within a week, life had returned to normal, and the sun and moon continued to run their course across the heavens.

Our ancient friends Luna, once thought to straddle the great frontier separating the corruptible from the incorruptible, and Sol, once thought to be a planet in its own right, a planet illuminating the heavens, have fallen on hard times. Modern science has demoted their place in the cosmos. They no longer inhabit one of the seven spheres of the universe. Instead, the moon is just a pockmarked satellite of the earth, a possible future staging area for man's exploration of the solar system, and the sun is not a planet at all. It's a star, and a rather ordinary one at that. Cosmically speaking, the sun, moon, and earth are insignificant. As theoretical physicist Sean Carroll describes, "On the very largest scales, the universe is extremely smooth and featureless. There is no center, no top or bottom, no edges, no preferred location at all."[41] The implication? "Cosmically speaking, there's no indication we matter at all."[42]

Even so, when nature draws attention to herself, we cannot help but be impressed. As the sun and moon aligned that August day, cheers erupted all over America. The heavenly pair waltzed their way across the sky throughout the day. In some places, such as Carbondale, Illinois, the heavenly dance

41. Sean Carroll, *The Big Picture: On the Origins of Life, Meaning, and the Universe Itself* (New York: Dutton, 2016), 50.

42. Carroll, *The Big Picture*, 49.

climaxed as the clouds parted in the closing minutes of the totality, revealing a ring of fire around the moon. While looking at the totality, there were no Democrats or Republicans, blacks or whites, haves or have-nots. There were just human beings, a sea of humanity united in awe. Not wanting to miss a teachable moment, the purveyors of disenchantment were quick to claim the "cosmic event of a lifetime" for themselves. Neil DeGrasse Tyson claimed a victory for science while tweeting, "The divided United States of America will unite today, sharing a cosmic event predicted by the methods and tools of science."[43] Bill Nye the Science Guy stated, "Experiencing an eclipse changes the way we feel about space and how we are connected. I hope this moment reminds us all that we share a common origin among the stars, and that we are all citizens of the same planet."[44]

We can agree that we share the earth and that we ought to learn how to get along. But it is not obvious how our emanating from a dead star, or even the knowledge that we emanated from a dead star, is supposed to unite humanity. The assumption underlying these comments is that science possesses unbridled power and potential to solve all mysteries, heal all problems, and usher in a utopian future for humanity (or whatever we evolve into). Yet when this unbridled power and potential is turned toward the question of God's existence, a common claim is that science somehow disproves God. The philosopher Alex Rosenberg, whom we met in chapter 5, claimed that science provides the best reason for atheism. But how exactly does science disprove God? The answer according to Rosenberg begins with one's theory of knowledge:

> If we're going to be scientistic, then we have to attain our view of reality from what physics tells us about it. Actually, we'll have to do more than that: we'll have to embrace physics as *the whole truth about reality*. Why buy the picture of reality that physics paints? Well, it's simple, really. We trust science as the only way to acquire knowledge. That is why we are so confident about atheism.[45]

43. Neil DeGrasse Tyson (@neiltyson), "The divided United States of America will unite today, sharing a cosmic event predicted by the methods and tools of science," Twitter, August 21, 2017, 7:02 a.m., https://twitter.com/neiltyson/status/899632684976046081.

44. Karen Kaplan, "Bill Nye on the Meaning of the Eclipse," *LA Times*, August 21, 2017, http://www.latimes.com/science/la-sci-great-american-eclipse-liveblog-bill-nye-on-the-meaning-of-the-eclipse-1503082111-htmlstory.html.

45. Alex Rosenberg, *The Atheist's Guide to Reality: Enjoying Life without Illusions* (New York: Norton, 2011), 20.

As we've seen, the answers atheism gives to life's deepest questions are pretty bleak. There is no hope, no meaning, no purpose, no freedom, no morality, and no justice in this life, and certainly none to be found in a nonexistent life hereafter. Unshackled from the chains of religion, humanity is cast adrift in a vast sea of nothingness.

Yet surprisingly, atheistic scientists think this is good news. The theoretical physicist Lawrence M. Krauss argues that the story science tells us is far more exciting than the gospel story. Science, not the Bible, provides us with "the greatest story ever told."[46] And what is the story science tells us? According to Krauss, science tells us "there is no obvious plan or purpose to the world we find ourselves living in. Our existence was not preordained, but appears to be a curious accident."[47] We should be grateful for the total solar eclipse and other marvels of the cosmos, not because they point us to the glory and majesty of God, but because Lady Fortune has smiled on us: "How lucky to have our brief moment in the Sun."[48]

I find all of this rather depressing. But we should not let these claims go unchallenged. Are these scientists and philosophers correct? Does science really disprove God? There are three replies we can make to this claim. First, as an exercise in pointing out the obvious, atheism does not give us good news; it gives us a *bad story*. This story does not offer hope nor does it understand us or our innate human dreams and longings. If science entailed atheism, and if atheism were true, then I think it would be better to simply admit that life stinks. Why should I be grateful to the universe for anything? Gratitude implies a gift given, a relationship between persons, yet no such relationship exists in an atheistic understanding of the world. All atheism offers is self-deception and a bad story. Why should I lie to myself and believe that a story that begins and ends in meaninglessness is somehow "the best story ever told—so far"? It's not a good story, even if it were true.

In addition, the atheist begins with an arbitrary limitation, assuming that science is the only source of knowledge. Those who argue that science disproves God usually adopt some version of a theory of knowledge called *scientism*, the idea that science is the only or best source of knowledge. This is why Rosenberg

---

46. Lawrence M. Krauss, *The Greatest Story Ever Told—So Far* (New York: Atria, 2017), 2.
47. Krauss, *The Greatest Story Ever Told*, 4.
48. Krauss, *The Greatest Story Ever Told*, 6.

thinks science entails atheism. Since physics tells us the *"whole truth about reality,"* and since the only things that exist according to physics are particles and force fields, which are physical entities one and all, it follows for him that God does not exist. Unfortunately for Rosenberg, scientism as a theory of knowledge is false. The view, as stated by Rosenberg, is self-refuting.

Consider a speaker uttering the following statement: "All English sentences are three words long." In the very act of making the claim, the speaker refutes himself, as his statement consists of seven words. In the same way, when Rosenberg states that science is "the only way to acquire knowledge," he refutes himself. How? *Because his claim is not a piece of knowledge delivered to us by science.* It is a philosophical statement about the nature of knowledge. Rosenburg limits acceptable forms of knowledge, but the rules do not seem to apply to his argument. While science is a wonderful source of knowledge, it is not the only one. We know things through history, logic and reasoning, mathematics, and even the so-called liberal arts (fields of study such as literature and language).

So is it true that science disproves God? The answer is no. In fact, once we understand how to incorporate the evidence from science into philosophical arguments, we find that science itself—or better, the deliverances of science—is neutral with respect to God's existence. But this does not make science useless in answering the question. We can employ the evidence from science to support premises we make in philosophical arguments, which can be used to support a theistic conclusion. Many cosmological and teleological arguments for the existence of God begin with empirical premises such as "the universe contingently exists" or "the universe began to exist" or "the universe is finely tuned for life" and reason from these empirical premises, supported by science, to theistic conclusions.

One of my favorite theistic arguments—simple enough to doodle on the back of a napkin over dinner yet profound in its implications—is the Kalam Cosmological Argument (KCA).[49] The argument can be stated as follows:

1. Whatever begins to exist has a cause.
2. The universe began to exist.
3. Therefore, the universe has a cause.

---

49. For the current state of play with respect to the Kalam Cosmological Argument, see William Lane Craig and James D. Sinclair, "The Kalam Cosmological Argument," in *The Blackwell Companion to Natural Theology*, ed. William Lane Craig and J. P. Moreland (Malden, MA: Blackwell, 2012), 101–201.

The scientific evidence comes into play with premise (2). In 1929, the discovery of redshift, the phenomenon where light from distant stars shifts to the red end of the visible spectrum, pointed scientists to an expanding universe. In 1965, cosmic microwave background radiation, radiation that permeates the universe, pointed scientists toward a cosmic origin event. The abundance of light elements such as hydrogen and helium at the early stages of the universe imply that the universe is temporally bound. Putting these pieces together, it leads us to conclude the universe has a beginning. Moreover, on the standard model of the Big Bang, the universe began a finite time ago out of a singularity, a mathematical point of infinite density equivalent to nothingness. Rather than conflicting with Christian theology and philosophy, science has discovered evidence for creation *ex nihilo*, just as Genesis 1:1 and Hebrews 11:3 proclaim. This evidence from science provides us with reasons to think premise (2) of the KCA true.

The conclusion of the KCA does not lead us directly to the Christian understanding of God, but it has theistic implications. It tells us that there is a first cause responsible for the existence of the universe. Since there was no physical reality *prior* to the beginning of the universe, this first cause must be nonphysical. Moreover, this first cause must be uncaused; otherwise it too would need a cause. Finally, when we add considerations related to the fine-tuning of the universe for life, we learn that the first cause is intelligent and thus a personal agent. Again, while an immaterial, uncaused, personal agent is not yet identified as the God of Abraham, Isaac, Jacob, and Jesus, this being is consistent with the God of the Bible. Further arguments, such as the argument from desire (chapter 3), the argument from reason (chapter 5), and the argument from morality (chapter 6), add further details about the nature of this transcendent cause of the universe. When taken together, these arguments point us compellingly to the God of the Bible. Science does not disprove God, as popularizers of atheism would have you believe. Rather, all of reality—including physical reality—points to God as Creator, Sustainer, and Redeemer.

Is God Really Good?

While visiting a museum in Nagasaki, the Japanese writer Shūsaku Endō encountered a bronze fumi-e, a portrait of Jesus that seventeenth-century

Christians were forced to step upon to confirm their apostasy.[50] This symbol of failed faith and the story of those Christians who betrayed Christ by stepping on it became the inspiration for Endō's 1966 novel, *Silence*.[51] In it Endō offers a beautiful and moving picture of the struggle of faith and the difficulty of bringing Christ to another culture.

Set in the early seventeenth century, Endō's book details the journey to Japan of the Portuguese priest Sebastian Rodrigues, based upon the historical figure of Giuseppe Chiara. Spurred by missionary zeal and the hope of discovering the truth about their beloved teacher and leader of the missionary order, Christovão Ferreira, who was rumored to have abandoned the faith, Rodrigues and his companions steal into Japan under cover of night and begin their ministry. Within a short time, Rodrigues is captured and taken to the Lord of Chikugo, Inoue. Known for ruthlessly persecuting Christians, Inoue sets out to destroy the faith of Father Rodrigues.

With Rodrigues watching, Inoue orders some Christian prisoners to step on the fumi-e. When they fail to comply, Inoue kills one of them. As Rodrigues watches, he thinks to himself, "So it has come to this."[52] Endō describes Rodrigues's internal struggle with God in the face of the senseless killing:

> What he could not understand was the stillness of the courtyard, the voice of the cicadas, the whirling wings of the flies. A man had died. Yet the outside world went on as if nothing had happened. Could anything be more crazy? Was this martyrdom? Why are you silent? Here this one-eyed man has died—and for you. You ought to know. Why does this stillness continue? This noonday stillness. The sound of the flies—this crazy thing, this cruel business. And you avert your face as though indifferent. This . . . this I cannot bear.[53]

In this moment of pain and anguish, Rodrigues looks to God for answers and comfort, but he is met with silence. God, why do you allow this evil? Where are you in the pain and suffering? Why are you silent and hidden?

---

50. Makoto Fujimura, *Silence and Beauty: Hidden Faith Born of Suffering* (Downers Grove, IL: InterVarsity Press, 2016), 36.

51. Shūsaku Endō, *Silence*, trans. William Johnston (New York: Picador, 2016). In 2016, Martin Scorsese directed a feature film based on the book.

52. Endō, *Silence*, 127.

53. Endō, *Silence*, 128.

Rodrigues is not alone in asking these questions. And when no answer is provided to these questions, people assume Christianity has no answer. God, if he exists, is cruel and unloving. Some walk away and never look back. If Christianity is to be seen as reasonable and desirable, we must be prepared to answer questions about the goodness of God rather than shrugging our shoulders in confusion. While this external barrier to belief takes many forms, the most pressing challenges to the goodness of God have to do with pain and suffering, divine hiddenness, and the portrayal of God as a moral monster, especially in the Old Testament. How might a cultural apologist respond to this family of objections?

Can the goodness of God be upheld in the face of pain and suffering? There are at least two reasons why the answer is yes. First, for any instance of evil, pain, or suffering, it is reasonable to think that God, a being worthy of worship and thus wholly good, has a morally sufficient reason for allowing it. To be clear, the evil itself is not good; it is an "ought-not-to-be."[54] Still, we can allow that God allows evil for some morally sufficient reason. What are God's reasons for allowing evil? Theists are split on how to reply to this question. Some say we can discern God's morally sufficient reason for evil. These theologians and philosophers offer a *theodicy*, a God-justifying reason for evil. Popular theodicies include the free will theodicy (God wants us to be self-determiners of our character and actions, and when we misuse our free will, evil results), the soul-making theodicy (God uses pain and suffering to grow our character), and the greater-goods theodicy (God brings about greater goods as a result of evil). The other camp thinks God has a morally justified reason for evil, but we just can't always know it. Moreover, we ought to expect that we won't know in all cases why God permits evil. These theologians and philosophers, called "skeptical theists," argue that human limitations prohibit us from discerning God's reason for evil in all cases.

Personally, I find theodicies helpful for understanding some of God's reasons for allowing evil. Ultimately, however, I do not believe we can know God's reason in every case, so I side with the "skeptical theists" on this issue (I am not skeptical of God's existence or goodness, but I do question whether or not we can fully know God's reason for evil). As fallible human beings limited in

---

54. Richard Gale, "Evil as Evidence for God," in *Debating Christian Theism*, ed. J. P. Moreland, Chad Meister, and Khaldoun A. Sweis (Oxford: Oxford University Press, 2013), 197.

knowledge, space, and time, we are not privy to all of God's reasons for allowing evil. This reply upholds both the goodness of God and the reality of evil.

What we can say, however, is that Jesus on the cross is God's answer to the problem of pain and suffering.[55] On the cross, Jesus took all pain and suffering, all sin and death, upon himself so we could find hope in this life and victory over sin and death's sting. Christianity goes beyond "mere theism" and offers a personal response to a personal problem. Because of the angst, pain, and suffering we all experience in a fallen world, God sent his Son so we might live. Thanks be to God! Pain and suffering does not get the last word. One day, all will be set right again, and for the redeemed, pain and suffering will be no more.[56]

Yet what about the problem of divine hiddenness or silence? Where is God in times of need? Does God care? And if God is perfectly loving as Christians claim, why is his existence not obvious to us? In a disenchanted world characterized by the felt absence of God, these questions have increasing existential force. For the believer, divine silence can be a source of doubt, as it was for Father Rodrigues. For the unbeliever, divine silence can be a source of nonbelief. Does divine hiddenness or silence provide good reason to think God doesn't exist?[57]

In reply, we can recall from chapter 2 that the evidence for God is both widely available and easily resistible. Part of the problem is our failure to perceive, and part of the problem is our fallen will. We no longer see reality as a signpost for God. Our will is disordered, crooked, and bent away from God and the transcendent and toward self and the mundane. God wants to genuinely transform fallen creatures, but he is not after mere belief in his existence. Rather, he has offered enough evidence so that we can find him if we seek him, while remaining hidden or elusive for those not willing to enter into a genuinely transformative relationship with him.

55. This point is beautifully argued in Peter Kreeft, *Making Sense Out of Suffering* (Ann Arbor, MI: Servant, 1986), 129–40.

56. For a more detailed discussion of the problem of pain and suffering, see Paul M. Gould, Travis Dickinson, and R. Keith Loftin, *Stand Firm: Apologetics and the Brilliance of the Gospel* (Nashville: B&H, 2018), ch. 9.

57. For an excellent discussion of the problem of divine hiding for the believer, see Saint John of the Cross, *Dark Night of the Soul*, trans. E. Allison Peers (New York: Image, 2005); John H. Coe, "Musings on the Dark Night of the Soul: Insights from St. John of the Cross on a Developmental Spirituality," *Journal of Psychology and Theology* 28, no. 4 (2000): 293–307; and Bruce Demarest, *Seasons of the Soul: Stages of Spiritual Development* (Downers Grove, IL: InterVarsity Press, 2009).

We can also argue that God *does* meet us in the silence. As the philosopher Michael Rea writes,

> Divine silence might just be an expression of God's preferred mode of interaction, and . . . we need not experience his silence as *absence*— especially if we see Biblical narratives and liturgies as things that in some sense mediate the presence of God to us, if we live out our lives in the conviction that God is ever present to us, and if we seek something more like communion with God rather than just communication.[58]

Endō's book is best understood as a work that explores and illustrates the nature of divine presence in the midst of suffering: "I did not write a book about the Silence of God; I wrote a book about the Voice of God speaking through suffering and silence."[59] His point is that even in divine silence God is present. Again, this provides us with a cultural apologetic of reenchantment, one that teaches us to see and delight in reality *as it is*. And when we do, we find Christ there with us. "In the mystery of silence and beauty God speaks through our broken lives facing our Ground Zero," writes Makoto Fujimura.[60] "In the layers revealed through the worn-smooth surface of a fumi-e is a true portrait of Christ."[61] God may have morally sufficient reasons for hiding, such as Rea's suggestion that silence is God's preferred mode of mediating his love and presence to creatures. Yet even in his hiding, even in his silence, God is present and active, seeking the good of free and fallen creatures.

The final objection of our disenchanted age concerns the apparent immoral actions and commands of God in the Old Testament. Over the past decades, New Atheists have forcefully vocalized their conviction that the God of the Old Testament is a moral monster. In an increasingly anti-intellectual and biblically illiterate culture, their rhetoric and arguments have raised doubts for many about one of the central claims of Christianity—the claim that the God of the Bible is wholly good and worthy of worship. Richard Dawkins is

---

58. Michael Rea, "Divine Hiddenness, Divine Silence," in *Philosophy of Religion: An Anthology*, ed. Louis P. Pojman and Michael C. Rea, 6th ed. (Boston, MA: Cenage, 2011), 274.

59. This quote by Endō is from a documentary on the writing of *Silence* by Yoichi Onaka, *The Voice of Silence* (Tokyo: President, 1992), quoted in Fujimura, *Silence and Beauty*, 143.

60. Fujimura, *Silence and Beauty*, 212.

61. Fujimura, *Silence and Beauty*, 212.

representative when he states in his 2006 *New York Times* bestseller, *The God Delusion*:

> The God of the Old Testament is arguably the most unpleasant char-
> acter in all fiction: jealous and proud of it; a petty, unjust, unforgiving
> control-freak; a vindictive, bloodthirsty ethnic cleanser; a misogynistic,
> homophobic, racist, infanticidal, genocidal, filicidal, pestilential, megalo-
> maniacal, sadomasochistic, capriciously malevolent bully.[62]

Space prohibits a detailed response to the charge that the God of the Old Testament is a moral monster. But I'll offer several suggestions for further study along with an outline of a way to respond. I recommend the work of philosopher Paul Copan, especially his book *Is God a Moral Monster?*, as well as the work of Old Testament scholar David Lamb in his *God Behaving Badly: Is the God of the Old Testament Angry, Sexist and Racist?*[63]

What can we say in response to this objection? Following Paul Copan's argument,[64] we should first note that the claim that God is evil is hard to sustain given atheism's inability to ground objective morality (as we argued in chapter 6). Ironically, *it is only if God exists that we can make such a claim about the moral status of God*. Dawkins himself denies objective morality, which under-cuts his ability to authoritatively assert the wickedness of God.[65] Historically, biblical theism—including the deliverances of the Old Testament—has served the opposite purpose, as a moral compass for a wayward culture. The burden of proof is surely on the shoulders of anyone who claims the God of the Bible is immoral. Arguably, as Copan and Lamb powerfully show in their books, a careful reading of the Old Testament reveals a God of love, justice, and com-passion. We need not assume that millions of readers of the Bible have erred on this fundamental claim. Finally, we can assert that biblical theism and its

---

62. Richard Dawkins, *The God Delusion*, First Mariner Books edition (New York: Houghton Mifflin, 2008), 51.

63. Paul Copan, *Is God a Moral Monster? Making Sense of the Old Testament God* (Grand Rapids: Baker, 2011); David Lamb, *God Behaving Badly: Is the God of the Old Testament Angry, Sexist and Racist?* (Downers Grove, IL: InterVarsity Press, 2011).

64. Paul Copan, "Is Yahweh a Moral Monster? The New Atheists and Old Testament Ethics," *Philosophia Christi* 10, no. 1 (2008): 34–37.

65. See, e.g., Richard Dawkins, *River Out of Eden: A Darwinian View of Life* (New York: Basic Books, 1995), 132–33, quoted in Copan, "Is Yahweh a Moral Monster?," 34.

claim that humanity is made in God's image is the best hope for grounding human dignity and value. While much more can and needs to be said on this point, this outlines the general direction to proceed to help others overcome this barrier to belief.

Is the Belief That Jesus Is the Only Way Intolerant?

With one voice, philosophers and theologians throughout intellectual history have affirmed the fundamental religiosity of man. In Yann Martel's book *Life of Pi*, a young boy named Piscine Molitor Patel embraces this impulse in spades, becoming (unbeknownst to his parents) a follower of Christ, Krishna, and Allah.[66] The first part of the book paints a portrait of "Pi" as a gentle, clean-hearted, and wise worshiper of the divine, as well as a contented zookeeper's son.

This serene existence is upset one day when Pi is walking in the town square with his parents and runs into his Christian priest, Muslim imam, and Hindu pandit. An awkward meeting ensues. To his parents' surprise, each of the religious leaders claim Pi as a devoted follower of their chosen religion. The discussion that follows is comical. The priest strikes first: "Piscine is a good Christian boy. I hope to see him join our choir soon."[67] Next the imam: "You must be mistaken. He's a good Muslim boy. He comes without fail to Friday prayers, and his knowledge of the Qur'an is coming along nicely."[68] Then the pandit: "You're both wrong. He's a good Hindu boy. I see him all the time at the temple coming for darshan and performing puja."[69] The conversation goes downhill from there. As the religious leaders argue, Pi wisely stands above them all. When challenged to pick one religion, Pi exclaims, "Bapu Gandhi said, 'All religions are true.' I just want to love God."[70] This honest and heartfelt admission diffuses the tension as everyone goes their own way.

The second half of the book initially seems disconnected from the first. Pi and his family and their zoo animals emigrate to Canada aboard a Japanese cargo ship. A few days into the voyage, the cargo ship sinks and Pi finds himself in a lifeboat, his only companions a hyena, an orangutan, a wounded zebra,

---

66. Yann Martel, *Life of Pi* (Orlando, FL: Harcourt, 2001).
67. Martel, *Life of Pi*, 66.
68. Martel, *Life of Pi*, 66.
69. Martel, *Life of Pi*, 66.
70. Martel, *Life of Pi*, 69.

and a 450-pound tiger named Richard Parker. For seven months, Pi survives in the lifeboat along with Richard Parker, whom Pi tames. They float hundreds of miles and eventually end up in Mexico. The tiger runs for the jungle never to be seen again; Pi is found and rescued.

It is the last few pages of Martel's tale that are the most shocking. Pi is being interviewed, interrogated even, by the owners of the Japanese ship that sank. They find his story of survival too fanciful to believe. A boy and a 450-pound tiger surviving together for seven months in a lifeboat? Nonsense! They challenge Pi's story until he finally blurts out an alternative. But this new tale is far more horrific: instead of a hyena, orangutan, zebra, and tiger, the initial survivors in the lifeboat were human. There was a cook (the hyena), Pi's mom (the orangutan), a crew member (the zebra) and Pi himself (the tiger). Pi relates an alternate story of tragedy, murder, brutality, and evil. The cook cuts off the leg of the crew member under the guise of saving him, intending to use it as bait for fish. The crew member (the wounded zebra) eventually dies. The cook (the hyena) kills Pi's mom, and Pi eventually kills the cook. The story ends with a choice. Pi tells his interrogators: "You can't prove which story is true and which is not. You must take my word for it. . . . So tell me, since it makes no factual difference to you and you can't prove the question either way, which story do you prefer? Which is the better story, the story with animals or the story without animals?"[71] Their answer is worth noting: "The story with animals. Yes. The story with animals is the better story."[72] Pi's response: "Thank you. And so it goes with God."[73]

In this response we see the connection between the second part of the book and the first. Martel's point is that religion, like Pi's story of his misadventure on the boat, is malleable, capable of multiple interpretations, even contradictory stories, since no religion has the whole truth. Yet in this book I've argued for a contrary thesis. I've argued that the Christian story is true to the way the world *is* and true to the way the world *ought* to be. In other words, the Christian story is the true story of the world, and to the extent that other religions disagree with Christianity, they are wrong. The idea that there is one religious truth is unpopular in our disenchanted age. Part of the problem is that religious claims,

---

71. Martel, *Life of Pi*, 317.
72. Martel, *Life of Pi*, 317.
73. Martel, *Life of Pi*, 317.

as we saw in chapter 1, are no longer viewed as knowledge claims. In this section I want to address a second problem, that Christianity's exclusive truth claims, like Jesus being the only way to God, are viewed as intolerant and thus intellectually and morally deficient.

Here we can offer two replies. First, it is important to understand that truth, by nature, is exclusive. If it is true that Jones is now mowing the lawn, then it is false that Jones is not now mowing the lawn. If it is true that Jesus is divine (as Christians claim), then it is false that Jesus is not divine (as Muslims believe). If it is true that Christianity is the only religion founded by God himself and in which salvation is found, then it is false that all other religions are valid paths to God. Truth obtains when a belief, thought, or statement corresponds to the way the world is; otherwise the belief, thought, or statement is false. Two contradictory beliefs, thoughts, or statements cannot both be true. Given the nature of truth, it is simply false to say that all religions are different expressions of the one true reality because each religion makes different and often contradictory claims about God, humanity's fundamental problem, and the solution.

Second, it does not follow that disagreement entails intolerance. We should tolerate—show love and respect to—*people*, not ideas. No one would call me loving if I persisted in tolerating my child's belief that rat poison is sugar. When my child reaches for the rat poison to sweeten his cereal, it would be unloving to allow him to persist in this falsehood. So too with religious beliefs. One of the most loving things we can do for each other as truth seekers is to submit our beliefs to others' examination. If at the end of the day we simply disagree, the loving thing is not to redefine truth in order to accommodate mutually exclusive beliefs. Rather, the loving thing is to respect those with whom we disagree and continue together to seek truth. As the philosopher Peter Kreeft helpfully explains, we ought to be egalitarian with people and elitist with ideas.[74]

Martel is correct about one thing, however. We long to tell and live the better story. But the better story is not that all religions contain a mixture of truth and error and that we are free to choose our own path. That story will not solve our fundamental problem with sin, nor is it true or tolerant. Only the gospel story enables us to be truly tolerant of others. For in it we read of a God who tolerates humanity even when we fail yet loves us enough to make us whole.

---

74. Peter Kreeft, *The Snakebite Letters*, 2nd ed. (San Francisco: Ignatius, 1998), 94.

Is the Ethic of the Bible Archaic, Repressive, and Unloving?

In a disenchanted age when the notion that people have a teleology or proper function is rejected, just about anything goes, or so it seems. We see this most clearly today in the rapidly changing views regarding sexuality. There is widespread belief today that there is no essence to marriage, our sexuality, or our gender. These are plastic and malleable. Sexuality, we are told, are points along a spectrum from heterosexual to bisexual to homosexual. Gender identity is fluid too, moving from man to androgyny to woman and anywhere in between. As Darwin famously wrote in *Origin of Species*, "I am fully convinced that species are not immutable."[75] This concept has been taken further in our post-Darwinian world, and today the idea that there are fixed natures, genders, or sexual identities is viewed as absurd. Decisions about sexual orientation and gender identity are largely determined by one's feelings.

Given this cultural mind-set, traditional Christian views regarding marriage, sexuality, and gender are viewed as implausible. Moreover, given contemporary views of happiness as the satisfaction of unfettered desires, traditional Christian teaching on sexuality is also seen as repressive and unsavory. How can the gospel get a fair hearing in such a context? How might a cultural apologist offer a way of addressing this barrier to Jesus and the gospel?

To focus our discussion, let's limit ourselves to consider the issue of homosexuality. We will use homosexuality as a case study, a model in which to address the other social concerns such as transgenderism, transhumanism, abortion, euthanasia, marriage, race, and poverty that also present themselves as obstacles to Jesus and the gospel.[76]

---

75. Charles Darwin, *On the Origin of Species: A Facsimile of the First Edition* (Cambridge, MA: Harvard University Press, 1964), 6.

76. For an introduction to the issue of transgenderism from a Christian perspective, see Mark A. Yarhouse, *Understanding Gender Dysphoria: Navigating Transgender Issues in a Changing Culture* (Downers Grove, IL: InterVarsity Press, 2015). For an introduction to transhumanism from a Christian perspective, see Denis Alexander, "Enhancing Humans or a New Creation?," *Cambridge Papers* 18, no. 2 (2009): 1–4. For an introduction to abortion and euthanasia from a Christian perspective, see Scott Klusendorf, *The Case for Life: Equipping Christians to Engage the Culture* (Wheaton, IL: Crossway, 2009); Robert P. George and Christopher Tollefsen, *Embryo: A Defense of Human Life* (New York: Doubleday, 2008); and Scott Rae, *Moral Choices: An Introduction to Ethics*, 4th ed. (Grand Rapids: Zondervan, 2018), ch. 8. For an introduction to marriage and a defense of the traditional view (called the conjugal view), see Sherif Girgis, Ryan T. Anderson, and Robert P. George, *What Is Marriage? Man and Woman: A Defense* (New York: Encounter, 2012). For an introduction to race from a Christian perspective, see Willie James Jennings, *The Christian Imagination: Theology and the Origins of Race* (New Haven, CT: Yale University Press, 2010). For an introduction to poverty from a Christian perspective, see Jay W. Richards, *Money, Greed, and God: Why Capitalism Is the Solution and not the Problem* (New York: HarperOne, 2009). Finally, in addition to Ed Shaw's book discussed in this section, see Sam

The traditional Christian view of sex and marriage sees marriage as a covenantal union between a man and a woman for life (Gen. 2:24; Matt. 19:3–6). Sex within marriage is appropriate and encouraged, while sex outside marriage, including homosexual sex, is prohibited (Lev. 18:22; 20:13; Mark 7:20–23; Rom. 1:26–27; 1 Cor. 6:9–10; 1 Tim. 1:9–10). The problem, as same-sex attracted Christian and pastor Ed Shaw notes, is that the traditional view of sex and marriage is no longer plausible or desirable.[77] The solution isn't to reject the church's traditional teachings, as some evangelical leaders have recently advocated.[78] Rather, Shaw argues the solution is "to make what the Bible clearly commands seem plausible [and desirable] again."[79] Importantly, the traditional view is largely implausible and undesirable because of "a whole number of missteps that the church itself has taken over the years; a whole host of ways in which evangelicals have become too shaped by the world around us."[80]

The missteps Shaw identifies can be organized around three familiar themes: anti-intellectualism, fragmentation, and an unbaptized imagination. And in order for Christians to address this barrier to the gospel (and others like it), we must embrace God's call to intellectual, moral, and imaginative virtue. First, in rejecting anti-intellectualism, we must seek to properly understand key Christian doctrines, such as the believers' union with Christ, original sin, celibacy, and the nature of the church. As Christians, our core identity is not found in our sexuality but in our status as God's children. This truth reminds those who are same-sex attracted that our identity is found in who we are under God (i.e., saints) and that our desires don't determine our destiny. As fallen creatures, the doctrine of original sin teaches us that every person enters the world damaged yet responsible. Even if we were to grant that there is such a thing as a gay gene and that some are born gay, what follows from this? Considering theological precedence, not as much as typically thought. The fall affects every aspect of humanity, so we should not embrace every actual or innate instinct.

Allberry, *Is God Anti-Gay?* (Purcellville, VA: The Good Book Company, 2013) for another introduction to the issue of homosexuality from a traditional Christian perspective.

77. Ed Shaw, *Same-Sex Attraction and the Church: The Surprising Plausibility of the Celibate Life* (Downers Grove, IL: InterVarsity Press, 2015).

78. See, e.g., Matthew Vines, *God and the Gay Christian: The Biblical Case in Support of Same-Sex Relationships* (New York: Convergent, 2014), and David P. Gushee, *Changing Our Mind*, 2nd ed. (Canton, MI: Read the Spirit, 2015).

79. Shaw, *Same-Sex Attraction and the Church*, 21.

80. Shaw, *Same-Sex Attraction and the Church*, 21–22.

As Shaw puts it, "Of all the people on the planet, we [i.e., Christians] should be the most comfortable with people being born gay (if that's really the case) and yet still think it wrong to express that sexually. It's been a massive misstep not to articulate this."[81] Given the "hook-up" mentality of the culture, celibacy as an alternative is largely seen as an unnecessary or repressive lifestyle. Even within the church, celibacy and singleness are usually viewed as temporary inconveniences or, if one is so "unlucky" to be over thirty and single, an unfortunate oddity. Scripture does say, after all, "It is not good for the man to be alone" (Gen. 2:18). But these are significant missteps. The absence of a sexual relationship doesn't entail a lack of healthy intimacy. Moreover, celibacy, like marriage, is a good thing. Celibacy is a gift, as Paul makes clear in 1 Corinthians 7. We find our fundamental family in our spiritual family, the church. Those who embrace celibacy are not renouncing sex as evil; they are acknowledging that there is something better in heaven and that the perfect union of Christ and the church will one day become a reality (Rev. 21:1–5).[82] Good theology helps make the traditional view on sexuality and marriage plausible and desirable.

The perceived plausibility of the traditional views on marriage and sex is determined by the way Christians live as well. The primary goal in our spiritual formation unto Christ is not heterosexuality but godliness.[83] Thus, while we should encourage same-sex attracted Christians to seek change regarding their sexual desires, this ought to be understood as a subset of the larger story of God's call to all to be like Christ. As the #MeToo and #ChurchToo movements testify, heterosexual sexuality does not guarantee godliness. Many Christians who are not same-sex attracted fall into sexual sin through adultery, pornography, lust, abuse, or masturbation. Yet there seems to be a double standard in which homosexual sin is treated worse than heterosexual sin. If we want the traditional view of sexuality to be plausible and desirable, heterosexual and homosexual Christians must seek godliness in their sexuality. "If same-sex attracted Christians feel they are being held to a higher standard than anyone else in the church," Shaw observes, "the plausibility problem will only get worse."[84]

---

81. Shaw, *Same-Sex Attraction and the Church*, 58. Shaw notes that the scientific evidence does not suggest there is a "gay gene." Thus, he is considering a hypothetical: If there is a gay gene, what follows biblically? Either there is or there isn't a gay gene. Either way, Shaw's point is it doesn't follow that we ought to act on our same-sex attraction given the Bible's clear prohibition against it.

82. Shaw, *Same-Sex Attraction and the Church*, 112.

83. Shaw, *Same-Sex Attraction and the Church*, 97.

84. Shaw, *Same-Sex Attraction and the Church*, 97.

Finally, we must seek to rebaptize our imagination with respect to marriage. Cultural views on marriage have shifted, and today marriage is viewed by many as an *emotional union* between consenting partners.[85] With growing frequency, Christians, inordinately shaped by a disenchanted culture, are adopting the same revisionist view of marriage. It's no accident that marriage, traditionally understood as a *union of body and soul* between a man and woman for life, is considered a sacrament of the church.[86] As a sacrament, it is a signpost, a symbol, "an earthly representation of a spiritual reality"[87]—the union between Christ and his bride, the church (Eph. 5:31–32). God created the institution of marriage, a unity within difference, to reveal the depth of his passionate love for us.

There is an essence to marriage. If we want the traditional Christian teaching of sexuality to be viewed as plausible and desirable, we must see marriage in its proper light: as a sacrament, a symbol of God's passionate, pursuing love in which sex is a gift and foretaste of the bliss we will experience with Christ for eternity.[88]

CONCLUSION

There is more that could be said about each of these internal and external barriers to the gospel. Undoubtedly, there are other barriers too. The cultural apologist should help seekers overcome these and similar barriers so that the seekers can genuinely consider the question of Jesus as an attractive possibility. The tools of the cultural apologist are many, offering multiple points of entry and contact with these barriers as well as ways of overcoming them. What we cannot do, however, is ignore them if we want others to see and understand Jesus as their only hope and greatest need.

---

85. Girgis, Anderson, and George, *What Is Marriage?*, 4.

86. Girgis, Anderson, and George, *What Is Marriage?*, 1.

87. Shaw, *Same-Sex Attraction and the Church*, 90.

88. For a powerful, imaginative expression of the sacramental view of marriage as a comprehensive union of body and soul between a man and a woman, see Edmund Spenser's poem "Epithalamion," written in 1595 to celebrate Spenser's marriage to Elizabeth Boyle, reprinted in Girgis, Anderson, and George, *What Is Marriage?*, xiii–xiv.

CHAPTER 8

HOME

In eternity this world will be Troy, I believe, and all that
has passed here will be the epic of the universe, the ballad
they sing in the streets. Because I don't imagine any reality
putting this one in the shade entirely, and I think piety
forbids me to try.

Marilynne Robinson[1]

But in keeping with his promise we are looking forward to a
new heaven and a new earth, where righteousness dwells.

2 Peter 3:13

Towering above the other summits in Rocky Mountain National Park, Longs Peak arouses in me a sense of conquest. Standing at 14,259 feet above sea level, she silently beckons even as she mocks my dreams. The climb to the top is dangerous and physically grueling: sixteen total miles, an elevation gain of 5,000 feet, the last 1.5 miles a treacherous climb (over the boulder field, through the Keyhole, around the Ledges, up the Trough, across the Narrows, and up the Homestretch). Twice, my son Austin and I have tried to summit Longs Peak. Two times we have failed. On our first attempt, Austin (then twelve years old) and I were turned back by altitude sickness and a good dose of fear as we scrambled to the top of the Trough, peered over the ledge, and met the Narrows, a slender

---

1. Marilynne Robinson, *Gilead* (New York: Picador, 2004), 57.

rock path supported by a thousand-foot cliff. Two years later, we made it through the Keyhole (1.5 miles from the summit), only to be turned back again by altitude sickness. When Austin asked to try again for his eighteenth birthday, I happily agreed. We both had unfinished business with the mountain.

Four days prior to our third summit attempt, we arrived at Estes Park, a quaint mountain city nestled at the base of Rocky Mountain National Park. Over the next few days we acclimated and trained, hiking six miles at 9,000 feet, then ten miles at 10,000 feet, and finally nine miles at 12,000 feet. We did all we could to prepare physically. As we lay in bed on the night before our climb, waiting for the 2:00 a.m. alarm, fear mounted in my heart. Seared into my mind from six years before was the image of that thousand-foot drop. It haunted me. What if I fall? Worse, what if Austin slipped? Lord, protect us, I prayed as sleep finally took me.

Embarking from the trailhead in the dark, we hiked by flashlight for three hours, making the base of the boulder field as the morning sun crested over the eastern horizon. William Wordsworth's poem "Stepping Westward" accurately captured my emotions that morning:

> The dewy ground was dark and cold;
> Behind, all gloomy to behold;
> And stepping westward seemed to be
> A kind of *heavenly* destiny;
> I liked the greeting, 'twas a sound
> Of something without place or bound;
> And seemed to give me spiritual right
> To travel through that region bright.[2]

As we passed through the Boulder Field and onto the Trough, guided by cairns left by those who had traveled before us, fear began to mount. Pulling ourselves over the ledge like we had done six years earlier, we faced our fear. After a harrowing quarter mile on the Narrows (or was it just five hundred feet?), we rounded the corner and saw for the first time the Homestretch. My heart sank. It was a near vertical climb. My lungs were burning. My legs were iron.

---

2. William Wordsworth, "Stepping Westward," in *Selected Poems* (London: Oxford University Press, 1919), lines 9–16 (p. 301).

I wavered, wanting to quit. Spurred on by the encouragement of my son and others with us, I pressed on. "One step at a time. You can do it." Thirty minutes later we climbed over the last boulder and reached the summit. It had taken us three tries over six years, but finally, we were standing atop Longs Peak.

I now realize that the hike on that mountain was more than a test of my physical abilities. It was a picture of a spiritual reality—a sacrament of life itself. The adventure at Longs Peak is a fitting metaphor for life's journey: we are not meant to travel alone; the safest way forward is to follow the path, and when the path is unclear, there are others who can point the way; life is full of struggle and doubt, exhale and fulfillment, radiant beauty and intolerable harshness. And by reflecting on the challenges of that journey, I see more clearly how my loves and longings motivate me. My love for my son and my longing for adventure compelled me up and onward. My longing for home sustained my weary legs on the path of return. On that thirteen-hour hike, I glimpsed the story of the world: wander and return; *home—away—home again*. As Frederick Buechner writes,

> Whether we're rich or poor, male or female . . . our stories are all stories of *searching*. We search for a good self to be and for good work to do. We search to become human in a world that tempts us always to be less than human or looks to us to be more. We search to love and be loved. And in a world where it is often hard to believe in much of anything, we search to believe in something holy and beautiful and life-transcending that will give meaning and purpose to the lives we live.[3]

Yet the paths of the nomads are well-trodden, leading many to despair and destruction. Corrupt or confused guides lead hungry hearts to plague-stricken fields that cannot sustain and thirsty souls to polluted waters that cannot satisfy. How can an apologetic of return help the lost find the path of life? How can we serve as faithful guides leading others home? In this concluding chapter, we shall explore the human quest for home, a quest that undergirds the pursuit of goodness, truth, and beauty and finds its fulfillment in God both now and in eternity. We will also explore how our lives and loves, our words and actions, can serve as cairns for weary travelers along the way.

---

3. Frederick Buechner, *The Longing for Home: Recollections and Reflections* (New York: HarperCollins, 1996), 66–67.

THE LONGING FOR HOME

After the ten-year war at Troy, Odysseus set out for Ithaca, a small island located in the Ionian Sea where his wife and son patiently waited for his return. What should have been a journey of weeks stretched into ten years. In vain, Odysseus tried to return home, but he was prevented at every turn by his own folly, tantalizing temptations, and terrifying monsters. We first encounter Odysseus as a prisoner of the beautiful goddess Calypso on a distant island "sitting on the shore . . . torturing himself with tears, groans and heartache, and looking out with streaming eyes across the watery wilderness."[4] Offers of immortality and sensual pleasure fail to erase his memory of home or his longing for it. Odysseus "would give anything for the mere sight of the smoke rising up from his own land."[5] He longs for home yet cannot find it on his own.

We, like Odysseus, must also face three jolting facts: we long for home, we are not home, and we can't find our own way home. These facts offer little comfort, at least initially, to the lost and weary. As we attend to this deep longing of the heart for home, we come to realize our feeble attempts to make the journey fall short. When all seems lost, we turn our souls away from ourselves and in desperation seek the help of Another. The good news is that our longing can find fulfillment; there is a way home. To get there, we must first grasp the bad news that we are lost and realize we are homeless. To help us unpack what this means as a cultural apologetic for a homesick culture, we will consider these three uncomfortable facts in greater detail. And as we better understand this longing, we will consider how to employ this deep longing of the human heart to point others to Jesus and the gospel.

We All Long for Home

While many don't come from an ideal home, we all intuitively have a sense of what home ought to be. Home is the *place* where you belong. It is a place where you are fully known and fully loved and where your identity is forged and your purpose discovered. It is also the place from which you are launched into the world to fulfill the unique purposes for which you were made. And when the work is done, home is waiting for your return. Buechner describes

---

4. Homer, *The Odyssey*, trans. E. V. Rieu and D. C. H. Rieu (New York: Penguin, 2003), 66–67.
5. Homer, *The Odyssey*, 4.

home as "a place where you feel you belong and which in some sense belongs to you, a place where you feel that all is somehow ultimately well even if things aren't going all that well at any given moment."[6]

Home is more than a place, however. It also represents a *path* that leads to life. We might put it this way: home is a place to stand and a story in which to live. It is a place of rest and return and a path of flourishing and delight. The Hebrew word describing this state of well-being is *shalom*. As theologian Cornelius Plantinga describes it, "Shalom means *universal flourishing, wholeness, and delight*—a rich state of affairs in which natural needs are satisfied and natural gifts fruitfully employed, a state of affairs that inspires joyful wonder as its Creator and Savior opens doors and welcomes the creatures in whom he delights."[7] In short, home is an apt metaphor for our hearts' deepest longings—for God, wholeness, meaning, and purpose; a place and path where life is experienced as it was meant to be. It is little wonder that the orphan Anne, as she rode to what she hoped would be her forever home, exclaimed to Matthew Cuthbert in L. M. Montgomery's classic *Anne of Green Gables*, "I'm glad to think of getting home. You see, I've never had a real home since I can remember. It gives me that pleasant ache again just to think of coming to a really truly home."[8] Before finding faith in Jesus, we are all orphans like Anne, aching for a place that is "really truly home."

We Are Not Home

We have this sense that something is not right with the world and our place in it. We long for rest and refuge yet find ourselves as strangers in a broken world that is not our own. We are painfully aware that our lives are temporally bound, and there is nothing we can do to prevent our death or the death of loved ones. As writer Julian Barnes describes the human experience, we travel with "the vicious awareness that this is a rented world."[9] We know in our guts that violence, murder, rape, misery, coercion, disease, loneliness, and the like are not how things ought to be. The consistent experience of life in this world can best be described as a shalom-violated experience. We are *not* home.

6. Buechner, *The Longing for Home*, 7.

7. Cornelius Plantinga Jr., *Not the Way It's Supposed to Be: A Breviary of Sin* (Grand Rapids: Eerdmans, 1995), 10.

8. L. M. Montgomery, *Anne of Green Gables* (New York: Bantam, 1987), 19.

9. Julian Barnes, *Nothing to Be Frightened Of* (New York: Knopf, 2008), quoted in Jen Pollock Michel, *Keeping Place: Reflections on the Meaning of Home* (Downers Grove, IL: InterVarsity Press, 2017), 28.

What accounts for the human condition of homelessness? The answer is found in the story of God. In Genesis 1 and 2, God creates a place and a people, and he gives his people a purpose. If Genesis 1 and 2 provide a description of home as a state of flourishing where humanity experiences God's presence and the blessings of place, then Genesis 3 can accurately be described as the beginning of man's story away from home. In Genesis 3, human beings take it upon themselves to try and meet their own needs in their own way. The result is the fall of humanity into sin, the "culpable disturbance of shalom,"[10] and Adam and Eve's subsequent banishment from the garden of Eden (Gen. 3:23–24). This state of fallenness or homelessness is now the common human experience as we take our place in the world. C. S. Lewis colorfully describes the elevation of self and the vandalism of shalom: "The golden apple of selfhood, thrown among the false gods, became an apple of discord because they scrambled for it. They did not know the first rule of the holy game, which is that every player must by all means touch the ball and then immediately pass it on. To be found with it in your hands is a fault: to cling to it, death."[11] This fatal turn toward self, Adam and Eve's eating of the "apple of discord," has led us into misery and displacement. Humanity is not home. But even in the midst of human tragedy, there is a glimmer of home and a hint of return.

We Can't Find the Way Home on Our Own

God knows humanity has tried. The nonreligious attempt to find their way home by pursuing this-worldly goods, such as pleasure, fame, accomplishment, or wealth. The religious seek the way home by performing good works. Both approaches are dead ends. These self-salvation plans don't work because they don't correctly diagnose our fundamental problem. Our problem is not a lack of stuff or accomplishment or good works. Our problem is sin: humanity is morally culpable to God and deserves judgment and reproach. The Bible is clear that the consequence of human sin is death—spiritual separation from God (Gen. 3:23; Rom. 6:23). This is the bad news. There is no self-salvation, no way home on our own.

But God, who is rich in mercy (Eph. 2:4), has acted on man's behalf. This is the good news, God's unexpected response to human tragedy. Even as the consequences for sin are set out in Genesis 3, God initiates his rescue plan.[12] This

---

10. Plantinga, *Not the Way It's Supposed to Be*, 16.

11. C. S. Lewis, *The Problem of Pain* (San Francisco: HarperCollins, 1996), 158.

12. "And I [i.e., the Lord] will put enmity between you [i.e., Satan] and the woman, and between your

plan culminates in the coming of Jesus and his death on the cross that paid the penalty of sin on man's behalf. Jesus provides us a way home. Jesus proclaims, "I am the way and the truth and the life. No one comes to the Father except through me" (John 14:6).

How can we find our way home? C. S. Lewis states the answer simply: "The thing you long for summons you away from the self. . . . Out of our selves, into Christ, we must go."[13] Paradoxically, if we aim for home and happiness, we won't find it. We must instead aim at something else—or better, *someone* else—and along the way, we will find shalom. As Jesus said in the Gospels,

> If anyone wishes to come after Me, he must deny himself, and take up his cross and follow Me. For whoever wishes to save his life will lose it; but whoever loses his life for My sake will find it. For what will it profit a man if he gains the whole world and forfeits his soul? Or what will a man give in exchange for his soul? (Matt. 16:24–26 NASB)

In Christ, life is full of paradox. We die in order to live. We seek another to find ourselves. We gain the whole world but lose our soul. In the end, you will either save your life by giving it away or lose it by trying to save it yourself; you will either find the happiness and home that God gives and enjoy it in creaturely response or eternally starve. As we allow Jesus to permeate every fiber of our being and allow the Holy Spirit to reveal our brokenness and need of a Savior, we are led to the cross. But we find home and happiness "along the way" as we die to self and look to Christ.

In the final words of the masterful work *Mere Christianity*, Lewis puts an exclamation point on the contemporary challenge to homelessness and sets out the path of return: "Look for yourself, and you will find in the long run only hatred, loneliness, despair, rage, ruin, and decay. But look for Christ and you will find Him, and with Him everything else thrown in."[14] The gospel brings us home. The journey begins when we turn from self and seek the living God.

---

offspring [i.e., the offspring of Satan] and hers [i.e., one of the offspring of Eve]; he will crush your head, and you will strike his heel" (Gen. 3:15). These words point to the future salvation of man, ultimately fulfilled in Christ, who saves while being crushed on a cross.

13. Lewis, *The Problem of Pain*, 154; and C. S. Lewis, *Mere Christianity* (New York: HarperCollins, 2001), 224.

14. Lewis, *Mere Christianity*, 227.

A STORY THAT UNDERSTANDS

In chapter 4 we noted that stories awaken our souls and invite participation. Stories draw us in. We long to live a dramatic life. Stories pull us out of ourselves and into a larger universe where we can aspire to be more or different or better. They call us to an allegiance and bid us to locate our lives within their narratives. One of the questions I've been pressing throughout this book is the question of story: Is there a story that understands you?[15]

We can think of the different worldviews prominent within a culture as competing stories, stories that compete for our allegiance and ask for our participation. The philosopher Alvin Plantinga boils down the major stories in the West to three narratives: naturalism, postmodernism, and the Christian story.[16] As we consider these various narratives, my hope is that by looking afresh at the Christian story in contrast to competing narratives you will see how the Christian story alone is both true and satisfying. Let's begin with naturalism.

Naturalism

The major plotline for the grand story of naturalism can be summarized as *material world—vulnerable selves—buffered selves*.[17] As the story usually goes, there are no nonnatural or nonphysical parts to reality. All the furniture, all the stuff, in the world is material, usually conceived as very small objects such as particles and force fields that compose bigger material objects like brains, buffaloes, boats, mountains, stars, and the Milky Way galaxy. This matter bumped into other bits of matter for billions of years. Eventually, atoms formed, then stars, and then a few billion years later we got lucky and life began: first single cells

15. This penetrating question and way of thinking about the story was first suggested to me through the teaching ministry of Tim Keller.

16. Alvin Plantinga, "When Faith and Reason Clash: Evolution and the Bible," *The Christian Scholar's Review* 21 (1991): 16. Plantinga labels the three competing stories as perennial naturalism, creative antirealism, and Christian theism.

17. Donald Opitz and Derek Melleby summarize the main story line of naturalism (the subject of this paragraph) and postmodernism (the next paragraph) in terms of these three main acts in *The Outrageous Idea of Academic Faithfulness*, 4th ed. (Grand Rapids: Brazos, 2009), 61–62. Opitz and Melleby summarize naturalism as *matter—ignorance—progress*. I think that the problem is slightly deeper than ignorance, however, and have modified the (now dominant) naturalistic story to accommodate that fact. Given naturalism, we are *vulnerable* to the ravages of the world, and the solution is not merely to make progress intellectually but ultimately to insulate ourselves from nature and the evil perpetrated by others. While there are other versions of naturalism, the version articulated here is the most popular, espoused by leading scientists and philosophers such as Stephen Hawking, Lawrence Krauss, Sean Carroll, and Alex Rosenberg.

and eventually you and me. In order to survive, we developed weapons to protect ourselves from wild beasts and each other. We cultivated tools to build habitats and produced food from the land. We invented languages and laws in order to communicate and relate to one another. As time progressed, we understood more and more of how the world works. In coming to understand more about the universe, we learned two basic facts: (1) the world is complex and awe-inspiring, and (2) humanity doesn't ultimately matter. Still, we should be thankful since our gaps in knowledge continue to close, and we hope that eventually we will understand everything, including how to master the universe technologically. Man's fundamental problem according to naturalism is our vulnerability to the world and each other. The solution to our problem is to buffer ourselves through progress and technology.[18] Our lives, while ultimately insignificant, can at least be enjoyed along the way toward our meaningless mastery of the cosmos.

Postmodernism

The plotline of the postmodern story is a bit different from the naturalist narrative. It can be summarized as *culture—majority oppression—individual expression*.[19] In this tale, reality is socially constructed. No single, overarching story explains and unifies reality. Instead, shorter narratives give meaning to various individuals and groups.[20] The postmodern story begins with a basic observation: there are over seven billion people in the world. Since each person has a unique viewpoint, it follows that there are lots of perspectives on reality too. A central question is how people can relate to one another given such diversity in perspective. One idea is to group together individuals who share a common interest or goal. In the postmodern story, the common interest that binds people together is *power*. Individually and collectively, we lust after power because when we attain it, we get to define the rest of the story and claim *our* truth is *the* truth about the world, to the neglect of others' truths. In the

18. Lest you doubt that naturalism is a story that invites participation, consider the February 21, 2011, issue of *Time* magazine. On the front cover, there is a picture of a human head connected to a computer cable. The cover reads, "2045: The Year Man Becomes Immortal*," and the asterisk (also on the front cover) notes, "If you believe humans and machines will become one. Welcome to the Singularity movement."

19. See for representative statements of postmodernism, the writings of Richard Rorty, Jean-François Lyotard, and, as a protopostmodern, Friedrich Nietzsche. The three-part narrative is summarized as *culture—oppression—expression* by Opitz and Melleby in *The Outrageous Idea of Academic Faithfulness*, 62–63.

20. "I define postmodern as incredulity toward metanarratives." Jean-François Lyotard, *The Postmodern Condition: A Report of Knowledge*, trans. Geoffrey Bennington and Brian Massumi (Minneapolis: University of Minnesota Press, 1984 and 1997), xxiv.

postmodern story, the lust for power leads to the oppression of the weak by the strong. The tension that ensues resolves itself when the weak give voice to their plight, find solace, and discover meaning in the telling of their own stories. Humanity's fundamental problem is oppression, and "salvation" is found through self- (or group) expression.

The Christian Story

Finally, we come to the Christian story, which has the familiar plotline we unpacked in chapter 2: *home—away—home again*. To further unpack the "away—home again" part of the storyline, Frederick Buechner's tripartite description of the gospel story in *Telling the Truth* is both profound and illuminating. It highlights the awe-inspiring beauty of God's love and action on our behalf.[21] Buechner unpacks this part of the story in terms of a three-act play: *tragedy—comedy—fairy story*. Let's explore each of these ideas to show how they come together to form a beautiful tapestry of God's love for man.

Buechner begins with tragedy, describing it as "the news that man is a sinner, to use the old word, that he is evil in the imagination of his heart, that when he looks in the mirror all in a lather what he sees is at least eight parts chicken, phony, slob. That is tragedy."[22] The tragedy of the fall is the vandalization of shalom. Every inch of creation is defiled by the fall, and the world is a "universal cemetery."[23]

But next, the divine comedy. God answers human tragedy.

The Tragic is the inevitable. The comic is the unforeseeable. How can Donald Duck foresee that after being run over by a steamroller he will pick himself up on the other side as flat as a pancake . . . but alive and squawking? How can Charlie Chaplin in his baggy pants and derby hat foresee that though he is stood up by the girl and clobbered over the head by the policeman and hit in the kisser with a custard pie, he will emerge dapper and gallant to the end, twirling his invincible cane and twitching

---

21. Frederick Buechner, *Telling the Truth: The Gospel as Tragedy, Comedy, and Fairy Tale* (New York: Harper One, 1977). This book, which can be read in one long sitting, is highly recommended for anyone who regularly preaches the gospel or shares his or her faith. In other words, I think this book is essential reading for Christians.

22. Buechner, *Telling the Truth*, 7.

23. David Naugle, *Reordered Love, Reordered Lives: Learning the Deep Meaning of Happiness* (Grand Rapids: Eerdmans, 2008), 26.

his invincible mustache? . . . The news [is] that [we are] loved anyway, cherished, forgiven, bleeding to be sure, but also bled for. That is comedy.[24]

God responds to human tragedy with the incarnation and atonement, and his response is unexpected and unforeseen—a high comedy. Who would have predicted that in the person of Jesus God would become man? Who would have expected that Jesus—God in the flesh—would die a horrible death on a cross to restore man's broken relationship with God? Not only is this a great story, it is the best possible story there could be![25]

The stage is set for the final act, the unending fairy story:

What gives [fairy tales] their real power and meaning is the world they evoke. It is a world of magic and mystery, of deep darkness and flickering starlight. It is a world where terrible things happen and wonderful things too. . . . Yet for all its confusion and wildness, it is a world where the battle goes ultimately to the good, who live happily ever after, and where in the long run everybody, good and evil alike, becomes known by his true name.[26]

Happily ever after—isn't this how all fairy stories go? They don't end; they continue forever. And this is the good news of the Christian story. God's overwhelming love and mercy to us on the cross is the sudden joyous turn that provides the means for human beings to live forever as intended.

C. S. Lewis beautifully captures this idea at the end of his Narnian tale. The Narnians had finally entered the real Narnia, heaven, where all is as it should be. Lewis concludes the series with these words, words that aptly describe the Christian hope in eternity with God: "All their life in this world and all their adventures in Narnia had only been the cover and the title page: now at last they were beginning Chapter One of the Great Story no one on earth has read: which goes on forever: in which every chapter is better than the one before."[27] It's the happy ending. Truth *is* better than fiction.

---

24. Buechner, *Telling the Truth*, 57 and 7.
25. Recall from chapter 2 Alvin Plantinga's suggestion that perhaps all the best possible worlds contain incarnation and atonement. See Alvin Plantinga, *Where the Conflict Really Lies: Science, Religion, and Naturalism* (Oxford: Oxford University Press, 2011), 59.
26. Buechner, *Telling the Truth*, 81.
27. C. S. Lewis, *The Last Battle* (New York: Harper Collins, 1984), 210–11.

Stories matter. They invite participation and move us to action. But not all stories are equally compelling. We judge a story according to its fidelity to reality and to our longings. A key question we should ask is which of our three competing stories (or the many lesser stories in our culture) correspond to the way things are and connect with our deep longings for how things *ought* to be? One of the burdens of this book is to remind you as the reader that the Christian story is both true and satisfying. But we can't stop there, of course. The gospel shouldn't be tucked away in the corner. Rather, it ought to be proclaimed throughout the earth.

Another burden of this book has been to unpack a model for how we might join with the Holy Spirit in helping others see Jesus and the gospel as reasonable and desirable. And this points to another thread of divine comedy woven throughout the Christian story: God has chosen us, his followers, to be his representatives. We find joy in the journey as we join with others in working to restore the Christian voice, conscience, and imagination within culture. We labor not because it feeds our ego but because it is God's plan for us as agents of shalom; we help erect signposts for others on the way.

THE JOURNEY HOME

We love to read of Don Quixote's comical attempts at romance and chivalry, Frodo's quest to dispose of the ring at Mount Doom, or Dorothy and Toto's search for the Wizard of Oz. We are drawn to adventure in stories and in life. The motif of journey captures our sense of destiny. "The idea of the journey," writes Os Guinness, "is the most nearly universal picture of our little lives on planet earth."[28] We have this sense that we are on a quest or pilgrimage and that "we are all at some unknown point between the beginning and the end."[29] This journey of life, I suggest, is an apt metaphor for the human search for God, including all that is wrapped up in finding him: union, happiness, heaven, eternal life, shalom, home. As apologists, it is crucial, according to Guinness, "to ponder the journey toward faith and know how it progresses as

---

28. Os Guinness, *Fool's Talk: Recovering the Art of Christian Persuasion* (Downers Grove, IL: InterVarsity Press, 2015), 229.

29. Guinness, *Fool's Talk*, 230.

well as its principles and its pitfalls along the way."[30] The hope is that we would be "trustworthy guides to those we meet who are at any stage of their search."[31]

Guinness is certainly correct; however, we can go further. We can develop the metaphor of humanity's journey home from the vantage point of the *cultural* apologist. A cultural apologist, as I've argued in this book, has local and global concerns. Locally, the cultural apologist seeks to help others hear and understand the gospel by building a bridge from some common starting point—such as our universal longings for truth, goodness, or beauty—and addressing barriers to belief along the way. The primary question each unbeliever needs to face is the question of Jesus: What do you make of Jesus Christ? Globally, the cultural apologist should be concerned with the collective mind-set, conscience, and imagination of the culture, including the people and institutions within the culture that shape this collective way of perceiving. His or her global concern is that the gospel will be viewed as reasonable and desirable.

So how might a cultural apologist become a skillful guide for those on the path of faith, as well as a creative curator of the path of faith itself? Let's consider some key questions and concerns for those on the journey home and how individuals and the church might serve as faithful guides for those who have lost their way.

First, let's return to Pascal's three types of people: the nonseeker, the seeker, and the found. Like the rest stops that dot American highways, these three kinds of people inhabit three rest stops or stopping points along our journey home to reenchantment. Each rest stop is different: some have clean bathrooms, others not so clean; some have a water fountain and single vending machine, others a veritable smorgasbord of restaurants with multiple choices for food and fun; some are stocked with information, guides, and maps, others with nothing at all. In a similar way, each stopping point, each *kind* of rest area on the journey to faith is different. And the rest areas at each stage of the journey are as various as the rest areas scattered across American highways: some are dark and grimy offering little by way of sustenance or relief, others are bright and clean offering refreshment and sustenance for the next leg of the journey.

Next, recall our two steps toward reenchantment: awakening longing and returning to reality. Let's think of these steps toward reenchantment as

---

30. Guinness, *Fool's Talk*, 231.
31. Guinness, *Fool's Talk*, 231.

transition points, moments of disruption that spur us ahead on the journey home. Putting these pieces together, we can picture the journey of faith as a three-stage journey with two transitions (see figure 8.1).

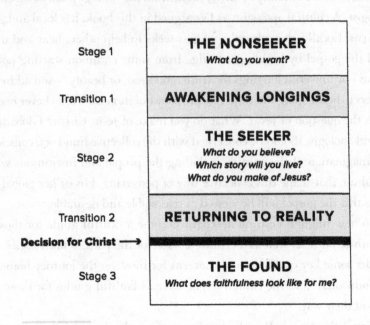

Stage 1	**THE NONSEEKER** *What do you want?*
Transition 1	**AWAKENING LONGINGS**
Stage 2	**THE SEEKER** *What do you believe?* *Which story will you live?* *What do you make of Jesus?*
Transition 2 **Decision for Christ** ⟶	**RETURNING TO REALITY**
Stage 3	**THE FOUND** *What does faithfulness look like for me?*

FIGURE 8.1: The Journey Home

The nonseeker in stage one is unaware or unresponsive to the deepest longings of his heart for God. The primary question the cultural apologist asks of the nonseeker is a question that awakens awareness of desire: *What do you want?* By attending to his loves and longings, whether through the way of imagination, reason, or morality, our hope is that the nonseeker will become cognizant of his deeper longings and set out on the path that eventually leads to Jesus. At the global level of culture, we do this by creating and cultivating beauty, goodness, and truth in the spaces we inhabit, the lives we live, and the things we make (and by supporting the Christian intellectuals, artists, and innovators who do this well). In this, we help the nonseeker see Jesus and the gospel as plausible and desirable, setting them on the path home.

In stage two the primary questions for the seeker, in addition to the question of longing, are questions of belief and meaning: *What do you believe?*

Which story will you live?[32] As Guinness describes the seeker, "The person for whom life has become a question mark is quite different. Such people are no longer complacent or satisfied with what they used to believe. Life has raised a question that acts like a pebble in a shoe or a bur under the saddle."[33] The seeker needs answers, and our task as cultural apologists is "to find out exactly where they are in the search."[34] We do this by listening, prodding, discussing, providing evidence, inviting, and serving the tangible needs of the seeker.

We do this in the hope that the seeker begins to view Christianity as reasonable and desirable and will set out on the road of "return" to reality. The seeker squarely and seriously faces the ultimate question as well: *What do you make of Jesus Christ?* He realizes the choice before him and weighs the cost of abandoning his old self and old ways and placing his faith in Another. Our job as cultural apologists at this stage is to walk with the seeker, praying that the Holy Spirit moves in his or her life. Of course, at this point or any before, a person is free to turn back or stall on the path, and many do. Knowing God is a gift that is freely given and must be freely received. "A key part of this moment of commitment," writes Guinness, "is when a person's seeking suddenly blossoms into knowing, knowing into trusting, and knowing and trusting into loving God and the unmistakable knowledge and experience of being loved by God."[35]

For those who bend their knee, the journey of *initial* discovery is finished. Of course, we will never cease exploring and discovering wonderful and beautiful truths about Jesus and the gospel story, but when the journey to God is over, the journey with God begins. Guinness describes this new reality for those who place their faith in Jesus. "When people take that step of committed faith and set out with us to be followers of Jesus, our task as Christian advocates is over, and from then on they join us as sisters and brothers on the long way home. The journey toward faith that is the quest for meaning is completed, though the journey of faith has only begun."[36] The adventure begins anew, but this time it is *with* and *for* God. The primary question for the found, the follower of Christ who embraces a cultural apologetic of return,

---

32. The question of longing (What do you want?) is not left behind at the seeker stage. Rather, what one desires is often in tension with the story one inhabits. As such, the seeker looks to his desires as a kind of guide, helping him to find a story that makes sense of the desires. Thanks to Ross D. Inman for this point.

33. Guinness, *Fool's Talk*, 235.

34. Guinness, *Fool's Talk*, 235.

35. Guinness, *Fool's Talk*, 249.

36. Guinness, *Fool's Talk*, 252.

is this: *What does faithfulness to Christ look like in my sphere of influence?* The found are "new in Christ," and in daily picking up the cross and individually and together as the church, they participate in the work that God prepared for them before the foundation of the world (Eph. 2:10).

MINISTRY IN FOUR DIMENSIONS

Is cultural renewal possible? Can the Christian voice, conscience, and imagination be reestablished within our culture? I'm hopeful. God's pursuing love for humanity gives us reason to think reenchantment is possible. But renewal won't happen overnight. There is no quick fix for culture or what ails it. A cultural apologetic of return will take time, and this fact pushes against the pragmatic utilitarianism that characterizes much that passes for Christian ministry these days. Instead, we must think about ministry in a new light, pushing our horizons beyond immediate needs to think years or even generations ahead. Our metrics should include more than conversions and baptisms—which are vital, of course. What is missing are metrics that measure the cultivation of the soil in which the seeds of the gospel are planted. As the artist Makoto Fujimura notes, "The tilling of the soil is the most important task we can do to prepare ourselves and our culture for the seeds of the gospel that God sows so lavishly."[37] If we neglect the soil of culture, belief will only continue to become more difficult for future generations.

In chapter 6 we looked at a three-dimensional ministry: going to every place on the map—length and height—as well as drilling deep within every point on the map. Let's add a fourth dimension. In addition to length, height, and depth, we add time.[38] Why time? Fujimura helps us see the importance of generational thinking:

> Our lives are directed or constrained by paths paved by the generations
> before us. Sometimes we can trace the paths. . . . Often they shape us
> unawares. What is true of legacies from our parents is true also for our
> communities and racial and national histories. Cultures are not created

37. Makoto Fujimura, *Culture Care: Reconnecting with Beauty for Our Common Life* (Downers Grove, IL: InterVarsity Press, 2017), 96.

38. Again, thanks to Greg Ganssle for the insight that ministry should be four-dimensional.

overnight. We are affected by layers of experiences, personalities, and works of previous generations. Cultural histories affect us far beyond what we are able to recognize—or, sometimes, admit.[39]

Since cultural formation is generational, an apologetic of return "can inspire us to work within a vision for culture," as Fujimura writes, "that is expressed in centuries and millennia rather than quarters, seasons, or fashions."[40]

A cultural apologist will be an iconoclast within the church, shattering images and the reductive and pragmatic impulses that define much of contemporary Christianity. He or she will also be an iconoclast within the institutions that shape the broader culture, pushing back against the dehumanizing impulses that inform the spirit of the age. Fujimura, speaking of artists in this way, calls these individuals "border walkers."[41] Existing at the edges of groups, border walkers "are *called* into the margins, into stalking the borders, moving between traditional tribes and the unknown"[42] in order to help us see reality in a different light. A cultural apologist is called to walk the borders between the mundane and the transcendent, helping others to see reality as sacred.

An apologetic of return requires the body of Christ to come together to work toward the good of all. The call to "return" calls patrons, visionaries, artists, intellectuals, cultural innovators, pastors, lawyers, business women and men, doctors and nurses, mothers and fathers, sons and daughters to each play their part in God's unfolding story.[43] In short, it will require the body of Christ being the hands and feet of Jesus to each other and helpful guides to those along the way.

AN INVITATION TO THE DANCE

I'll admit I'm a bit envious of Matt Harding. He has traveled the world and made a few videos along the way. One day in 2003, he quit his day job and embarked on a journey of exploration. To document the trip, Matt videotaped himself dancing

39. Fujimura, *Culture Care*, 20–21.
40. Fujimura, *Culture Care*, 19–20.
41. Fujimura, *Culture Care*, 58.
42. Fujimura, *Culture Care*, 81.
43. For more on how you might join with other cultural apologists for the good of all, visit the Two Tasks Institute at https://twotasksinstitute.org/.

with a group of locals at each location he visited, often in front of a well-known building or natural formation. He posted a video of his first trip on the internet and the video went viral. Stride Gum sponsored a couple more trips resulting in two more videos released in 2006 and 2008. To date, there are five major videos documenting Matt's dancing exploits at hundreds of locations around the globe.

While I love all of them, I'm particularly moved by his 2008 video.[44] Watching it, I'm reminded of the passage in Revelation 7:9 where "a great multitude . . . from every nation, tribe, people and language" stand before the throne of God in worship. The video gives us a taste of what heaven will be like as we view frame after frame, in Prague, Moscow, London, Auckland, Seattle, Toronto, Timbuktu, Soweto, and on and on, and see the diverse people of the world moving together in rhythm and laughing with delight. Watching, I'm struck by our universal love of dance. Human beings love to dance, and we love to join others in dance. It's as if we were *made* to dance.

In this, we have another way to think of God's invitation to locate our lives within his story. We can think of finding our way home on the journey as an invitation to dance with God. The music is playing. The story is unfolding. God extends an invitation to jump in and join him, along with others, and simply dance. God the Father, Son, and Holy Spirit have been engaged in this dance from eternity past, enjoying a life of mutual self-giving love. C. S. Lewis provocatively describes this Trinitarian dance: "In Christianity God is not a static thing—not even a person—but a dynamic, pulsating activity, a life, almost a kind of drama. Almost, if you will not think me irreverent, a kind of dance."[45] In creation, the triune God's love bursts forth, inviting us to join the eternal dance and share in God's own joy and delight: "The whole dance, or drama, or pattern of this three-Personal life is to be played out in each one of us: or (putting it the other way round) each one of us has got to enter that pattern, take his place in that dance. There is no other way to the happiness for which we were made."[46]

So, *what are you waiting for?* Do you hear the music? Join with God and others in the dance and continue on the journey. Find the happiness he offers and then go and invite others to sing the beautiful song of grace, savor the goodness of the gift, and find the truth that sets us free.

---

44. To see the 2008 video, as well as the others, go to http://www.wheretheheckismatt.com.

45. Lewis, *Mere Christianity*, 175.

46. Lewis, *Mere Christianity*, 176.

APPLYING THE MODEL TO NON-WESTERN CULTURES

F ollowing Paul's example at Mars Hill, this book has unpacked a model of cultural apologetics that seeks to address the primary barriers to belief in Jesus and the gospel that are characteristic of Western culture at the beginning of the twenty-first century. The crux of the issue, as I've argued, is that Christianity is often seen as unreasonable or undesirable or both in a disenchanted world. Can this model be applied to non-Western contexts, contexts where disenchantment and its ills are not the dominant way of perceiving? I think so. In this appendix I offer thoughts on how to apply the model of the book to different cultures, whether Eastern or animistic, for example, or subcultures within the West that might have their own set of concerns and issues that warrant fresh insight.

Recall, in broad outline, Paul's method at Mars Hill:

- First, Paul sought to understand the culture.
- Second, Paul identified a starting point from which to build a bridge to Jesus and the gospel.
- Third, Paul set out his case for Jesus and the gospel, addressing barriers to belief along the way.
- Finally, in a way his listeners could understand, Paul brought them to a place where they could consider the ultimate question: *What do you make of Jesus Christ?*

These four bulleted "steps" can serve as a guide in applying the model set forth in this book to other cultures or subcultures.

Faithful and meaningful evangelism and apologetics begin with understanding. Like Paul, we must seek to understand those we hope to reach. Toward that end, Newbigin's question is as good as any: What is the culture's dominant way of perceiving, thinking, and living? We must also recognize the dominant culture-shaping institutions within any particular culture, as well as its sacred beliefs and plausibility structure. We must apply the insight of four-dimensional ministry to each culture we seek to reach. Importantly, the third (depth) and fourth (time) dimension point to the importance of global concerns and the call to "faithful presence" within the culture-shaping institutions, whatever they may be. This, of course, requires time, compassion, vision, money, cooperation, intellectual and moral virtue, and the grace of God.

By understanding a culture, possible starting points from which to build a bridge to Jesus and the gospel will become apparent. Paul started with the statues in Athens, where worship was offered to "an unknown god." Paul affirmed the religious impulse behind the idolatry and then redirected that impulse to Jesus and the gospel. In this book, I've chosen the universal longings for goodness, truth, and beauty as starting points from "our Athens" to build bridges to Jesus and the gospel along the planks of the human conscience, reason, and the imagination. Since I've identified three universal longings, these starting points and the planks built upon them may be used in any context. I suspect that any other starting points will eventually use some or all of the "planks" of reason, conscience, and imagination, especially if we are to help others see and delight in reality as Jesus does. Still, there are other possible starting places that might be better. The point is to start somewhere!

Even if the starting points in non-Western contexts are the same as those I've chosen in this book, the barriers will often be different. The primary barriers to belief in the West might also be barriers to belief in some other context, but they might not. And there will undoubtedly be different barriers to belief in those contexts. For example, in the West, belief in one true religion is seen as intolerant. Not so, however, in the Middle East. In the Far East, science might not be viewed as much of a barrier to belief in God, but the belief that there is one true God is. We must learn to be good diagnosticians so we can address the actual barriers to belief within each culture. I suspect that this is where a cultural apologetic of return in non-Western context will look the most different: in responding to the actual barriers to belief—internal and external—that hinder people along the way to Jesus and the gospel. In all cases, the goal remains the same: we want the gospel to get a fair hearing. We want each person within a culture to grasp the meaning and significance of the ultimate question: *What do you make of Jesus Christ?* We want Christianity to be viewed as reasonable and desirable, a viable option among all competing options for allegiance.

My challenge to you, the reader: go and be like Paul as you follow Christ's call to take the gospel to all nations.

BIBLIOGRAPHY

Alexander, Denis. "Enhancing Humans or a New Creation?" *Cambridge Papers* 18, no. 2 (2009): 1–4.

Allberry, Sam. *Is God Anti-Gay?* Purcellville, VA: Good Book Company, 2013.

Alston, William. *Perceiving God: The Epistemology of Religious Experience*. Ithaca, NY: Cornell University Press, 1991.

Anderson, Conor R. "Desire and the Failure of Evolutionary Naturalism." *Philosophia Christi* 17, no. 2 (2015): 369–82.

Anderson, James N. and Greg Welty. "The Lord of Noncontradiction: An Argument for God from Logic." *Philosophia Christi* 13, no. 2 (2011): 321–38.

Anderson, M. T. *Symphony for the City of the Dead: Dmitri Shostakovich and the Siege of Leningrad*. Somerville, MA: Candlewick, 2015.

Aquinas, Thomas. *On Evil*. Edited by Brian Davies. Translated by Richard Regan. Oxford: Oxford University Press, 2003.

———. *The Treatise on the Divine Nature: Summa Theologiae I, 1–13*. Translated by Brian J. Shanley, OP. Indianapolis: Hackett, 2006.

Aristotle. *Metaphysics*. In *The Complete Works of Aristotle*. Edited by Jonathan Barnes. Vol. 2. Princeton, NJ: Princeton University Press, 1984.

Augustine. *Confessions*. Translated by Henry Chadwick. Oxford: Oxford University Press, 1998.

Axe, Douglas. *Undeniable*. New York: HarperOne, 2016.

Bacon, Francis. *The Advancement of Learning*. Oxford: Clarendon Press, 1891.

Baggett, David and Marybeth Baggett. *The Morals of the Story*. Downers Grove, IL: InterVarsity Press, 2018.

Balcomb, A. O. "Re-Enchanting a Disenchanted Universe: Post Modern Projects in Theologies of Space." *Religion & Theology* 16 (2009): 77–89.

Barnes, Julian. *Nothing to Be Frightened Of*. New York: Knopf, 2008.

Barrett, William. *Irrational Man*. New York: Anchor, 1962.

Block, Ned. "Do Causal Powers Drain Away?" *Philosophy and Phenomenal Research* 67 (2003): 133–50.

Berger, Peter. *A Rumor of Angels: Modern Society and the Rediscovery of the Supernatural.* New York: Doubleday, Anchor, 1970.

———. *Facing Up to Modernity.* New York: Basic Books, 1977.

Beversluis, John. *C. S. Lewis and the Search for Rational Religion.* Grand Rapids: Eerdmans, 1985.

Boersma, Hans. *Heavenly Participation.* Grand Rapids: Eerdmans, 2011.

Buechner, Frederick. *Telling the Truth: The Gospel as Tragedy, Comedy, and Fairy Tale.* New York: HarperCollins, 1977.

———. *The Longing for Home: Recollections and Reflections.* New York: Harper Collins, 1996.

Brentano, Franz. *Psychology from an Empirical Standpoint.* New York: Routledge, 1995.

Brown, Peter. *Power and Persuasion in Late Antiquity: Towards a Christian Empire.* Madison: University of Wisconsin Press, 1992.

Byerly, T. Ryan. *Introducing Logic and Critical Thinking.* Grand Rapids: Baker, 2017.

Cahill, Thomas. *How the Irish Saved Civilization.* New York: Anchor, 1995.

Calvin, John. *Institutes of the Christian Religion.* Edited by John T. McNeill. Translated by Ford Lewis Battles. Louisville: Westminster John Knox, 1960.

Carpenter, Humphrey. *W. H. Auden: A Biography.* Boston: Houghton Mifflin, 1981.

Carroll, Sean. *The Big Picture: On the Origins of Life, Meaning, and the Universe Itself.* New York: Dutton, 2016.

Carr, Nicholas. *The Shallows: What the Internet Is Doing to Our Brains.* New York: W. W. Norton, 2010.

Carson, D. A. *Christ and Culture Revisited.* Grand Rapids: Eerdmans, 2008.

Classen, Albrecht. *Handbook of Medieval Studies: Terms—Methods—Trends.* Vol. 1. Berlin: De Gruyter, 2010.

Coleridge, Samuel T. *Biographia Literaria.* New York: Leavitt, Lord & Co., 1834.

Collins, Robin. "The Anthropic Teleological Argument." In *Philosophy of Religion: Selected Readings,* edited by Michael Peterson et al., 5th ed., 187–96. New York: Oxford University Press, 2014.

Collins, Suzanne. *The Hunger Games.* New York: Scholastic, 2008.

Coe, John H. "Musings on the Dark Night of the Soul: Insights from St. John of the Cross on a Developmental Spirituality." *Journal of Psychology and Theology* 28, no. 4 (2000): 293–307.

Cooper, John W. *Body, Soul, and Life Everlasting: Biblical Anthropology and the Monism-Dualism.* Grand Rapids: Eerdmans, 2000.

Copan, Paul and Kenneth D. Litwak. *The Gospel in the Marketplace of Ideas.* Downers Grove, IL: InterVarsity Press, 2014.

Copan, Paul. "Is Yahweh a Moral Monster? The New Atheists and Old Testament Ethics," *Philosophia Christi* 10, no. 1 (2008): 7–37.

———. *Is God a Moral Monster? Making Sense of the Old Testament God*. Grand Rapids: Baker, 2011.

Coppenger, Mark. *Moral Apologetics*. Nashville: B&H, 2011.

Cowan, Steven B., ed. *Five Views on Apologetics*. Grand Rapids: Zondervan, 2000.

Craig, William Lane. *Reasonable Faith*, 3rd. ed. Wheaton, IL: Crossway, 2008.

Craig, William Lane and James D. Sinclair, "The Kalam Cosmological Argument." In *The Blackwell Companion to Natural Theology*, edited by William Lane Craig and J. P. Moreland, 101–201. Malden, MA: Blackwell, 2012.

Craven, S. Michael. *Uncompromised Faith: Overcoming Our Culturalized Christianity*. Colorado Springs: NavPress, 2009.

Crouch, Andy. *Culture Making: Recovering Our Creative Calling*. Downers Grove, IL.: InterVarsity Press, 2008.

Cushman, Philip. "Why the Self Is Empty." *American Psychologist* 45 (May 1990): 599–611.

Darwin, Charles. *On the Origin of Species: A Facsimile of the First Edition*. Cambridge, MA: Harvard University Press, 1964.

Dawkins, Richard. Afterward to *A Universe from Nothing: Why There is Something Rather Than Nothing*, by Lawrence M. Krauss. New York: Atria, 2012.

———. *The Blind Watchmaker*. New York: Norton, 1986.

———. *River Out of Eden: A Darwinian View of Life*. New York: Basic Books, 1995.

———. *The God Delusion*. New York: Mariner, 2008.

Demarest, Bruce. *Seasons of the Soul: Stages of Spiritual Development*. Downers Grove, IL: InterVarsity Press, 2009.

Dennett, Daniel. *Darwin's Dangerous Idea*. New York: Touchstone, 1995.

DeYoung, Rebecca Konyndyk. "Sloth: Historical Reflections on Laziness, Effort, and Resistance to the Demands of Love." In *Virtues and Their Vices*, edited by Kevin Timpe and Craig A. Boyd, 177–98. Oxford: Oxford University Press, 2014.

Dillard, Annie. *Pilgrim at Tinker Creek*. New York: Harper Perennial, 2007.

Dostoevsky, Fyodor. *The Idiot*. Hertfordshire: Wordsworth, 1996.

Dougherty, Trent, ed. *Evidentialism and its Discontents*. New York: Oxford University Press, 2011.

Dow, Philip E. *Virtuous Minds: Intellectual Character Development*. Downers Grove, IL: InterVarsity Press, 2013.

Dreher, Rod. *The Benedict Option: A Strategy for Christians in a Post-Christian Nation*. New York: Sentinel, 2017.

Endō, Shūsaku. *Silence*. New York: Picador, 2016.

English, JT. "Finding Your Way Home." Sermon given at the Village Church, Flour Mound, Texas, March 26, 2017. http://www.tvcresources.net/resource-library/sermons/finding-our-way-home.

Evans, C. Stephen. *Natural Signs and the Knowledge of God*. Oxford: Oxford University Press, 2010.

Feser, Edward. *Philosophy of Mind*. Oxford: Oneworld, 2006.

Ferry, Luc. *A Brief History of Thought: A Philosophical Guide to Living*. New York: Harper Perennial, 2011.

Fish, Stanley. *Save the World on Your Own Time*. Oxford: Oxford University Press, 2008.

Foster, Richard J. *Celebration of the Disciplines*. Rev. ed. San Francisco: HarperSan Francisco, 1988.

Fujimura, Makoto. *Silence and Beauty*. Downers Grove, IL: InterVarsity Press, 2016.

———. *Culture Care: Reconnecting with Beauty for Our Common Life*. Downers Grove, IL: InterVarsity Press, 2017.

Gale, Richard. "Evil as Evidence for God." In *Debating Christian Theism*, edited by J. P. Moreland, Chad Meister, and Khaldoun A. Sweis, 197–207. Oxford: Oxford University Press, 2013.

George, Robert P. and Christopher Tollefsen. *Embryo: A Defense of Human Life*. New York: Doubleday, 2008.

Gillespie, Michael Allen. *The Theological Origins of Modernity*. Chicago: University of Chicago Press, 2008.

Girgis, Sherif, Ryan T. Anderson, and Robert P. George. *What Is Marriage? Man and Women: A Defense*. New York: Encounter, 2012.

Giubilin, Alberto and Francesca Minerva. "After-Birth Abortion: Why Should the Baby Live." *Journal of Medical Ethics* 39, no. 5 (May 2013): 261–63.

Gould, Paul M. *The Outrageous Idea of the Missional Professor*. Eugene, OR: Wipf & Stock, 2014.

Gould, Paul M., Travis Dickinson, and R. Keith Loftin. *Stand Firm*. Nashville: B&H, 2018.

Guinness, Os. *Fool's Talk: Recovering the Art of Christian Persuasion*. Downers Grove, IL: InterVarsity Press, 2015.

Gushee, David P. *Changing Our Mind*. 2nd ed. Canton, MI: Read the Spirit, 2015.

Harris, Sam. *The End of Faith: Religion, Terror, and the Future of Reason*. New York: Norton, 2004.

Hasson, Peter. "Michigan School Let Students Pick Gender, Name, and Bathroom." The Daily Caller, March 21, 2016. http://dailycaller.com/2016/03/21/michigan-schools-to-let-students-choose-gender-name-and-bathroom/#ixzz43YnMWaV0.

Henderson, David W. *Tranquility*. Grand Rapids: Baker, 2015.

Hitchens, Christopher. *God Is Not Great: How Religion Poisons Everything*. New York: Twelve Publishers, 2007.

Hoang, Bethany Hanke and Kristen Deede Johnson. *The Justice Calling: Where Passion Meets Perseverance*. Grand Rapids: Brazos, 2016.

Hodgson, Leonard. *The Doctrine of the Trinity*. London: Nisbet and Co, 1955.

Hoffman, Ken, "Ordering up some food for thought." *Houston Chronicle*, January 15, 2008. http://www.chron.com/life/hoffman/article/Ordering-up-some-food-for -thought-1627633.php.

Holyer, Robert. "The Argument from Desire." *Faith and Philosophy* 5, no. 1 (1988): 61–71.

Homer. *The Odyssey*. Translated by E. V. Rieu and D. C. H. Rieu. New York: Penguin, 2003.

Hume, David. *A Treatise of Human Nature*. Edited by David Fate Norton and Mary J. Norton. Oxford: Oxford University Press, 2005.

———. *An Enquiry Concerning Human Understanding*. Indianapolis: Hackett, 1993.

Hunter, James Davison. *To Change the World*. Oxford: Oxford University Press, 2010.

Istvan, Zoltan. *The Transhumanist Wager*. Reno, NV: Futurity Image Media, 2013.

Jacobs, Alan. *The Narnian: The Life and Imagination of C. S. Lewis*. New York: HarperCollins, 2005.

Jacobsen, Douglas and Rhonda Hustedt Jacobsen. "Postsecular American: A New Context for Higher Education." In *The American University in a Postsecular Age*, edited by Douglas Jacobsen and Rhonda Hustedt Jacobsen, 3–15. Oxford: Oxford University Press, 2008.

Jennings, Willie James. *The Christian Imagination: Theology and the Origins of Race*. New Haven, CT: Yale University Press, 2010.

John of the Cross. *Dark Night of the Soul*. Translated by E. Allison Peers. New York: Image, 2005.

Johnson, Keith E. "Hearing the Music of the Gospel." *Critical Concepts Series*. Vol. 1. Orlando: CruPress, 2008.

Kaplan, Karen. "Bill Nye on the Meaning of the Eclipse." *LA Times*, Aug. 21, 2017. http://www.latimes.com/science/la-sci-great-american-eclipse-liveblog-bill-nye -on-the-meaning-of-the-eclipse-1503082111-htmlstory.html.

Kant, Immanuel. *Critique of Practical Reason*. Translated by Mary Gregor. Cambridge: Cambridge University Press, 1997.

———. *Anthropology from a Pragmatic Point of View*. Translated by R. Louden. Cambridge: Cambridge University Press, 2006.

Keener, Craig S. *Miracles: The Credibility of the New Testament Accounts*. 2 vols. Grand Rapids: Baker, 2011.

Keller, Timothy. "Why We Need Artists." In *It Was Good: Making Art to the Glory of God*, edited by Ned Bustard, 117–24. Baltimore, MD: Square Halo, 2006.

———. *The Reason for God*. New York: Riverhead, 2008.

Kilner, John F. *Dignity and Destiny*. Grand Rapids: Eerdmans, 2015.

Kim, Jagewon. *Mind in a Physical World*. Cambridge, MA: MIT Press, 1998.

———. *Physicalism, or Something Near Enough*. Princeton: Princeton University Press, 2005.

Kind, Amy. "Introduction: Exploring Imagination." In *The Routledge Handbook of Philosophy of Imagination*, ed. Amy Kind, 1–11. New York: Routledge, 2016.

Kinnaman, David and Gabe Lyons. *Unchristian: What a New Generation Really Thinks about Christianity . . . and Why It Matters*. Grand Rapids: Baker, 2007.

Kirsch, Arthur. *Auden and Christianity*. New Haven, CT: Yale University Press, 2005.

Klusendorf, Scott. *The Case for Life: Equipping Christians to Engage the Culture*. Wheaton, IL: Crossway, 2009.

Koperski, Jeffrey. *The Physics of Theism*. Malden, MA: Wiley Blackwell, 2015.

Kort, Wesley A. *C. S. Lewis: Then and Now*. Oxford: Oxford University Press, 2001.

Koukl, Greg. *Tactics: A Game Plan for Discussing Your Christian Convictions*. Grand Rapids: Zondervan, 2009.

Krauss, Lawrence M. *The Greatest Story Ever Told—So Far*. New York: Atria, 2017.

Kreeft, Peter. *Making Sense out of Suffering*. Ann Arbor, MI: Servant, 1986.

———. *Heaven: The Heart's Deepest Longing*. San Francisco: Ignatius, 1989.

———. *Back to Virtue: Traditional Moral Wisdom for Modern Moral Confusion*. San Francisco: Ignatius, 1992.

———. *The Snakebite Letters*. 2nd ed. San Francisco: Ignatius, 1998.

Kurzweil, Ray. *The Age of Spiritual Machines: When Computers Exceed Human Intelligence*. New York: Penguin, 1999.

Lamb, David. *God Behaving Badly: Is the God of the Old Testament Angry, Sexist and Racist?* Downers Grove, IL: InterVarsity Press, 2011.

Lewis, C. S. *An Experiment in Criticism*. Cambridge: Cambridge University Press, 1961.

———. "Bluspels and Flalansferes: A Semantic Nightmare." In *Selected Literary Essays*, edited by Walter Hooper, 251–65. Cambridge: Cambridge University Press, 1969.

———. *Christian Reflections*. Grand Rapids: Eerdmans, 1967.

———. "Image and Imagination." In *Image and Imagination: Essays and Reviews*, edited by Walter Hooper, 34–53. Cambridge: Cambridge University Press, 2013.

———. *Letters to Malcolm Chiefly on Prayer*. Orlando: Harcourt, 1992.

———. "Meditation in a Toolshed." In *God in the Dock: Essays on Theology and Ethics*, edited by Walter Hooper, 212–15. Grand Rapids: Eerdmans, 1970.

———. *Mere Christianity*. New York: HarperColllins, 2001.

———. *Miracles*. New York: Touchstone, 1996.

———. "Modern Man and his Categories of Thought." In *Present Concerns*, edited by Walter Hooper, 61–66. New York: Harcourt, 1986.

———. *Surprised by Joy: The Shape of My Early Life*. Orlando: Harcourt, 1955.

———. *The Abolition of Man*. New York: HarperCollins, 2001.

———. *The Four Loves*. New York: Harcourt Brace Jovanovich, 1960.

———. *The Last Battle*. New York: HarperCollins, 1984.

———. *The Magician's Nephew*. New York: HarperCollins, 1983.

———. "Man or Rabbit?" In *God in the Dock*, edited by Walter Hooper, 108–13. Grand Rapids: Eerdmans, 1970.

———. *The Pilgrim's Regress*. Grand Rapids: Eerdmans, 2002.

———. *The Problem of Pain*. New York: HarperCollins, 2001.

———. *The Screwtape Letters*. Westwood, NJ: Barbour, 1990.

———. *The Weight of Glory*. New York: HarperCollins, 2001.

Lewis, David. *Philosophical Papers*. Vol. 2. Oxford: Oxford University Press, 1986.

Linville, Mark D. "The Moral Argument." In *The Blackwell Companion to Natural Theology*, edited by William Lane Craig and J. P. Moreland, 391–448. Malden, MA: Wiley Blackwell, 2012.

Locke, John. *The Reasonableness of Christianity*. Oxford: Oxford University Press, 1999.

Lyotard, Jean-François. *The Postmodern Condition: A Report of Knowledge*. Translated by Geoffrey Bennington and Brian Massumi. Minneapolis: University of Minnesota Press, 1997.

Machen, J. Gresham. *What Is Christianity?* Grand Rapids: Eerdmans, 1951.

MacIntyre, Alasdair. *After Virtue*. 3rd ed. Notre Dame: University of Notre Dame Press, 2007.

Malik, Charles. *A Christian Critique of the University*. Waterloo, ON: North Waterloo Academic Press, 1987.

Martel, Yann. *Life of Pi*. Orlando: Harcourt, 2001.

Marx, Karl. "Toward a Critique of Hegel's *Philosophy of Right*." In *Karl Marx: Selected Writings*, edited by David McLellan. New York: Oxford University Press, 1977.

Matherne, Samantha. "Kant's Theory of the Imagination." In *The Routledge Handbook of Philosophy of Imagination*, edited by Amy Kind, 55–68. New York: Routledge, 2016.

Mattison II, Willian C. "Hope." In *Being Good: Christian Virtues for Everyday Life*, edited by Michael W. Austin and R. Douglas Geivett, 107–25. Grand Rapids: Eerdmans, 2012.

McCleary, Mary. "The Work of Our Hands." In *It Was Good: Making Art to the Glory of God*, edited by Ned Bustard, 125–40. Baltimore: Square Halo, 2006.

McDowell, Josh and Sean McDowell. *Evidence That Demands a Verdict: Life-Changing Truth for a Skeptical World*. Nashville: Nelson, 2017.

McDowell, Josh. *The Resurrection Factor: Compelling Evidence Which Proves the Resurrection of Jesus Christ*. San Bernardino, CA: Here's Life, 1989.

McGinn, Colin. *Mindsight: Image, Dream, Meaning*. Cambridge, MA: Harvard University Press, 2004.

Meyer, Stephen C. *Signature in the Cell: DNA and the Evidence for Intelligent Design*. New York: HarperOne, 2010.

Michel, Jen Pollock. *Keeping Place: Reflections on the Meaning of Home*. Downers Grove, IL: InterVarsity Press, 2017.

Milbank, Alison. "Apologetics and the Imagination: Making Strange." In *Imaginative Apologetics: Theology, Philosophy and the Catholic Tradition*, edited by Andrew Davison, 31–45. Grand Rapids: Baker Academic, 2012.

Mill, John Stuart. *Utilitarianism*. Edited by George Sher. Indianapolis: Hackett, 2001.

Modrak, Deborah K. W. "Aristotle on Phantasia." In *The Routledge Handbook of Philosophy of Imagination*, edited by Amy Kind, 15–26. New York: Routledge, 2016.

Montgomery, L. M. *Anne of Green Gables*. New York: Bantam, 1987.

Moreland, J. P. and William Lane Craig. *Philosophical Foundations for a Christian Worldview*. Downers Grove, IL: InterVarsity Press, 2003.

Moreland, J. P. *Scaling the Secular City: A Defense of Christianity*. Grand Rapids: Baker, 1987.

———. *The Recalcitrant Imago Dei: Human Persons and the Failure of Naturalism*. London: SCM, 2009.

———. "A Reluctant Travelers Guide for Slouching Toward Theism." *Philosophia Christi* 14, no. 2 (2012): 429–38.

———. *Love Your God with All Your Mind*. Rev. ed. Colorado Springs: NavPress, 2012.

———. *The Soul*. Chicago: Moody Press, 2014.

Morley, Brian K. *Mapping Apologetics: Comparing Contemporary Approaches*. Downers Grove, IL: InterVarsity Press, 2015.

Moser, Paul K. "Cognitive Idolatry and Divine Hiding." In *Divine Hiddenness: New Essays*, edited by Daniel Howard-Snyder and Paul K. Moser, 120–48. Cambridge: Cambridge University Press, 2002.

Muehlhoff, Tim and Richard Langer. *Winsome Persuasion: Christian Influence in a Post-Christian World*. Downers Grove, IL: InterVarsity Press, 2017.

Nagel, Thomas. *The Last Word*. New York: Oxford University Press, 1997.

———. *Mind and Cosmos: Why the Materialist Neo-Darwinian Conception of Nature is Almost Certainly False*. Oxford: Oxford University Press, 2012.

Naugle, David K. *Worldview: The History of a Concept*. Grand Rapids: Eerdmans, 2002.

———. *Reordered Love, Reordered Lives: Learning the Deep Meaning of Happiness*. Grand Rapids: Eerdmans, 2008.

Niebuhr, H. Richard. *Christ and Culture*. New York: Harper & Row, 1951.

Nietzsche, Friedrich. *The Gay Science*. Translated by Walter Kaufmann. New York: Vintage, 1974.

———. *Beyond Good and Evil*. Translated by R. J. Hollingdale. London: Penguin, 2003.

Newbigin, Lesslie. *Foolishness to the Greeks: The Gospel and Western Culture*. Grand Rapids: Eerdmans, 1986.

Newman, Randy. *Bringing the Gospel Home: Witnessing to Family Members, Close Friends, and Others Who Know You Well*. Wheaton, IL: Crossway, 2011.

Noll, Mark A. *The Scandal of the Evangelical Mind*. Grand Rapids: Eerdmans, 1994.

Novalis. *Henry von Ofterdingen*. Translated by Palmer Hilty. Long Grove, IL: Waveland, 1990.

Oldenburg, Henry. *Correspondence*. Edited and translated by A. R. Hall and M. B. Hall. Madison: University of Wisconsin Press, 1965.

Onaka, Yoichi. *The Voice of Silence*. Tokyo: President Publishing, 1992.

Opitz, Donald and Derek Melleby. *The Outrageous Idea of Academic Faithfulness*. 4th ed. Grand Rapids: Brazos, 2009.

Oppy, Graham. "Conflict Model." In *Four Views on Christianity and Philosophy*, edited by Paul M. Gould and Richard Brian Davis, 21–47. Grand Rapids: Zondervan, 2016.

Ordway, Holly. *Apologetics and the Christian Imagination: An Integrated Approach to Defending the Faith*. Steubenville, OH: Emmaus Road, 2017.

Pascal, Blaise. *Pensées*. Translated by A. J. Krailsheimer. New York: Penguin, 1995.

Paley, William. *Natural Theology*. Oxford: Oxford University Press, 2006.

Pearcey, Nancy. *Total Truth: Liberating Christianity from Its Cultural Captivity*. Wheaton, IL: Crossway, 2004.

———. *Saving Leonardo: A Call to Resist the Secular Assault on Mind, Morals, and Meaning*. Nashville: B&H, 2010.

Pinsent, Andrew. "Humility." In *Being Good: Christian Virtues for Everyday Life*, edited by Michael W. Austin and R. Douglas Geivett, 242–64. Grand Rapids: Eerdmans, 2012.

Plantinga, Alvin. "When Faith and Reason Clash: Evolution and the Bible." *The Christian Scholars Review* 21 (1991): 8–31.

———. *Warranted Christian Belief*. Oxford: Oxford University Press, 2000.

———. *Where the Conflict Really Lies: Science, Religion, and Naturalism*. Oxford: Oxford University Press, 2011.

Plantinga, Cornelius Jr. *Not the Way It's Supposed to Be: A Breviary of Sin*. Grand Rapids: Eerdmans, 1995.

Plato. *Theaetetus*. Translated by M. J. Levett and Rev. Myles Burnyeat. In *Plato: The Complete Works*. Edited by John M. Cooper and D. S. Hutchinson. Indianapolis: Hackett, 1997.

———. *The Republic*. Translated by G. M. A. Grube and Rev. C. D. C. Reeve. In *Plato: The Complete Works*. Edited by John M. Cooper and D. S. Hutchinson. Indianapolis: Hackett, 1997.

Polkinghorne, John. *Science and Creation: The Search for Understanding*. West Conshohocken, PA: Templeton Foundation Press, 2006.

Poor, Michael. "A Primer: Cultural Apologetics . . ." *The Humanitas Forum on Christianity and Culture*. November 7, 2013. http://humanitas.org/?p=2552.

Postman, Neil. *Amusing Ourselves to Death: Public Discourse in the Age of Show Business*. New York: Penguin, 1985.

Prothero, Stephen. *American Jesus: How the Son of God Became a National Icon*. New York: Farrar, Straus and Giroux, 2003.

Puckett Jr., Joe. *The Apologetics of Joy: A Case for the Existence of God from C. S. Lewis's Argument from Desire*. Eugene, OR: Wipf & Stock, 2012.

Rae, Scott. *Moral Choices: An Introduction to Ethics*. 2nd ed. Grand Rapids: Zondervan, 2000.

Rea, Michael. "Divine Hiddenness, Divine Silence." In *Philosophy of Religion: An Anthology*, edited by Louis P. Pojman and Michael C. Rea, 6th ed, 266–75. Boston, MA: Wadsworth/Cenage, 2011.

Reppert, Victor. *C. S. Lewis's Dangerous Idea*. Downers Grove, IL: InterVarsity Press, 2003.

———. "The Argument from Reason." In *The Blackwell Companion to Natural Theology*, edited by William Lane Craig and J. P. Moreland, 344–90. Malden, MA: Wiley Blackwell, 2012.

Richards, Jay W. *Money, Greed, and God: Why Capitalism Is the Solution and Not the Problem*. New York: HarperOne, 2009.

Rickabaugh, Brandon and Todd Buras. "The Argument from Reason, and Mental Causal Drainage: A Reply to van Inwagen." *Philosophia Christi* 19, no. 2 (2017): 381–98.

Rieff, Philip. *My Life Among the Deathworks: Illustrations of the Aesthetics of Authority*. Charlottesville, VA: University of Virginia Press, 2006.

Ritchie, Angus. *From Morality to Metaphysics: The Theistic Implications of Our Ethical Commitments*. Oxford: Oxford University Press, 2012.

Roberts, Vaughn. *God's Big Picture: Tracing the Storyline of the Bible*. Downers Grove, IL: InterVarsity Press, 2002.

Robinson, Marilynne. *Gilead*. New York: Farrar, Straus and Giroux, 2004.

———. *When I Was a Child I Read Books*. Thorndike, MA: Center Point, 2012.

Rosenberg, Alex. *The Atheist's Guide to Reality: Enjoying Life Without Illusion*. New York: Norton, 2011.

Ruse, Michael. *Taking Darwin Seriously: A Naturalistic Approach to Philosophy*. Amherst, NY: Prometheus, 1998.

Russell, Bertrand. *Introduction to Mathematical Philosophy*. London: Routledge, 1919.

———. *Why I Am Not a Christian*. New York: Touchstone, 1957.

Sagan, Carl. *Pale Blue Dot*. New York: Random House, 1994.

Schaeffer, Francis. *How Should We Then Live? The Rise and Decline of Western Thought and Culture*. 50th L'Abri Anniversary Ed. Wheaton, IL: Crossway, 2005.

———. *Art and the Bible*. Downers Grove, IL: InterVarsity Press, 2006.

Schmidt, Alvin J. *Under the Influence: How Christianity Transformed Civilization*. Grand Rapids: Zondervan, 2001.

Scruton, Roger. *Beauty: A Very Short Introduction*. Oxford: Oxford University Press, 2011.

———. *The Soul of the World*. Princeton: Princeton University Press, 2014.

Shaw, Ed. *Same-Sex Attraction and the Church: The Surprising Plausibility of the Celibate Life*. Downers Grove, IL: InterVarsity Press, 2015.

Sheiman, Bruce. *An Atheist Defends Religion: Why Humanity is Better Off with Religion Than Without It*. New York: Penguin, 2009.

Shelley, Mary. *Frankenstein*. London: Penguin, 1985.

Shellnutt, Kate. "Cambodia Rising." *Christianity Today*, June 2017, 27–32.

Siemon-Netto, Uwe. "J. S. Bach in Japan." *First Things*, June 2000. https://www.first things.com/article/2000/06/j-s-bach-in-japan.

Simpson, William M. R. "Knowing Nature: Beyond the False Dilemma of Reduction or Emergence." In *Knowing Creation: Perspectives from Theology, Philosophy, and Science*, edited by Andrew B. Torrance and Thomas H. McCall, 237–259. Grand Rapids: Zondervan, 2018.

Singer, Peter. *Practical Ethics*. 2nd ed. Cambridge: Cambridge University Press, 1993.

Sire, James W. *The Universe Next Door*. 5th Ed. Downers Grove, IL: InterVarsity Press, 2009.

———. *Apologetics Beyond Reason: Why Seeing Really Is Believing*. Downers Grove, IL: InterVarsity Press, 2014.

Smith, Christian and Melinda Lundquist Denton. *Soul Searching: The Religious and Spiritual Lives of American Teenagers*. Oxford: Oxford University Press, 2005.

Smith, James K. A. *Desiring the Kingdom: Worship, Worldview, and Cultural Formation*. Grand Rapids: Baker, 2009.

———. *Imagining the Kingdom: How Worship Works*. Grand Rapids: Baker, 2013.

———. *You Are What You Love*. Grand Rapids: Brazos, 2016.

———. *Awaiting the King: Reforming Public Theology*. Grand Rapids: Baker, 2017.

Spurlock, Morgan. *Don't Eat This Book: Fast Food and the Supersizing of America*. New York: Putnam, 2005.

Stark, Rodney. *The Victory of Reason: How Christianity Led to Freedom, Capitalism, and Western Success*. New York: Random House, 2005.

———. *God's Battalions: The Case for the Crusades*. New York: HarperOne, 2009.

Stevenson, Robert Louis. *The Strange Case of Dr. Jekyll and Mr. Hyde*. Mineola, NY: Dover, 1991.

Strobel, Lee. *The Case for Christ: A Journalist's Personal Investigation of the Evidence for Jesus*. Grand Rapids: Zondervan, 1998.

Stokes, Dustin. "Imagination and Creativity." In *The Routledge Handbook of Philosophy of Imagination*, edited by Amy Kind, 247–61. New York: Routledge, 2016.

Strom, Stephanie. "McDonald's Seeks Its Fast-Food Soul." *New York Times*, March 7, 2015. http://www.nytimes.com/2015/03/08/business/mcdonalds-seeks-its-fast -food-soul.html?_r=0.

Stump, Eleonore. *Wandering in Darkness: Narrative and the Problem of Suffering*. Oxford: Clarendon, 2010.

Tannen, Deborah. *The Argument Culture: Moving from Debate to Dialogue*. New York: Random House, 1998.

Taylor, Charles. *A Secular Age*. Cambridge, MA: Belknap, 2007.

Taylor, David O., ed. *For the Beauty of the Church: Casting a Vision for the Arts*. Grand Rapids: Baker, 2010.

Tirosh-Samuelson, Hava. "Transhumanism as a Secularist Faith." *Zygon* 47 (2012): 710–34.

Tolkien, J. R. R. "On Fairy-Stories." In *The Tolkien Reader*, 33–99. New York: Del Rey, 1986.

Tooley, Michael. "Abortion and Infanticide." *Philosophy and Public Affairs* 2, no. 1 (1972): 37–65.

Torres, Hazel. "Legendary U. S. Swimmer Michael Phelps Reveals How 'Purpose Driven Life' by Rick Warren Saved Him From Suicide." *Christian Today*, August 3, 2016. http://www.christiantoday.com/article/legendary.u.s.swimmer.michael. phelps.reveals.how.purpose.driven.life.by.rick.warren.saved.his.life/92191.htm.

Tozer, A. W. *The Knowledge of the Holy*. New York: HarperCollins, 1961.

Turnau, Ted. *Popologetics: Popular Culture in Christian Perspective*. Phillipsburg, NJ: P&R, 2012.

Turner, Steve. *Imagine: A Vision for Christians in the Arts*. 2nd ed. Downers Grove, IL: InterVarsity Press, 2017.

Tyson, Neil DeGrasse (@neiltyson). "The divided United States of America will unite today, sharing a cosmic event predicted by the methods and tools of science." Twitter, August 21, 2017, 7:02 a.m. https://twitter.com/neiltyson/status/899632684 976046081.

Tyson, Paul. *Returning to Reality: Christian Platonism for Our Times*. Eugene, OR: Cascade, 2014.

Vanhoozer, Kevin J. *Pictures at a Theological Exhibition: Scenes of the Church's Worship, Witness, and Wisdom*. Downers Grove, IL: InterVarsity Press, 2016.

Vicini, Andrea, S. J. and Agnes M. Brazal. "Longing for Transcendence: Cyborgs and Trans- and Posthumans." *Theological Studies* 76, no. 1 (2015): 148–65.

Vines, Matthew. *God and the Gay Christian: The Biblical Case in Support of Same-Sex Relationships*. New York: Convergent, 2014.

Volf, Miroslav. *Flourishing: Why We Need Religion in a Globalized World*. New Haven, CT: Yale University Press, 2015.

Ward, Michael. "The Good Serves the Better and Both the Best: C. S. Lewis on Imagination and Reason in Apologetics." In *Imaginative Apologetics: Theology, Philosophy and the Catholic Tradition*, edited by Andrew Davison, 59–78. Grand Rapids: Baker, 2012.

Wayne, Teddy. "The End of Reflection." *New York Times*, June 11, 2016. https:// www.nytimes.com/2016/06/12/fashion/internet-technology-phones-introspection .html?_r=0.

Weaver, Richard M. *Ideas Have Consequences*. Chicago: University of Chicago Press, 1948.

West, Ryan and Adam C. Pelser. "Perceiving God through Natural Beauty." *Faith and Philosophy* 32, no. 3 (July 2015): 293–312.

Wielenberg, Erik J. *God and the Reach of Reason: C. S. Lewis, David Hume, and Bertrand Russell.* Cambridge: Cambridge University Press, 2008.

———. "In Defense of Non-Natural Non-Theistic Moral Realism." *Faith and Philosophy* 26, no. 1 (2009): 23–41.

———. *Robust Ethics: The Metaphysics and Epistemology of Godless Normative Realism.* New York: Oxford University Press, 2014.

Watts, Isaac. *Logic: The Right Use of Reason in the Inquiry after Truth.* Grand Rapids: Soli Deo Gloria, 2013.

Wilder, Thornton. *Our Town.* New York: HarperCollins, 1998.

Wilkinson, Alissa. "How 'Stranger Things' Re-Enchants the World." *Christianity Today*, July 26, 2016. http://www.christianitytoday.com/ct/2016/july-web-only/stranger-things.html?start=1.

Willard, Dallas. *The Divine Conspiracy: Rediscovering our Hidden Life in God.* New York: HarperCollins, 1998.

———. *The Spirit of the Disciplines: Understanding How God Changes Lives.* San Francisco: HarperSanFrancisco, 1991.

Wirzba, Norman. *From Nature to Creation: A Christian Vision for Understanding and Loving Our World.* Grand Rapids: Baker, 2015.

Wolfe, Gregory. *Beauty Will Save the World: Recovering the Human in an Ideological Age.* Wilmington, DE: ISI Books, 2011.

Wooddell, Joseph D. *The Beauty of the Faith.* Eugene, OR: Wipf & Stock, 2011.

Wordsworth, William. "Stepping Westward." In *Selected Poetry*, edited by Stephen Gill and Duncan Wu, 146–47. New York: Oxford University Press, 2008.

Wright, N. T. *The Resurrection of the Son of God.* Minneapolis: Fortress, 2003.

———. *Paul for Everyone: Romans, Part One; Chapters 1–8.* Louisville: Westminster John Knox, 2004.

Yarhouse, Mark A. *Understanding Gender Dysphoria.* Downers Grove, IL: InterVarsity Press, 2015.

SCRIPTURE INDEX

SUBJECT INDEX